D1598414

UNITY AND DIVERSITY IN NEW TESTAMENT THEOLOGY

George Eldon Ladd

UNITY AND DIVERSITY IN NEW TESTAMENT THEOLOGY

Essays in Honor of George E. Ladd

EDITED BY
Robert A. Guelich

WILLIAM B. EERDMANS PUBLISHING COMPANY
GRAND RAPIDS, MICHIGAN

LIBRARY
McCORMICK THEOLOGICAL SEMINARY
1100 EAST 55th STREET
CHICAGO, ILLINOIS 60615

BS
2397
.A1
U54

Copyright © 1978 by Wm. B. Eerdmans Publishing Co.
255 Jefferson Ave. S.E., Grand Rapids, Mich. 49503
All rights reserved
Printed in the United States of America

Library of Congress Cataloging in Publication Data

Main entry under title:

Unity and diversity in New Testament theology.

Bibliography: p. 214.
CONTENTS: Hubbard, D. Biographical sketch and appreciation.—Meye, R. Psalm 107 as horizon for interpreting the miracle stories of Mark 4:35-8:26.—Martin, R. P. The pericope of the healing of the centurion's servant/son (Matt. 8:5-13 par. Luke 7:1-10).—Harrison, E. F. A study of John 1:14. [etc.]
1. Bible. N.T.—Theology—Addresses, essays, lectures. 2. Ladd, George Eldon, 1911- Addresses, essays, lectures. I. Ladd, George Eldon, 1911- II. Guelich, Robert A.
BS2397.A1U54 230 78-16426
ISBN 0-8028-3504-X

Contents

Editor's Preface

George Eldon Ladd has left a lasting imprint in the area of biblical studies and biblical theology both through his classroom and his pen. A lucid style, fairness toward all sides of the issue, and an openness to the biblical text in particular and biblical scholarship in general have marked his lectures and his writings. Aware of the diversity within the biblical witness to God's redemptive activity in history, he has constantly sought to underline the unity this witness reflects, a unity anchored in the consistency of the God who acts and speaks. In keeping with this perception of the nature of biblical theology, the title *Unity and Diversity in New Testament Theology* was chosen and the articles written accordingly.

I want to express my thanks to each of the contributors for their time and efforts to make this *Festschrift* a reality. The list of contributors represents both former students and fellow colleagues in the common task of biblical scholarship. I also thank the publishers, William B. Eerdmans, for their interest in this project. We offer this as an expression of appreciation and gratitude to George Eldon Ladd, Senior Professor of New Testament, Fuller Theological Seminary.

ROBERT A. GUELICH

Abbreviations

AB	*Anchor Bible*
BA	*Biblical Archaeologist*
BibS	*Bibliotheca Sacra*
BJRL	*Bulletin of the John Rylands University Library of Manchester*
CBQ	*Catholic Biblical Quarterly*
CJT	*Canadian Journal of Theology*
EBT	*Encyclopedia of Biblical Theology*
EvT	*Evangelische Theologie*
ExpTim	*Expository Times*
HKNT	*Handkommentar zum Neuen Testament*
HNT	*Handbuch zum Neuen Testament*
HNTC	*Harper's New Testament Commentaries*
HTCNT	*Herder's Theological Commentary to the New Testament*
HTKNT	*Herder's theologischer Kommentar zum Neuen Testament*
HTR	*Harvard Theological Review*
HUCA	*Hebrew Union College Annual*
IDB	*The Interpreter's Dictionary of the Bible*
IDBSup	*The Interpreter's Dictionary of the Bible, Supplementary Volume*
IEJ	*Israel Exploration Journal*
Int	*Interpretation*
JBL	*Journal of Biblical Literature*
JBR	*Journal of the Bible and Religion*
JSJ	*Journal for the Study of Judaism*
JTS	*Journal of Theological Studies*
LCC	*Library of Christian Classics*
LTK	*Lexikon für Theologie und Kirche*
MeyerK	Meyer: *Kritische-exegetischer Kommentar über das Neue Testament*
MGWJ	*Monatsschrift für Geschichte und Wissenschaft des Judentums*
NA	*Neutestamentliche Abhandlungen*
Neot	*Neotestamentica*
NICNT	*New International Commentary on the New Testament*

NIDNTT	*New International Dictionary of New Testament Theology*
NovT	*Novum Testamentum*
NovTSup	*Novum Testamentum, Supplements*
NRT	*Nouvelle Revue Théologique*
NTD	*Das Neue Testament Deutsch*
NTS	*New Testament Studies*
OTL	*Old Testament Library*
OTS	*Oudtestamentische Studiën*
RB	*Revue Biblique*
RevExp	*Review and Expositor*
RevQ	*Revue de Qumran*
RGG	*Die Religion in Geschichte und Gegenwart* (3rd edition)
RHPhR	*Revue d'histoire et de philosophie religieuses*
SBT	*Studies in Biblical Theology*
SE	*Studia Evangelica*
SJT	*Scottish Journal of Theology*
SNTSMS	*Society for New Testament Studies Monograph Series*
TDNT	*Theological Dictionary of the New Testament*
TLZ	*Theologische Literaturzeitung*
TRu	*Theologische Rundschau*
TSF Bulletin	*Theological Students Fellowship Bulletin*
TU	*Texte und Untersuchungen*

Biographical Sketch and Appreciation

DAVID ALLAN HUBBARD

In joining the Fuller faculty in the fall of 1950, George Ladd missed our first graduating class. He has been part of the life and history of every Fuller graduate in the twenty-eight classes that have received degrees since that first one.

Harrison, Henry, Lindsell, Smith—these charter faculty members were joined in 1948 and 1949 by Archer, Carnell, and LaSor. They were the crew to whose name Ladd's was added as the early faculty began to take its full shape and size. Thin, eager, demanding, George Ladd dived into his work at the Seminary with the enthusiasm which has been his trademark ever since. In those early classes, we saw him as a great complement to the more reserved style of his New Testament colleague, Everett Harrison. His probing manner, his driving style, his restless curiosity, his passionate fervor for the subject kept every class alive during the lecture session and awake far into the night trying to pass muster.

One of the striking things about George Ladd's early contribution to Fuller was the great heart for missions that he brought with him. Some of the most stirring addresses of those early years were delivered by him. He held before the student body the challenge of missions in the context of New Testament exegesis and its demand to proclaim the gospel of the kingdom. For those of us who may have been tempted to view the call to world mission and the task of biblical scholarship as separate subjects barely in conversation with each other, George Ladd's ability to integrate them was a thing of beauty and challenge. In the intervening years scores of men and women have gone out from Fuller inspired to take the gospel to the ends of the earth by the deliberate and intense presentation of the missionary task which they gained at his feet.

This zeal for the spreading of the gospel was sparked by George's conversion experience. Born in Alberta, Canada, on July 31, 1911, he had moved with his parents to New Hampshire, where his father served as a country doctor. George was impressed by some words written in his father's New Testament—"Born again, August 10, 1910." At the time he did not know what that meant. But in 1929, when living in Maine, he attended a Methodist church that was too small to have a resident pastor.

A young woman graduate of Moody Bible Institute received permission from the superintendent to preach on Sundays. It was during this year that he received Christ as Savior and learned the meaning of his father's note.

It was his urge to write that brought George Ladd to Fuller. He was already a seasoned pastor, teacher, and scholar when he arrived. His apprenticeship began even before he completed his undergraduate work at Gordon College. He had commuted for two years from Boston to Gilford, New Hampshire, where he served as a student pastor. After his graduation from Gordon and his ordination in 1933 as a Northern Baptist minister (now American Baptist), he continued at Gilford and was joined by Winnie, his bride. Together they settled in the parsonage and George traveled to Boston two days a week to complete his Bachelor of Divinity degree at Gordon Divinity School. From 1936 to 1942 he and Winnie served the First Baptist Church of Montpelier, Vermont. During this time, restless for further study, George sought a pastorate where he could carry on his ministry of teaching and at the same time pursue his work at a university to prepare him for a career of teaching in a college or seminary.

Finally in 1942 he and Winnie moved to the Blaney Memorial Church in Boston, and almost immediately he enrolled in the department of classics at Boston University and completed more than a year of study. This academic endeavor led to his acceptance at Harvard University in 1943 where he pursued a Ph.D. program in classics, completing the exams in 1947 and receiving the degree in 1949. He supported himself during this graduate period by teaching Greek at Gordon College and a little later serving in the New Testament department at Gordon Divinity School. It was from there that he accepted the call to Fuller in fulfillment of his desire to teach in an institution where the schedule and environment would encourage substantial writing in theological and exegetical studies.

George Ladd's experience with New England congregations, going back to the difficult days of the depression, gave him a strong sense of realism about the struggles that young ministers would face. He has told stories, for instance, of the frugality of the congregation, a frugality which resulted in a salary of $22 a week at Montpelier plus $1.80 for conducting a midweek service at a church in South Northfield, Vermont. In one of his congregations there was a prominent laymen who, though fairly successful by New England depression standards, limited his philanthropy to something like ten cents a week. Those were the times that tried the soul of a young Baptist pastor and helped to whet his appetite for a life in the more sheltered halls of academia.

This is not to say that George was looking for a life of idle meditation. Indeed he had always worked uncommonly hard. From the gravel pits near his home in Maine, where he was working in 1929, to the dining hall in Gordon where he waited on tables, from the creamery where he cut butter and cracked eggs to the student pastorates, from the Greek and Latin classes at Boston University to the advanced seminars at Harvard, hard work had always been part of George Ladd's life. Nothing changed for him when he came to Fuller. It did change some for the rest of us. We were encouraged by his example and forced by his requirements to work harder than we ever had before.

But all this happened with great good will. One of his contributions through the years has been an incredible ability to stimulate graduate students. His rigorous standards, often expressed in a no-nonsense way, cured all temptation to bluff. His comments on our papers were penetrating, and his rebuttal to our arguments was often overpowering. We found him to be a passionate advocate of his theories, not so much because they were *his* theories, but because he viewed them as biblical. And for what the Bible teaches, George Ladd has always shown extraordinary concern.

Carefully prepared, ardent in his presentation, and relevant to the needs of the church—these are the kinds of phrases that have often been used of George Ladd's teaching ministry. It is a ministry that has been expanded through his increasing personal openness. Many a student has wept with him as he shared the joy and suffering of his own spiritual pilgrimage.

For his students through the years, George Ladd has been an effective bridge between evangelical faith and contemporary scholarship. He has refused to compromise either his commitment to the basic doctrines of the Christian church or to sound technical study. Devout and critical, critical because of the devoutness and devout because of what he had learned from biblical criticism—these have been the measured adjectives in George Ladd's life and witness.

As much as anyone in our generation, he has sought consciously to make evangelical scholarship credible in the universities of the world. *Jesus and the Kingdom* (1964), republished under the title *The Presence of the Future* (1974), and *A Theology of the New Testament* (1974) have been his major attempts along this line. Students who went abroad to do graduate study often discovered that the name of George Ladd brought instant recognition from theological faculties which either ignored or were not aware of North American evangelical scholarship. This burning desire to make our evangelical understanding of the faith believable in the general world of scholarship was not without its price. The success of his teaching and writing ministry has, on occasion, been accompanied by wounding sometimes at the hands of reviewers that seemed to him almost too painful to bear.

George Ladd has always shown a kind of impatience with topics that he considered trivial or obscure. As his bibliography will indicate, he almost always went for the throat of an issue. He realized, for instance, the crucial importance of the credibility of the gospel in the face of the attacks by form critics and particularly the restructuring of the New Testament faith at the hands of Rudolf Bultmann. Beyond that, he has understood better than most of our generation the importance of eschatology to the whole of Christian theology. Probably no contemporary Christian scholar has done more to help us understand the future and present aspects of the kingdom of God than George Eldon Ladd.

His work in these areas has received widespread recognition. Through the years he has served as guest lecturer at seminaries like Western Conservative Baptist, Bethel, Southwestern Baptist, and North Park. A particular honor that came his way was to be asked to be one of a handful of contributors to the twenty-fifth anniversary issue of the journal of biblical scholarship, *Interpretation* (January 1971). In addition he received a particularly touching tribute when his faculty colleagues at Gordon Divinity School awarded him a Doctor of Divinity degree in memory of his contribution to that institution and in appreciation of his service to Fuller and the church around the world. That worldwide church, by the way, has profited from his books on the kingdom of God which have been translated into Japanese and Spanish and his important book on scholarly methods, *The New Testament and Criticism,* which has appeared in Norwegian and Spanish.

George and Winnie Ladd were the parents of two children, Larry who lives in Pasadena, and Norma who is married to Dr. William Parker and resides in Manhattan, Kansas. Bill and Norma Parker presented the Ladds with two grandchildren, Terry and Daniel.

No appreciation of George Ladd's ministry and particularly his contribution to life at Fuller during the nearly thirty years he has served among us would be complete without some words for Winnie. Until her untimely death in the spring of 1977, Winifred Webber Ladd served as an outstanding member of the Seminary community. In graciousness, in faithfulness, in servanthood, her life was exemplary. Probably no wife of any faculty member has rendered more steady and significant service through the history of the institution than Winnie Ladd. Beyond that, in her quiet way, she rendered stellar service to the entire church by her participation in the typing, editing, and preparing of indices for George's books. This word of appreciation and the essays of this volume pay tribute to her alongside her husband.

George Ladd's work is as close to my own heart as that of any scholar whom I know. He not only had the patience, grace, and aggressiveness to help me hone my tools as a young student, but his writings furnish part of the equipment that I use regularly in my present ministry. It is a rare week that I do not use one of George Ladd's books in the preparation of a sermon or in background reading for a class lecture. *A Theology of the*

New Testament sits on my shelf with a handful of books that I keep most readily available for consultation.

But beyond the actual training and the legacy of his books is a theological perspective that continues to inform my thinking and preaching. His understanding of the relationship between this age and the age to come, his insights into the interpretation of the parables of Jesus as they explicate the truths of the kingdom of God, his perspective on the present and future significance of the book of Revelation, his appreciation of the centrality of the resurrection of Jesus—these and a cluster of other doctrinal emphases have been absorbed into my blood and marrow.

In this I am not alone. George Ladd missed the first graduating class at Fuller. He arrived on our campus just three months after they left, but for those who were here when he came and have continued to come during the years that he has been here, there is no one who has shaped the preaching and teaching of the men and women of Fuller more than the professor whose scholarship we admire, whose character we salute, and whose person we love. These essays are an attempt to capture in essence something of that admiration, that salute, that love.

1: Psalm 107 as "Horizon" for Interpreting the Miracle Stories of Mark 4:35-8:26

ROBERT MEYE

I

INTRODUCTION

The thesis argued in this essay is that Psalm 107 provides the "horizon" for interpreting the miracle stories of Mark's Gospel, especially the miracle stories of Mark 4:35-8:26.[1] The term "horizon" is used rather than other familiar terms such as "background" or "key" both in view of its contemporary utilization in New Testament interpretation, and its aptness for the present essay. It stands for "that which was, consciously or unconsciously, in the author's intention." Being aware of this, one is able to make proper inferences regarding the meaning of an author's material, and is guarded from improper inferences. The horizon, for all its distance or vagueness, is "there," and it is there in a certain configuration which determines our perspective on that which lies before it.[2]

It is worth belaboring the question of a proper reference point for interpretation in view of the varied, seemingly antithetical, meanings which have been attached to the miracle stories of the Gospels, and more particularly of Mark's Gospel. As we shall see, it is apparent that the miracles of Jesus were important for the evangelist of the second Gospel; the history of interpretation, particularly the more recent history, rather accentuates the question of the *meaning* Mark attached to the mighty deeds of Jesus. Although it is not the intention of this essay to provide a *Forschungsbericht,*[3] it is well to note in passing at least three representative perspectives on the "horizon" for understanding the Markan miracle stories.

The first perspective, perhaps the most important, is whether the miracle stories are to be understood within the horizon of the Hebrew scriptures, our Old Testament, and within the locus of a first-century piety which oriented its life to those scriptures, or whether the essential horizon is rather to be found within the context of Hellenistic culture and religion. Although scholars are generally aware of the manifold crossing points of these two worlds, both in geographical and in other terms, the fact is that the two worlds were *two,* and the differences were often experienced as a matter of life and death for those who worshipped the God of Israel. Rudolf

Bultmann, whose work on *The History of the Synoptic Tradition* pointed in the direction of preponderant Hellenistic influence in the shape and horizon of the gospel miracle stories, has left a legacy which, though often debated and modified, remains strong in New Testament scholarship.[4]

A second perspective, which has been widely discussed in more recent times, views the miracles of Mark as representative of an objectionable theological perspective, so far as the evangelist himself is concerned. Thus, Theodore Weeden's study *Mark: Traditions in Conflict* concludes that the evangelist Mark was engaged in a sharp polemic against an ecclesiastical group who gloried in the miraculous, were identified with the disciples of Jesus, and who, like the disciples, failed to perceive that the way of Jesus Christ and the gospel was the way of humility and suffering.[5]

A third important perspective for gaining insight into the Markan miracle stories comes from Alan Richardson's widely used study *The Miracle Stories of the Gospels.*[6] In an effort to make the strongest possible case for the theological moment of the gospel miracle stories, Richardson downgrades the element of *compassion:*

> In all the Gospels Jesus is unwilling to work miracles as mere displays, but the motive of compassion is not prominent and certainly is not primary either in the Synoptists or in St. John. . . . The truth would seem to be that the Synoptists and St. John alike present the miracles of Jesus neither as motived nor unmotived.[7]

Each of the three studies noted has been influential in the ongoing work of gospel interpretation; each would need correction if the present essay presents a valid thesis.

II

THE IMPORTANCE OF MIRACLE IN MARK'S PERSPECTIVE

Although it is commonplace in Markan study to describe Mark's Gospel as a Gospel of "the deeds of Jesus," it is well to reestablish the actual importance of miracle stories in the narrative. In terms of quantity, the emphasis is obvious: According to Alan Richardson's tally (and the tallies vary somewhat), "some 209 verses out of a total of 666" are devoted in one way or another to miracles.[8] This amounts to about a third of the Markan material—one might say, the dominant material of Mark. In the first ten chapters of the narrative (prior to Jesus' entry into Jerusalem), almost half of the material pertains to Jesus' mighty works. In other words, Mark's description of the course of Jesus' ministry is weighted heavily with miracle stories, which provide a crucial perspective from which to understand the gospel of Jesus Christ which Mark proclaims (1:1).

The miraculous works of Jesus, as Mark displays them, are greatly varied. There are extended stories, as well as the briefest summary statements. There are healings, nature miracles, the raising of a dead girl, and the feeding, on two occasions, of a great multitude. Although exorcisms represent a very specific manifestation of Jesus' power, they have a formal and substantial relationship to the miracle stories and may be included with them; the demonic power represents a disordering of one's life in the same fashion as other elements from which a person must be delivered. Through extended and varied presentation of Jesus' mighty deeds, the evangelist shows that they are a decisive manifestation of the reign of God (1:14-15); at the same time they are a display of the power of the Spirit of God (see 1:9-13; 3:22-26).

The importance of the miracles of Jesus is also underlined by the way in which they figure in the narrative structure of the Gospel. At this point, Mark 4:35-8:26 claims our attention as a discrete narrative unit. In a number of ways this narrative section is set off in Mark from that which precedes and that which follows. Rudolf Bultmann, who is skeptical regarding the presence of any patterned structure in the second Gospel, views 8:27-10:52 as a Markan unit.[9] But the case is equally strong for dividing up the material prior to 8:27 as material in which the hand of the evangelist is evident. Basically, 4:1-34 and 4:35-8:26 may be divided into two parallel sections over which one may write respectively "The Word (Parables) of Jesus" and "The Deeds of Jesus." The former has its focus on "the mystery of the kingdom" (4:10-12) in a *parabolic* setting; the latter in a setting of *miracle stories.* Although there are many ways of partitioning the Markan material, so that no one way seems wholly justified, the following paragraphs suggest the validity of viewing 4:35-8:26 as a unit.

Mark 4:35-8:26 is unique in the synoptic tradition in that it represents seventeen successive units in the parallel traditions which are present either in Matthew or in Luke. All these units but one, or possibly two, consist of miracle stories or units such as 8:14-21 whose focus is on miracle stories. There are one or two seeming surd elements, so far as any view of the unitary nature of this "section" is concerned. The long parenthesis on the death of John (6:17-29) is one such element. However, this parenthesis exists in close connection with the mention of Herod's response to the powers at work in Jesus through his disciples (6:13-16). Because of the importance of John for Mark's understanding of Jesus' ministry, Herod's name and his notice of Jesus are important points for commentary on the death of John.[10] Mark 7:1-23, with its focus on "What Defiles a Man," does not readily fit into a collection of miracle stories—and one should not force a fit where none is apparent. The safer procedure would be rather to point to the remarkable concentration on miracle, to the extent that there is only one exception (as it seems) to the rule. Those who are familiar with the abruptness of the Markan narrative and its propensity for surprises will not expect perfect symmetry and development in the narrative. On the other hand, they will be all the more impressed with evidences of narrative pattern.[11] It is to be noted that, at the least, the evangelist Mark should not be forced into modern categories of analysis—even when we are often reduced to describing him through such categories.

The importance of the miracle stories in 4:35-8:26 is made especially evident in 8:14-21, wherein Jesus shows that the cumulative impact of the two feeding miracles should have brought the disciples to an understanding, an understanding in which they are apparently woefully lacking.[12] Similarly, 6:45-52 connects the first feeding of the multitude, Jesus' walking on the water, and the stilling of the storm. Again, what is important is the implicit/explicit note that there should be a "carry-over," in terms of understanding, from one miracle to the next. This is ultimately suggested by the movement in the narrative from 4:35-41 to 8:27-31.

The narrative section begins with the question posed by the disciples: "Who then is this, that even wind and sea obey him?" (4:41). This question is not answered until the completion of the long succession of miracle stories (8:27-30). At that point, the narrative provides an analogy to the response of Herod and others to Jesus' mighty works in 6:14-16. The difference is that Jesus himself now poses the question of his identity to his disciples. They first answer the question of Jesus' identity in terms of the answers being given by others—and then are directed to answer their own question by Jesus himself: "But who do you say that I am?" (8:29*b*). Peter responds by affirming that Jesus is the Christ (8:29), in accordance with the true identity of Jesus as announced in the Gospel's superscription (1:1).

The Gospel of Mark otherwise parallels this strong stress on the role of Jesus as the Lord who is Teacher, through vocabulary, structure, themes, etc.[13] Commentaries on Mark need to be aware of the elevation of *both* the teachings *and* the miracles of Jesus as complementary manifestations in Jesus of the reign of God.

One other Markan note illustrates the urgency of miracles in Mark. In the apocalyptic discourse of chapter 13, Jesus warns the disciples concerning the future as follows: "And then if anyone says to you, 'Look, here is the Christ!' or 'Look, there he is!' do not believe it. False Christs and false prophets will arise and show signs and wonders, to lead astray, if possible, the elect" (vv. 21-22). This text makes a direct and an indirect statement about miracles. The direct statement is, of course, that false Christs will display signs and wonders. False Christs are false and dangerous precisely because they mimic the true Christ in an effort to deceive the faithful. Signs and wonders, or miracles, are thus given a christological value. The indirect statement of the text is that the route chosen by the false Christs is urgent in that it follows the dominant pattern evident in the very ministry of Jesus, as we see it displayed in the first ten chapters of Mark. This datum alone requires a major revision of Weeden's critique of miracle in Mark's Gospel.[14]

III

THE OLD TESTAMENT AS HORIZON FOR MARK: SOME GENERAL COMMENTS

Once the importance of miracle stories for Mark is established, the question of the "horizon" for their interpretation is made the more urgent. The evangelist himself provides the strongest possible indication, as we shall see, that the Old Testament scriptures, with Jesus and "the gospel" in the foreground, provide a literary and religious horizon for understanding first the miracles of Jesus, and then Jesus himself. Initially, it is well to take note of the following:

1. The dominant territorial, religious, and cultural context in which the mission of Jesus was carried out was that of a Judaism consciously ordering its life in accordance with the Hebrew scriptures enshrined in our Old Testament.

2. Jesus himself consistently interpreted his mission to Israel in relation to the Old Testament, whether directly or indirectly, typologically or literally.

3. Jesus called disciples who were conditioned by that Old Testament background, and likewise interpreted his mission to them in relation to it.

4. The disciples, and then the primitive church after Easter, interpreted Jesus' coming, death, and resurrection in terms of the promise and fulfillment of the Old Testament. There would be an initial presumption that Mark, a member of that community in terms of its confession of faith and pattern of life, would be one with it in this pattern of reference to the Old Testament.

That the Jewish scriptures did provide a horizon for Mark's understanding and presentation of Jesus in his Gospel is abundantly evident. The evangelist begins his Gospel with an extended quotation from the Old Testament (1:2-3), and he concludes by highlighting an Old Testament text (16:7; cf. 14:27 and Zech 13:7). Quotations from and references to the Old Testament abound throughout. The debates between Jesus and the religious leaders of Judaism in his time, so important in the Markan narrative, are a part of that thrust. In *The Riddle of the New Testament,* Hoskyns and Davey suggest that specific references to the Old Testament are only the tip of the iceberg.[15] Howard Clark Kee speaks of "the hundreds of allusions to and quotations from scripture that this little book contains."[16]

Is there a way of bringing together the Markan emphasis on the miracles of Jesus with his strong reference to the Old Testament? A chief problem facing the interpreter here is that of a methodology which allows one to encounter the Old Testament in its expansiveness while maintaining a manageable specificity: Where does one find a specific reference point which truly suggests that the Old Testament provided the horizon for Mark's understanding of and presentation of miracle stories? Scholars are wont to point to the Exodus events or to the Elijah stories as a likely, if not evident, horizon for understanding Mark, or at least the tradition which Mark utilizes. Without debating the merits of the two suggestions noted, the procedure followed here is rather to search for evidences of an Old Testament locus apparently familiar to the evangelist, wherein miracle stories are handled in a comparable fashion.

IV

ON ESTABLISHING PSALM 107 AS HORIZON FOR MARK'S MIRACLE STORIES

A number of clues point to the Psalms, and specifically to Psalm 107, as a horizon for Mark's miracle stories; once this possibility is tested and then attested as a thesis, the visible clues increase.

The Psalms generally figured strongly in the faith, life, and worship of the church from the very beginning. Indeed, the church inherited this pattern from Judaism before it. An example of this background is included in Mark's narrative where it is noted that the disciples and Jesus sang after table fellowship and before the departure to Gethsemane (Mark 14:26). It is probable that the songs came from the second half of the Hallel Psalms (Psalms 115ff.).[17] This familiarity with and use of the Psalms is variously reflected in the New Testament (see 1 Cor 14:15; Eph 5:19; Col 3:16). Mark was familiar with texts from the Psalter which were most important in the preaching and teaching of the church. More important, Mark specifically shows familiarity with the fifth book of the Psalter, drawing from Psalm 110 (cf. 12:36; 14:62) and Psalm 118 (11:9, 10; 12:10, 11). It is therefore of special interest to note that Psalm 107, which begins the fifth book of the Psalter (which book contains Psalms 110 and 118), is a systematic recital and interpretation of the miracles wrought by the hand of God the Lord of Israel.

Psalm 107 celebrates the mighty acts of God, the miracles experienced by the people of God. It begins with a call to thanksgiving because of the steadfast love (*chesed*) of the Lord. The redeemed of the Lord are called upon to proclaim what he has done (v. 2); he has gathered them from the lands (v. 3). The psalm then celebrates four typical experiences of deliverance in which God intervened upon hearing the cry of the people:

1. Deliverance from hunger and thirst in the wilderness (107:4-9)
2. Deliverance from dark and distressing imprisonment (107:10-16)
3. Deliverance from sickness (107:17-22)
4. Deliverance from peril at sea (107:23-32)

As Weiser's commentary on the Psalms describes it, the second part of this psalm glorified the divine saving rule which "continually manifests itself in the baffling ups and downs of life."[18] Weiser goes on to sum up its hortatory conclusion as follows:

> Prudence demands that the gracious acts of God be heeded and remembered, so that they become a lasting possession of faith . . . this parenetic warning . . . emphasizes the educational aspect of the appropriation of salvation.[19]

There is an obvious affinity between Psalm 107 and Mark 4:35-8:26. The analysis of the psalm given above is a generally valid description of the types of miracle stories presented in the Markan section. To the types of deliverance in the psalm, the following passages in Mark may be compared:

1. From hunger and thirst (6:30-44; 8:1-10, 14-21)
2. From imprisonment (5:1-20; 6:13; 7:24-30)
3. From sickness (5:21-6:5, 13, 53-56; 7:31-37; 8:22-26)
4. From peril at sea (4:35-41; 6:45-52)

With respect to the second category, namely, deliverance from dark and distressing imprisonment, it should be noted that the dominant view of demon-possession was as a sort of bondage from which one had to be released.[20]

There are other points of comparison beyond the common presentation of God, and Jesus the Son, as being mighty to deliver. It is important that the manifestation of divine power has a common object: persons in distress. There is no question of a willy-nilly display of power, as one sometimes sees in nonbiblical sources. The manifestation of divine power also has this in common, that it may happen directly through the spoken word (cf. Ps 107:20 and Mark 4:39; 5:41; 7:29).

Several other incidental points of comparison may be noted here. In Psalm 107:11 God is named "the most High"; this same name is attached to Jesus in Mark 5:7 (and only here in the entire synoptic tradition—Luke 8:28 being a parallel). Both the Psalm and the Gospel feature the name in the comparable unit, reporting the experience of deliverance from bondage. The sick in Psalm 107:17-22 can take no food, drawing near to the gates of death. After Jesus raises Jairus' daughter, he commands that she be given something to eat (5:43). In both, the great deliverance from hunger is a *community* experience, whereas the other instances of deliverance, though repeated, are the experiences of individuals. These and other notes are not unimportant suggestions—to be amplified in the following comments—that

Mark 4:35-8:26 and Psalm 107 are energized by the same spirit.

V

THE MOTIF OF COMPASSION IN PSALM 107 AND IN MARK 4:35-8:26

Psalm 107 is notable and remembered for its repeated (vv. 1, 15, 21, 31, 43) praise of God for his steadfast love (*chesed;* LXX ἔλεος). After each account of God's deliverance, there is a priestly call to praise Yahweh for his steadfast love and wonderful works (vv. 8, 15, 21, 31). Mark uses a correspondent term, in this case the verbal form ἠλέησεν (5:19), to describe what Jesus has done for the exorcised demoniac: "Go home to your friends, and tell them how much the Lord has done for you, and how he has had mercy [ἠλέησεν] on you" (5:19). Although this is the only instance where Mark 4:35-8:26 uses a cognate of ἔλεος to describe Jesus' miracles (but see 10:47, 48), the synonymous root σπλαγχ- is used in 6:34 and 8:2 (cf. also 1:43; 9:22). Helmut Koester's article on this term in the *Theological Dictionary of the New Testament* demonstrates that the roots ἐλεο- and σπλαγχ- were basically paired and synonymous Greek translations of the Hebrew *chesed* during this period, leaving the interpreter free to consider the two expressions together.[21] It is of first importance in understanding Mark that

1. Jesus' miracles are described therein by Jesus himself directly (8:2) and indirectly (5:19) in terms of compassion, and

2. Mark speaks of Jesus' miracles from the same perspective (6:34).

Mark moves far beyond the other synoptists in emphasis upon compassion as the motive for Jesus' miracles. Mark 4:38, 5:19, 6:34, and 8:2 feature the compassion motif; Matthew lacks the first two notes, and Luke lacks the first three notes and has no material paralleling the setting of the fourth reference. In view of this thrice-repeated note, not to mention other Markan notes outside this narrative section (1:43; 9:22; 10:47, 48), it simply will not do, with Richardson, to speak lightly of the motif of compassion in Jesus' miracle-working—at least with respect to the second evangelist.[22] One should be skeptical of Richardson's note that the evangelists "lived in an age unaffected by the humanistic approach and the humanitarian attitude." One should speak either of a "new humanism" in Jesus, or at least make the point that the theological and compassionate motives are not antithetical but rather linked in Jesus, on the model of Psalm 107!

VI

THE MOTIF OF UNDERSTANDING IN PSALM 107 AND MARK 4:35-8:26

There is another motif which binds the Psalm and the Gospel together. It is of the greatest importance for our analysis to note that Psalm 107 concludes with a call to *understanding.*

> *Whoever is wise, let him give heed to these things;*
> *let men consider the steadfast love of the Lord.*
> (Ps 107:43)

We may repeat the summary of Weiser:

> Prudence demands that the gracious acts of God be heeded and remembered, so that they become a lasting possession of faith . . . this parenetic warning . . . emphasizes the educational aspect of the appropriation of salvation.[23]

Psalm 107 is unique among the psalms in its parenetic conclusion (107:43), following the recapitulation of the "wonderful works" and "steadfast love" of Yahweh. Psalm 106, immediately preceding, provides a substantial and helpful parallel in its review of the salvation of God experienced by Israel:

> *Our fathers, when they were in Egypt,*
> *did not consider thy wonderful works;*
> *they did not remember the abundance of thy steadfast love,*
> *but rebelled against the Most High at the Red Sea.*
> (Ps 106:7)

Psalm 107:43, together with its counterpart in Psalm 106, parallels the parenetic statement and warning of Jesus to the disciples in Mark 8:14-21, which looks backward at the mighty deeds of Jesus displayed in the preceding part of the narrative. Here Jesus chides the disciples for their failure to remember and to understand despite their seeing and experiencing his mighty works. The same Greek word συνίημι signifying "understanding," appears in the Septuagintal translation of the Hebrew *bîn* of Psalm 107:43, and in Mark 8:17, 21. The works of Yahweh, Lord of Israel, and the works of Jesus the Christ, call forth *understanding* as their issue. The focus on understanding in Mark is pervasive, and has been especially underscored by the discussion of the so-called "messianic secret" in Mark, generated by the monograph on Mark of Wilhelm Wrede.[24] The comparability of the call to understanding gains importance in the presence of the similarities already discussed, but also, because of its uniqueness, gives the more significant weight to the comparability of those elements.

VII

OTHER PARALLELS BETWEEN PSALM 107 AND MARK 4:35-8:26

If one perceives Psalm 107 as the horizon from which Mark 4:35-8:26 is to be understood, there are yet other elements of Mark which seem to be worthy of note, at least in passing.

1. Wrede's discussion of the "messianic secret" has directed scholarly attention to the constant public disclosure of the deeds of Jesus in Mark. Such disclosures occur even when Jesus expressly commands the person healed or exorcised to keep silence. One cannot help but note that Psalm 107 calls those who have been the object of the mighty works of Yahweh to *proclaim* that fact:

O give thanks to the Lord,
for he is good;
for his steadfast love endures for ever!
Let the redeemed of the Lord say so,
whom he has redeemed from trouble
and gathered in from the lands,
from the east and from the west,
from the north and from the south.
(107:1-3)

Tell of his deeds in songs of joy!
(107:22*b*)

Let them extol him in the congregation of the people,
and praise him in the assembly of the elders.
(107:32)

The repeated and urgent call to keep silent is most meaningful when read against a horizon of expectation (as in Psalm 107) that one *should* proclaim the deed. The call to silence against the horizon of an expected proclamation has the effect of bringing the specific nature of Jesus' ministry and Messiahship into sharpest focus.

2. Mark's Gospel is notable for the fact that Jesus is always besought by the widest array of followers. Thus, Mark 3:7-8 lists in detail the areas from which people have come to Jesus: ". . . a great multitude from Galilee followed; also from Judea and Jerusalem and Idumea and from beyond the Jordan and from Tyre and Sidon a great multitude, hearing all that he did, came to him." This text has its parallels in 1:37, 45, and 7:24—to mention but a few. This dominating motif of Jesus as the sought-for redeemer has its parallel at the very outset of Psalm 107:2:

Let the redeemed of the Lord say so,
whom he has redeemed from trouble,
and gathered in from the lands,
from the east and from the west,
from the north and from the south.

Each set of texts suggests that the mighty deeds cannot be confined to a small circle, but have an ever-widening audience as their proper sphere.

This also corresponds to the Markan reflection of the universal outreach of the gospel (13:10; 14:9).

3. The cry for deliverance is typical. Neither Yahweh nor Jesus the Son of God is cast first of all in the role of seeking occasions and objects for the exercise of miraculous divine power. Rather, they respond to man's *cry* for deliverance; each biblical unit makes this abundantly clear, according to its own literary genre and statement.

VIII

PSALM 107 AS THE HORIZON FOR UNDERSTANDING MARK'S MIRACLE STORIES

Psalm 107 provides a dominant, well-profiled horizon against which to interpret Mark 4:35-8:26. Mark displays Jesus as eschatological deliverer (see esp. 1:1-15) who performs the works of the Lord God of Israel, his Father, in the time of the kingdom's manifestation. Jesus, who is presented early on as the divine Son of God (1:1)—and throughout the narrative (3:11; 5:7; 9:7; 12:6-9; 13:32; 14:61; 15:39)—is a true representation and agent of the Father. In the language of John's Gospel, the Father is working still, and Jesus is working (John 5:17). One sees and experiences in the Son the same manifestation of saving power and compassion, and, because of this, becomes object of the same urgent call to understanding.

Viewed in this light, the horizon (Psalm 107) provides the following perspectives:

1. God's action in the world has not come to an end, but was manifest in Jesus of Nazareth (1:24!), and will be manifest in Jesus the Risen Lord (16:7).

2. God, in Jesus, is mighty to deliver those who call upon him, and upon whom he has compassion (5:19!).

3. There is a unity of God's working in Israel and in Jesus, the messianic Son sent to Israel (12:1-9).

4. Jesus, the Lord, is worthy of praise and worship and faith (4:35-41!), as the Son and Redeemer come down from above (14:62!).

5. Because Jesus is identified with God as the divine Son, salvation is dependent upon obedient response to Jesus, the incarnate manifestation of the Father (see esp. 8:38; 9:7).

Mark 13, whose emphasis upon the urgent (messianic) meaning of Jesus' miracles has already been noted, gives some indication that the Christian community which the evangelist addressed was either involved in or facing imminent persecution.[25] (The question of the historicity of the material in Mark 13 does not alter this observation; what is important is that the evangelist clearly demonstrates by inclusion of this lengthy section that the church needed this exhortation from the Lord for its *present* life.) What could be more instructive or encouraging to the Markan community than to receive a gospel (proclamation) of the deeds of Jesus, the Deliverer from every kind of distress. This gospel declares that Jesus is the power over every evil power. There is no peril or evil of which Jesus is not Lord. The church has every reason to trust in Jesus, who does the works of God. In the words of the apostle Paul, "neither death, nor life, . . . nor things present, nor things to come, nor powers, nor height, nor depth, nor anything else in all creation" can separate the believer from Christ the Lord.

It is entirely likely that the Markan congregation had long since sung the praises of God, and of Jesus the Son, through the medium of Psalm 107. If early Christian history is thus conceived, then Mark's Gospel is faithful to the faith of the community, to the Old Testament horizon against which that faith was being formed, and to Jesus, who brings faith into being by his proclamation of the reign of God and his manifestation of the deed of God.

There is no need to scour heaven and earth looking for the appropriate historical setting, or horizon, for understanding the deeds of Jesus in Mark. The effort to understand the *Markan* Jesus in terms of Hellenistic "divine man" categories is historically interesting, important, and instructive, but ultimately of secondary value. (One could say that it is Mark's intention to point beyond such categories to the true categories for understanding Jesus.) Whether consciously or unconsciously, the Psalm provided the evangelist and the Christian community a horizon for understanding Jesus' miracles which both invited and commanded attention.

Faith in Jesus was enriched, and hope in him was made strong, as Jesus' ministry was viewed against the horizon of Psalm 107. The rule of interpretation, then and now, was provided by the evangelist in Mark 4:24:

> *The measure you give will be the measure you get,*
> *and still more will be given to you.*

IX

SOME CONCLUDING REMARKS

Even though Markan commentators over many decades have sporadically taken note of parallels between elements in Mark and Psalm 107, most of the harvest has remained standing in the field. Almost certainly, much remains to be gleaned, if not harvested. At the very least, the preceding study suggests that whatever the value of extrabiblical sources and references may be, interpreters must continue to focus on scripture as the richest, and ultimate, horizon for the interpretation of scripture. In so doing, they will receive understanding in the measure they give attention to that word. The two testaments continue to illuminate each other, and reveal the wisdom embodied in the faith of the church which received both into one canon. That one canon is *the* horizon for biblical interpretation.

Notes to Chapter 1

1. This essay has been presented in earlier configurations to the Chicago Society of Biblical Research and the Institute for Biblical Research.
2. For a discussion of this term in New Testament studies see Howard Clark Kee, *Community of the New Age: Studies in Mark's Gospel* (Philadelphia: Westminster, 1977) 1-3. The quotations are from E. D. Hirsch's study, *Validity in Interpretation* (New Haven: Yale University, 1967) 222-223.
3. For such a study, see Hendrick van der Loos, *The Miracles of Jesus* (Leiden: Brill, 1965).
4. Rudolf Bultmann, *The History of the Synoptic Tradition* (Oxford: Blackwell, 1963) esp. 239-240, 346-347.
5. Theodore Weeden, *Mark: Traditions in Conflict* (Philadelphia: Westminster, 1971). For a strong rejoinder to Weeden's conclusions, see William Lane, *"THEIOS ANER* Christology and the Gospel of Mark," in *New Dimensions in New Testament Study* (edd. Richard N. Longenecker and Merrill C. Tenney; Grand Rapids: Zondervan, 1974) 144-161.
6. Alan Richardson, *The Miracle Stories of the Gospels* (London: SCM, 1959) 31.
7. Ibid., 31. See William Lane, *The Gospel According to Mark* (*NICNT;* Grand Rapids: Eerdmans, 1974) 176-177.
8. Ibid., 36.
9. Weeden, *Traditions,* 350.
10. The so-called "sandwich" style in the Markan narrative has often been noted.
11. For a more recent example of interpreting Mark in terms of a well-developed structural pattern see the work of the late Norman Perrin in *Christology and a Modern Pilgrimage* (ed. Hans Dieter Betz; Claremont: New Testament Colloquium, 1971) 1-78.
12. There is adequate base to develop a more extended study of the parallel between Mark 4:10-12 and Mark 8:14-21. Each underlines the point that an encounter with Jesus (whether in word or deed) so reveals Jesus that one's openness in that encounter becomes the measure for true understanding in any future encounter (see esp. 4:24-25).
13. For extended discussion of the didactic element in the Gospel of Mark, see Robert P. Meye, *Jesus and the Twelve* (Grand Rapids: Eerdmans, 1968).
14. Weeden, *Traditions,* 70-100, does not address the explicit and implicit understanding evident in Mark 13:21-22.
15. Sir Edwyn Hoskyns and Noel Davey, *The Riddle of the New Testament* (London: Faber and Faber, 1958) 60-62.
16. Kee, *Community,* 45-49.
17. See Lane, *Mark,* 509.
18. Arthur Weiser, *The Psalms* (*OTL;* Philadelphia: Westminster, 1962) 687.
19. Ibid., 688.
20. See Lane, *Mark,* 143.
21. Helmut Koester, "σπλάγχνον," *TDNT* 7 (1971) 552.
22. Richardson, *Miracle Stories,* 32.
23. Weiser, *Psalms,* 688.
24. Wilhelm Wrede, *The Messianic Secret* (Cambridge: J. Clark, 1971).
25. On this see Ralph Martin, *Mark: Evangelist and Theologian* (Grand Rapids: Zondervan, 1973) 164-166; and Lane, *Mark,* 12-17.

2: The Pericope of the Healing of the "Centurion's" Servant/Son (Matt 8:5-13 par. Luke 7:1-10): Some Exegetical Notes

RALPH P. MARTIN

Writing in a book that has been hailed as opening a new era in evangelical biblical studies, George Ladd invites his readers to consider the following passages of the New Testament:

> If the reader opens two Bibles to . . . the healing of the centurion's servant in Matthew 8:5-13 and Luke 7:1-10, he will find both a striking identity of wording, accompanied by numerous variations, particularly in the addition or omission of material. Thus Luke 7:3-5 is lacking in the parallel account in Matthew; Matthew 8:11-12 is not found in the parallel passage in Luke 7, but in Luke 13:29-30.[1]

This short essay proposes to take a second look at this gospel section, and to ask some obvious questions in the hope that the exegetical task that confronts the modern interpreter may be, at least partially, illuminated.

I

THE PROBLEM

In fact, as we come to this gospel pericope we encounter not one single problem but a group of difficulties, all of which are closely related to the question of the central issue of the passage's exegesis.

First, there are some textual problems which on the surface appear easily disposed of, for the MSS readings with their slight variations are sufficiently homogeneous to require no extended comment. There is one exception, however; at Matthew 8:10*b* the original texts read, "With no one [else] in Israel have I found such faith"[2] in place of "Not even in Israel have I found such faith."

Two points of translation also need mention. What was the exact designation of the Roman officer's rank: centurion or chiliarch? G. Zuntz argues for the latter.[3] And, more importantly for the exegetical task before us, what value is to be accorded to the preposition ὑπό in the phrase ὑπὸ ἐξουσίαν, especially in the light of the Lukan expansion (at 7:8, which reads ὑπὸ ἐξουσίαν τασσόμενος). Again, Zuntz[4] submits that the evidence of the Syriac versions is decisive in showing that the earliest recoverable form of what the centurion said was represented by the Aramaic phrase *bᵉšûlṭānā'* ("having authority"). The full statement would be translated into Greek as ἄνθρωπός εἰμι ἐν ἐξουσίᾳ, in which the phrase ἐν ἐξουσίᾳ means quite simply, "I am a man *having authority,*"[5] with the following addition "and have soldiers under my hand." The Greek translator of Q has misunderstood this idiom and rendered the semitic phrase by ὑπὸ ἐξουσίαν. It is Luke who then makes the man utter two strangely conflicting statements by the addition of τασσόμενος, namely, Luke thought that "under authority" meant "having superiors over me," and completed the sentence with ὑπὸ ἐξουσίαν τασσόμενος. If this conclusion is sound, it indicates one further sign of Luke's editorializing work on a *Vorlage* which is better represented in Matthew.

Then, as a minor point of translation difficulty, we may raise the issue of the punctuation of the sentence ἐγὼ ἐλθὼν θεραπεύσω αὐτόν in Matthew 8:7, where there is general agreement that the sentence should be in the interrogative: "Am I to come and heal him?"[6] The decisive argument in favor of this view is that only as an astonished question on the part of Jesus, who is thus asked to enter the house of the Gentile and so incur defilement, does the emphatic ἐγώ gain significance[7] and the renewed appeal in verse 8 make sense.

But the vital question is that forced upon us by the parallel accounts, with their verbal identity in part,[8] and yet their peculiarities both in emphasis and wording. As a test-case for the resolution of the synoptic problem, this passage is often praised as a classic demonstration of a common source, and it stands out as unique as the only narrative portion in Q. Vincent Taylor and Alan Richardson classify it as a paradigm rather than a miracle story. The punch-line, which is the saying recorded in Matthew 8:10 (cf. Luke 7:9), seems, however, to be the climax of what is better classified as a pronouncement story.[9]

The points of distinctiveness within the two accounts can be quickly tabulated.

1. Matthew is consistent with his use of παῖς for the sufferer, while Luke varies between παῖς (v. 7, Q) and δοῦλος (normally), and "in *v.* 8 the centurion speaks of his 'slave' as if the slave were another person than his 'boy'."[10] But we should note that δοῦλος and ἄξιος are Lukan terms,[11] while παῖς and ἱκανός are preferred in those passages where Matthew and Luke overlap (i.e., in Q). It seems that we should interpret the centurion's παῖς as his son (as in John 4:46-54, which has several interchangeable terms for the nobleman's needy one),[12] for it is unlikely that a Roman official would show great concern for a subordinate, especially in view of his own confession of possessing authority. Luke has justified his preference for δοῦλος by adding ὃς ἦν αὐτῷ ἔντιμος, so "boy" is to be taken in the military sense of subaltern, "batman."[13]

2. In Matthew's account the Roman comes personally to Jesus and addresses him face to face, whereas in Luke the elders of the Jews are the intermediaries who carry the request with a special recommendation of clemency and favor. Presumably they shared the conviction that Jesus could be prevailed upon to help and had the power to heal. If so, their part hardly tallies with the comment of Jesus that the centurion's faith was unrivalled in Israel. We must ask why they are introduced.

The same difficulty is posed by the role played by the "friends" whom the centurion sends (7:6) before Jesus can reach his house. They relate the centurion's message, using direct speech in a way that leads Wellhausen to comment that it seems as if they have committed to memory the centurion's personal confession of unworthiness.[14]

3. The center of interest in the two stories is different. In Matthew the focus of attention is the man's personal faith, on which Jesus passes the encomium of verse 10 with a note of amazement. His efficacious faith is commended again in verse 13. In the Lukan version faith is not accented, but the reader's interest is attracted to the man's sense of unworthiness and the key phrase lies in verse *7a:* διὸ οὐδὲ ἐμαυτὸν ἠξίωσα πρὸς σὲ ἐλθεῖν (L), i.e., the unworthiness and disadvantage of being a Gentile are stressed.[15]

4. Certain amplifications in Matthew contribute to the purpose of this evangelist. For instance, he adds μόνον to Q's ἀλλὰ εἰπὲ λόγῳ, and so emphasizes the importance of the Gentile's confidence in the mere utterance of Jesus.[16] The Gentile leader, unlike the Jews, seeks no confirming sign or visible prop for his faith. Then, as though to indict unbelieving Israel for its faithless desire for legitimating signs (Matt 12:38-42; 16:1-4), Matthew inserts verses 11 and 12, which are found in another context in Luke at 13:28, 29.

II

SOME PROPOSED SOLUTIONS

1. Bultmann's form-critical approach can find no basis for this story in fact. The scenes, he says, are imaginary and are the creation of the church. Even if there were a modicum of historical value, it would be unhistorical to give credence to telepathic healing![17]

2. Attempts at harmonization are not without their difficulties. G. Zuntz comments that the desire to fit the narratives into a coherent whole is a most fertile source of corruption in the transmission of the text, and he dryly remarks that theological motivation has played its part in seeking to secure a verbally exact and consistent account, with all the difficulties ironed out.[18]

J. N. Geldenhuys[19] endeavors to bring the two accounts together by proposing that both accounts tell the same story, but in lesser (Matthew) and greater (Luke) detail. He suggests that, first, the delegation of the elders went to Jesus, to be followed later by the Roman himself, so that both records preserve a part of the whole. Similarly, in the note in the *New Bible Commentary*[20] the legal principle (traced to Augustine, *De consensu evangelistarum* 2.20) *qui per alios facit, ipse facit* is invoked, and it is submitted that the Greek ἀποκριθεὶς . . . ἔφη (Matt 8:8) means not that the man himself said anything, but that the report of his statement was relayed to Jesus by the elders mentioned in Luke. Matthew 11:3 is called in as a supporting witness of this use of the verb "to say"; but the use of ἀποκριθείς is decisively against this attempt at harmonization. The commentator's remark that "the centurion was not personally present" in verse 8 is difficult to reconcile with verse 13, where Jesus speaks to him as though he were there.

In another attempt at dovetailing the two narratives, Z. C. Hodges[21] endeavors to secure what he calls "an absolute harmony" between the two accounts. This entails, on his self-admission, a reading of the two versions as consecutive, so that the Lukan narrative (7:1-8) breaks off at verse 8, at which point Matthew's narrative (8:5*b*-9) is to be inserted. But this arrangement of the text requires that Jesus must speak the same words twice, first to the people who followed (Luke 7:9) and then (Matt 8:10) to the same group once the centurion had joined them. The Matthean insertion must then be interlaced with the Lukan account in view of the divergent endings of the two accounts (Matt 8:13: the centurion is bidden to return; Luke 7:10: the delegation of Jewish elders returns to verify the healing). This attempted harmonization is weakened by recourse to a psychologizing explanation, which professes to read into the centurion's *psyche* by suggesting that he changed his mind several times as a "man of vacillation and uncertainty" and that he did *not* return as he was bidden to do.[22] This attempt only confirms our impression that the writer is seeking to do the impossible, namely, to force the scriptural verses into a preconceived mold of precise harmony by an illegitimate filling of *lacunae* and by imaginative reconstruction.

3. So, it must be fairly stated that the two versions are not in verbal agreement, nor can they justifiably be run together without forcing the data. And they are thus disparate[23] because their *motives* are different. The intention of the evangelists is one of selective emphasis,[24] each writer inserting and highlighting the details which will give point and purpose to his overruling theological *Tendenz*.

III

CONCLUSION

A conclusion from the data would then be as follows. Luke's account is clearly secondary, and his detail of the elders and friends who act as intermediaries is given, not primarily to pick up the theme of the Gentiles' indebtedness to Israel,[25] but to give an independent attestation of the Roman's integrity, worthiness, and humility as a part of his (that is, Luke's) interest in presenting the Gentiles in a favorable light.[26] He has an eye on a ruling purpose, stated in his preface (Luke 1:1-4), to commend the Christian message to Theophilus. But, at a deeper level, in order to endorse the legitimacy of the preaching to the Gentiles, he wants to demonstrate how the church of his generation came genetically out of "true Israel," of which this Gentile soldier, like Cornelius in Acts, is an illustrious example (cf. Acts 10:34, 35). Luke has phrased the Lord's word in 7:9 in a way that could conceivably be an implied compliment to Israel: "Not even in Israel (where I would most expect it) have I found such faith." Matthew's version of this logion (8:10: "With no one in Israel have I found such faith") is radically different, and leaves no room for a complimentary attitude to the Jews. It is in keeping with Matthew's emphasis on the failure of Israel to respond to the Messiah's call and claim (Matt 8:12).[27]

The Matthean account is most markedly emphatic in the special *Tendenz* which the evangelist has sought to underline. Chiefly by his accentuation of faith in Jesus' naked word and by his addition of the universalistic verses 11 and 12 he is a champion of the Pauline gospel. As the Gentiles were crowding into the church of his day, he finds in the teaching and actions of Jesus in this Gentile-oriented story precisely the emphases which were needed. We may remark on the way in which his addition of μόνον and his conclusion at verse 10 correspond to the Pauline *sola fide*, and his citation of verses 11 and 12 (as illuminated by the Old Testament and rabbinical metaphors of the eschatological pilgrimage of the Gentiles[28] to the Mount of God at the time of the Last Judgment)[29] is calculated *both* to defend the gospel against the bitter insinuations of Jewish and Jewish-Christian particularism which was opposing the entry into the church of uncircumcised Gentiles *and* to justify the rejection of Israel which was still insisting on signs (1 Cor 1:22) and had thereby cut itself off from the divine purpose. In fact, these two developments of (a) Gentile interest and inclusion within God's covenant (Matt 2:1-12; 4:15; 12:18, 21; 13:38; 21:43; 22:9, 10; 28:18-20), and (b) Jewish rejection and exclusion from the kingdom (Matt 3:9, 10; 8:11, 12; 21:43; 22:7, 8; 27:25) proceed *pari passu* throughout the Matthean Gospel. These data are some additional evidence for N. A. Dahl's thesis, so succinctly stated in terms of Matthew's church as composed of liberalized Jewish-Christians who saw that "God's people of the new covenant is the church embracing all nations," because in God's design the gospel produces a church which is "not Jewish-Christian, but universal."[30]

Notes to Chapter 2

1. G. E. Ladd, *The New Testament and Criticism* (Grand Rapids: Eerdmans, 1967) 126-127.
2. Παρ' οὐδενὶ τοσαύτην πίστιν ἐν τῷ 'Ισραὴλ or its equivalent is read in B W it sy[c pal hark. marg.] sah boh fam 1 22 892 a g1 k q.

The implication is that there was not one example of this kind of faith present in the nation, and this Gentile believer in his uniqueness is held up to praise and to the condemnation of Israel.

The reading offered in the other body of witnesses (Byzantine texts, ℵ C, and most of the Latin and Syriac versions) conforms to Luke 7:9, reading οὐδὲ ἐν τῷ 'Ισραὴλ in place of παρ' οὐδενί. The standard comparison is less severe, and the former reading may even contain a tribute to the man as exemplifying such faith as Jesus expected to find within the Jewish nation. It says nothing about the presence or absence of faith, and this reading probably reflects Luke's redaction of the Matthean "radicalized form" (W. Grundmann, *Das Evangelium nach Matthäus* [*HKNT* 1; Berlin: Evangelische Verlaganstalt, 1968] 252).

In this way Luke has made it possible to include the faith of "the elders" and the "friends" (7:6), who presumably shared the Gentile's confidence in Jesus' ability to heal. The alternative Matthean reading demonstrates the tendency to osmosis with the "easier reading," and it attempts to soften the stark original form: παρ' οὐδενὶ τοσαύτην πίστιν, κτλ (see H. Schürmann, *Das Lukasevangelium* [*HTKNT* III; Freiburg: Herder, 1969] 397).

3. G. Zuntz, "The 'Centurion' of Capernaum and his Authority (Matth. VIII. 5-13)," *JTS* 46 (1945) 183-190 (reprinted in *Opuscula Selecta: Classica, Hellenistica, Christiana* [Manchester: University Press, 1972] 181-188). The pagination that follows is that of Zuntz's collected essays.

His argument is that χιλίαρχος (chiliarch) (which is attested by sy[s] and sy[hark. marg.], Eusebius, Ps.-Clem., and Hilary [*quidam tribunus*]) represents a rank higher than ἑκατοντάρχος (centurion) and that the wide distribution of its attestation as well as its suitability to indicate a man of commanding authority (once the additional phrase ὑπὸ ἐξουσίαν τασσόμενος is understood as a Lukan expansion) argues in favor of the presence of "an original text which has escaped the overpowering tendency to harmonize Matthew and Luke" (p. 185).

Luke, with his ὑπὸ ἐξουσίαν τασσόμενος, has "demoted" the Roman soldier whose higher rank should be restored in our translations. We may, however, continue to use the familiar term "centurion" without placing it in quotation marks where they are strictly required, as in the title of this essay.

4. Zuntz, "The 'Centurion'," 182-183. M. Black, *An Aramaic Approach to the Gospels and Acts* (3rd ed.; Oxford: Clarendon, 1967) 158-159, is in agreement independently.
5. As noted by J. Jeremias, *Jesus' Promise to the Nations* (*SBT* 1/24; London: SCM, 1958) 30 n. 4. Jeremias' later discussion in his *New Testament Theology: The Proclamation of Jesus* (New York: Scribners, 1971) II, 163-164, pursues a different tack. His later conclusion emphasizes the centurion's modesty in spite of his claim to authority—a paradoxical association, to be sure, and not cogent in the Lukan context.
6. So R. Bultmann, *The History of the Synoptic Tradition* (Oxford: Blackwell, 1963) 38; H. J. Held, "St. Matthew's Understanding of the Law," *Tradition and Interpretation in Matthew* (edd. G. Bornkamm *et al.;* Philadelphia: Westminster, 1963) 194-195; and J. Jeremias, *Jesus' Promise,* 30, who observes that the sentence is to be read as a question in the light of (1) John 4:48, and (2) Luke's recasting of the narrative introduction in order to eliminate the refusal of Jesus, which is in turn countered by the Gentile's persistent plea (Matt 10:8). This snatch of lifelike dialogue, comparable with Matthew 15:21-28/Mark 7:24-30, is absent from Luke, for whom the Gentile is accounted "worthy," if not in his own eyes, then at least in the esteem of the Jewish elders (vv. 4, 5), and Jesus does not delay to come (v. 6).
7. The point at issue in the question of defilement is emphasized in the centurion's perception: "Lord, I am not worthy that *you should enter my roof.*" This sentiment is repeated in Luke 7:6 (Q), but then transformed in verse 7: "nor did I esteem myself worthy (cf. v. 4) *to come to you,*" to explain why there is no direct contact between Jesus and the Gentile.
8. The close correspondence is seen in Matthew 8:6-10/Luke 7:6*b*-9 (the dialogue section). But even here there are significant changes, usually in the direction of Luke's alterations and additions to a *Vorlage* which is more faithfully (because more consistently) preserved in Matthew's account.

9. Taylor, *The Formation of the Gospel Tradition* (2nd ed.; London: Macmillan, 1935) 75; A. Richardson, *The Miracle Stories in the Gospels* (London: SCM, 1941) 78 n. 1. M. Dibelius, *From Tradition to Gospel* (London: Clarke, 1971 repr.) 244-245, thinks that the original Q story had little narrative, not even a mention of the cure. But this suggestion seems implausible, since the point of the Gentile's faith is that it is rewarded. However, the miracle element is not emphasized in the synoptic tradition where the reader's interest centers on the Gentile's faith. In the Johannine version, in keeping with the purpose of that Gospel, the locus of faith is shifted (John 4:46-54) and the climactic logion is omitted, thus diminishing the Gentile interest, and heightening the miraculous element (e.g., it is seen in the mention of actual death implied in John 4:47, 49, 50, 53, in place of near-death in Luke 7:2 and "grievously tormented" in Matt 8:6. John 4:50, 53 recall 1 Kings 17:23, and this shows Jesus' word to be a formula by which the dead are raised to life).

10. T. W. Manson, *The Sayings of Jesus* (London: SCM, 1949) 64. But this is by no means certain, since δοῦλος has already been used in verse 2 of the sufferer. It is more interesting to see the parallel with John 4:47-54 where the nobleman's son (υἱός) is called also παῖς (4:51) and παιδίον (4:49) in an account which Manson regarded as a later version of the synoptic pericope. One reason why παῖς in Q may well be a translation-equivalent of παιδίον/υἱός (in John) is provided if we postulate an underlying semitic term (*'ebed*).

On the entire question of the relation between the synoptic pericope and the Johannine story, see the judicious discussion of R. Schnackenburg, *The Gospel According to St. John* (*HTCNT;* New York: Herder, 1968) I, 464-477, concluding that the assumption that both sets of narrative portray a common story is "highly probable" (p. 475). For a *Forschungsbericht,* see E. F. Siegman, "St. John's Use of the Synoptic Material," *CBQ* 30 (1968) 182-198.

11. And it is part of Luke's style to ring the changes stylistically by substituting closely similar or synonymous terms. See H. J. Cadbury's list of examples in "Four Features of Lucan Style" in *Studies in Luke-Acts: Essays in Honor of Paul Schubert* (edd. Leander E. Keck and J. Louis Martyn; London: SPCK, 1968) 87-102, esp. 93-94.

The peculiarity of Lukan usage would support once again the originality of Matthew's consistent use of παῖς (from Q). Perhaps Luke's intention in departing from the Q designation was to highlight the military aspect of the centurion-slave relationship, in keeping with an underlying purpose to draw the parallel between the story here and that involving another Gentile centurion, Cornelius. See in particular Acts 10:1 (a centurion), 10:2, 22 (a Gentile God-fearer, pious and generous), 10:22 (well-spoken of by the entire Jewish people), and 10:24 (having "friends"). Then, the bond mentioned in 7:2 of a slave "who was valued by him" (see C. F. Hogg, "Luke VII. 2," *ExpTim* 29 [1917/18] 475) is meant to soften the harshness that otherwise could be associated with δοῦλος, a term in the sociological sense Luke avoids in the Acts of the Apostles.

12. See n. 10.

13. Batman: "an orderly of a British military officer" (Webster's *Dictionary*).

14. J. Wellhausen, *Das Evangelium Lucas* (Berlin: Reimer, 1904) *ad loc.* Moreover, Luke has recorded these words for recital at a later point in the narrative (cf. J. M. Creed, *The Gospel According to St. Luke* [London: Macmillan, 1930] 100). They are prefaced by "Lord, do not trouble yourself" (v. 6*c*, L). With this change of person in the verb a Markan influence (from Mark 5:35; cf. Luke 8:49) has been suspected. See T. Schramm, *Der Markus-Stoff bei Lukas* (*SNTSMS* 14; Cambridge: University Press, 1971) 42-43.

But when Jesus hears the transmitted message (although set in the form of *oratio recta*), he speaks as though the centurion were personally present (v. 9)—a fact denied by verse 10. We may contrast Matthew 8:13 where the centurion is personally on the scene to hear Jesus' words.

15. This conclusion is clinched by the Lukan insertion of αὐτόν into the statement of Jesus' reaction: "He marvelled (ἐθαύμασεν) *at him.*" The verb is found only once again in the synoptic tradition (Mark 6:6, used there in reference to Jesus' utter astonishment at the absence of faith among his kinsfolk: See R. P. Martin, *Mark: Evangelist and Theologian* [Grand Rapids: Zondervan, 1973] 124).

16. As Calvin recognized ("he believes that He can heal his servant by His Word alone," *A Harmony of the Gospels* [Grand Rapids: Eerdmans, 1972] I, 249); see too J. Schniewind, *Das Evangelium nach Matthäus* (*NTD* 2; Göttingen: Vandenhoeck & Ruprecht, 1964) 109.

In that the Gentile recognizes the efficacy of Jesus' word he is ranged with "true Israel," even if it is not warrantable to read into his self-confession (οὐκ εἰμὶ ἱκανός κτλ) a tacit confession of belief in Jesus' Messiahship, as K. Rengstorf, "ἱκανός," *TDNT* 3 (1965) 294-295, wishes to do. Simple confidence in Jesus' word stands opposed to Jewish unbelief in Matthew, whereas in John the official's trust in Jesus' word (4:50, 53) may be a polemic against a false faith that despises the earthly Jesus and seeks a sign, not Jesus himself. But this is not the same kind of sign as was required by the Jewish enemies of Jesus in the synoptics. That was an accrediting "sign." In John, false faith is "something" that takes the place of Jesus, the gift rather than the giver (so E. Schweizer, "Die Heilung des Königlichen, Joh. 4, 46-54," *EvT* II [1951-52] 64-71, esp. 69-70).

17. Bultmann, *History,* 39. It was this kind of skeptical treatment that gave form criticism a bad reputation, since it lost an opportunity to exploit constructively the gains of the new approach to the Gospels, and turned precipitately to an excessively negative attitude to the historical question. There are signs that some of the more extreme judgments in the latter area are being reevaluated. See E. Earle Ellis, "New Directions in Form Criticism," *Jesus Christus in Historie und Theologie: Festschrift for H. Conzelmann,* ed. G. Strecker; Tübingen: Mohr, 1975) 299-315, esp. 300.

18. G. Zuntz, "The 'Centurion,'" 186.

19. J. N. Geldenhuys, *Commentary on the Gospel of Luke* (*NICNT;* Grand Rapids: Eerdmans, 1950) 220. He concludes: "the two Gospels supplement each other."

20. *The New Bible Commentary* (edd. F. Davidson *et al.;* London: Tyndale, 1953) 783. In the revised edition (edd. D. Guthrie, J. A. Motyer *et al.*; 1970, 826) no such dovetailing process is recognized and it is conceded that "each [evangelist] has given the setting in his own words."

21. Z. C. Hodges, "The Centurion's Faith in Matthew and Luke," *BibS* 121 (1964) 321-332.

22. See Hodges, "The Centurion's Faith," 331-332; cf. Schürmann's comment (*Das Lukasevangelium*, 393) on the attempt at psychologizing. It is a procedure that marred the *Leben Jesu* school of liberal Protestantism.

23. Their individual distinctiveness is so pronounced, as we have observed, that some reason(s) must be found for the several ways in which they diverge from each other. This search for reasons to account for the individual *Tendenz* of the evangelists is the task set before the gospel student in the era of *Redaktionsgeschichte.* For what criticism that does not avail itself of *redaktionsgeschichtlich* insights makes of this story, see H. van der Loos, *The Miracles of Jesus* (*NovTSup* 9; Leiden: Brill, 1965) 530-550. And for the maximum value to be gleaned from the various *Tendenzen* in the three accounts (Matt, Luke, John), see E. Haenchen, "Faith and Miracle," *SE* (*TU* 73; Berlin: Akademie Verlag, 1959) 495-498.

24. To use B. Reicke's phrase in his *The Gospel of Luke* (London: SPCK, 1965) 72-74.

25. As A. Richardson, *The Miracle Stories*, 79, suggests.

26. See S. G. Wilson, *The Gentiles and the Gentile Mission in Luke-Acts* (*SNTSMS* 23; Cambridge: University Press, 1973) 31-32. He comments on how closely Luke's narrative parallels the story of Cornelius. See earlier, n. 11. Luke, he believes, is interested in both stories in establishing the right of the Gentile mission on the basis of the evangelist's pragmatic approach to the Jew-Gentile problem in Acts.

27. As George Ladd also observes (*Jesus and the Kingdom* [New York: Harper and Row, 1964] 243-245), where the Matthean texts are cited. He concludes: "The Jewish nation which has rejected the offer of the Kingdom of God has therefore been set aside as the people of God and is to be replaced by a new people" (p. 245).

For the universalism implied in "the sons of the kingdom" being thrown into outer darkness, see P. Richardson, *Israel in the Apostolic Church* (*SNTSMS* 10; Cambridge: University Press, 1969) 59, who argues that Israel's rejection is not absolute. Presumably the patriarchs are still inside the banqueting hall to receive the "many" who enter, but those who do enjoy the feast are there, not on the basis of natural privilege but as true sons of Abraham (Matt 3:7-9)—a typical Pauline statement (Rom 2:28, 29; Gal 3:29).

28. We are dissenting at this point from Dahl's one-sided conclusion (*Das Volk Gottes* [Oslo: J. Dybwad, 1941] 150) that Matthew 8:11, 12 speaks exclusively of Israel's judgment. The other side is surely implied, namely, that Israel's refusal to hear opens the door to a mission to non-Jews.

29. See the data in J. Jeremias, *Jesus' Promise,* 62-63: "The fact that the Gentiles participate with the patriarchs in the Messianic feast indicates that they have been incorporated into the people of God at the consummation of all things. . . . To sit at table with them no longer causes defilement." The last thought reverts to Matthew 8:7 ("Am I to come and heal him?"), and shows how Jewish exclusiveness is at an end in the gospel age and how Jesus' mission, in Matthew's church, embraces those whom the Jews regarded as ritually impure. The connection between 8:7 and 8:11, 12 also indicates how Matthew has kept the Q logion in its logical place (contrast Luke 13:28, 29, which says nothing about Jew-Gentile tensions; it derives from Luke's tradition: see I. H. Marshall, *Luke: Historian and Theologian* [Grand Rapids: Zondervan, 1970] 140-141). And the order of events in Matthew (Gentiles included; the sons of the kingdom cast out) is inverted in Luke 13:28-29. See my essay in *Int* 30 (1976) 375.
30. N. A. Dahl, "Die Passionsgeschichte bei Matthäus," *NTS* 2 (1955-56) 17-32, esp. 23.

3: A Study of John 1:14

EVERETT F. HARRISON

The fourth Gospel is such a well-explored area, particularly its Prologue, that one might well ask, Why should it be investigated yet once more? Why not move off the beaten track and find some neglected nook of scripture and delve into it with the zest of a discoverer? The reason is fairly evident. Where the trees are well marked one may be confident that the trail leads to abundant treasure. Furthermore, students of the fourth Gospel are well aware that this portion of the gospel tradition exemplifies to an unusual degree the ingredients of unity and diversity which the title of the present volume invites the reader to expect.

In recent years there has been much discussion about the form of the Prologue and about its integrity. This is not the place to investigate such matters in any detail. One may grant the possibility that this portion should be understood as a hymn and that it may have been used in the worship of the ancient church. Further, it may have been composed after the body of the Gospel was written. If so, this could help to explain the allusion to John the Baptist, which need not then be regarded as an interpolation but rather as deliberate preparation for the more explicit information about the forerunner and his work that is supplied in the following chapters.

Although our study is primarily centered on a single verse, which can with some justice be considered the key verse of the Prologue, it is impossible to deal with this segment without reference to the remainder of the passage and indeed in some measure to the entire Gospel. In addition, other portions of the New Testament and even of the Old can hardly be ignored if we are to gain the proper focus on some key words and concepts.

Central to the Prologue is the term λόγος. Used as a personal designation, it is confined in New Testament usage to the Johannine literature (Luke 1:2 is not an exception). The four occurrences can be set out in this arrangement: (1) as pre-existent (John 1:1), (2) as becoming incarnate (1:14), (3) as encountered in his earthly life and ministry (1 John 1:1-3), and (4) as coming again in triumph (Rev 19:13). This progression need not be taken as certain evidence for the comparative dating of the books in question, though this may well have been the order in which the various documents appeared.

Since the Greek language has another term for "word," namely, ῥῆμα, one that is used not infrequently in the New Testament, it is in order to inquire why λόγος alone stands in the passages we have noted. While there is some overlapping in usage, the basic difference lies in the fact that ῥῆμα is the suitable term for indicating a statement, whereas λόγος stresses meaning. The latter is therefore the more suitable vehicle for indicating revelation, which is John's concern in the Prologue.

This term also had the advantage of being familiar to students of Greek philosophy, where it had long been used in the sense of principle or reason, the integrating element in the cosmos, the mind or soul of the universe that gives order and cohesion to the whole. Philo also made generous use of the word, giving it the nuance of mediation. The inacessible, incomprehensible Deity needs the λόγος (which Philo equated with many things) in order to have relationship to and exercise control over the world without having to come into direct contact with it. Genesis 1 introduces the various stages of creation with the phrase, "And God said." Apparently out of this background developed the concept of the word as the medium of God's will and activity in creation (Ps 33:6; Isa 55:11). The divine word was dynamic. It produced whatever was announced (Gen 1:3). More fully developed was the notion of wisdom as an intermediary between God and the world, created by God before heaven and earth were formed (Prov 8:22-31). However, no creative activity is postulated here for wisdom. There are hints of such a function in the intertestamental literature (Wis 8:4; Sir 1:9). Something that on the surface appears to resemble Johannine thought occurs in the Hermetica: "Holy art thou, who by the word (λόγος) hast constructed all that is" (Poimandres 31). Summarizing the λόγος concept in the Poimandres, C. H. Dodd describes it as "the spoken word or command of God. . . . The Hermetist is acquainted with the doctrine that the world was created by the Son of God, His Logos, and he is prepared to accept that doctrine, but only in the sense that he carefully defines, that a word is the offspring of a mind."[1] The Hermetic literature dates from a time somewhat later than the New Testament and doubtless owes something to that source, especially to the fourth Gospel.

From this brief survey it is apparent that when John wrote, both Jew and Gentile were familiar with the concept of λόγος in its mediatorial aspect. It is equally apparent that John went beyond his predecessors and contemporaries by claiming for his λόγος figure actual being, indeed, divine and eternal being. In him was creative power, an expression of his self-existence shared with God. Beyond the furthest reaches of the past, he was not only in fellowship with God but was God. Here in the opening verse of his Gospel, by the device of using θεός without the article, John announces the deity of the λόγος and at the same time avoids confusing him with God the Father, which could not be the case anyway, since the λόγος was *with*

God. John is not indulging in theologizing, but giving expression to what he has learned through personal contact with Jesus of Nazareth. "Before Abraham was, I am" (8:58). The sphere of time and finitude has been entered by the timeless and the infinite.

Moving on now to verse 14, it is helpful to observe that John describes the coming of the λόγος into the world not as a birth, in the fashion of Matthew and Luke, but as an incarnation. He is one with them regarding the central fact of the emergence of a new life that could be identified as Jesus of Nazareth, but he presents the matter differently, leaving aside the details of time and place, of circumstances and personalities involved. Yet his account is fully congruent with the truth contained in Matthew 1:23: Jesus is Emmanuel, God with us.

We might have expected John to pass more directly from the opening statements of the chapter (1:1-4) to the incarnation. Why should the witness of John the Baptist be given a place in the Prologue (1:6-8), when it did not begin until long after the birth of Jesus? Similarly, why is the lack of faith in Jesus on the part of the bulk of the nation included here before the account of the incarnation (1:11)? Possibly these items are thrust into the foreground for no more profound reasons than that they turn out to be two leading motifs of the fourth Gospel. Inclusion of these elements presents, in miniature, the fact that Israel was not without witness concerning the importance of the one who came to dwell in their midst, and that the witness resulted both in faith and unbelief. This latter contrast can be traced in page after page of the Gospel.

Believers become children of God by receiving the one whom he has sent (1:12). This is followed by the unexpectedly elaborate description of such people (1:13), of which the most arresting feature is the statement that these were not born of blood. The word "blood" appears here in the plural, which is quite remarkable and calls for explanation. It is easier to apply this description to the Son than to the children of God, since he was not the product of the commingling of paternal and maternal strains. There is some textual evidence among the Fathers and ancient versions for the singular ("was born"), though the Greek manuscripts unite in using the plural. The expression "born of God" is a typically Johannine term, used repeatedly of believers in the first letter. Our conclusion probably should be that John has deliberately described the new birth of believers in language that is also fitting for the Son of God. The writer shows his knowledge of the virgin birth without placarding it.

We move on to give attention specifically to verse 14. Here we have a repetition of the term λόγος, which invites comparison with the first mention of it in verse 1. In addition to continuity there is contrast. The λόγος who was pictured as being with God prior to the creation is now seen as coming to be with men. And whereas the λόγος has been described as divine (in the highest sense), here he is represented as truly human, for he has entered the ranks of mankind. But lest the reader leap to the conclusion that by entering humanity the λόγος has divested himself of deity (something inherently impossible), John adds the observation that the incarnate one still possessed the divine glory in a unique sense as μονογενής. He is more than a prophet, more than the greatest of the prophets (v. 9; cf. Matt 11:11; Luke 7:28).

And the Word became flesh. John has already made generous use of the verb "become" in regard to creation (vv. 3, 10) and the new creation wrought in the case of believers (v. 12). Here it marks a new stage in the history of the λόγος, one which will never be renounced or revoked. The language will not fit the docetic idea that the λόγος came upon a man, identified with him for a season, and then abandoned the human form prior to the crucifixion by a return to spirit existence. John was fully aware of this notion associated with the teaching of Cerinthus, a fellow-townsman of Ephesus, and was denouncing it without naming it, content to state positive truth.

How startling is the use of "flesh" in this passage, especially after its occurrence in the previous verse, where it is one of three elements set over against God and may be said to denote "the purpose which comes from the animal nature."[2] So, even though there is no antagonism regarding the meaning of σάρξ in the two contiguous verses, there is enough dissimilarity to provoke thought and careful analysis. One of the distinctives of the fourth Gospel is the employment of a single word in more than one sense. Some nuances are fairly easy to distinguish, such as "world," used of mankind as both the object of God's love (3:16) and as the world system in revolt against him (14:30). The double use of "lifted up" (12:32) is more subtle. As to the use of "flesh" in John, at least two meanings need to be differentiated. One speaks of limitation, though not necessarily of sin (1:13; 3:5-6; 6:63; 8:15). It is akin to Paul's use of "flesh and blood." The other denotes man or mankind simply from the standpoint of humanity (1:14) and is similar in force to Paul's use in Romans 1:3. It is the equivalent of his statement that Christ, in taking the form of a servant, came to be (γίνομαι as in John 1:14) in the likeness of men (Phil 2:7). See also 1 Timothy 3:16.

And dwelt among us. The verb can be rendered more pointedly, "tented" or "tabernacled." Since the consonants of the verb "to dwell" are *skn,* and these bear a strong resemblance to the radicals in the corresponding Hebrew *škn,* some have concluded that John has in mind a concept of late Judaism, namely, the use of the term Shekinah to denote the presence of God. However, Shekinah did not of itself suggest the idea of glory. John's language is sufficiently explained in terms of the Old Testament tabernacle, with its visible display of glory symbolizing the divine presence and majesty.

One cannot help wondering whether the dwelling is to be construed as temporary or permanent. From the standpoint of language alone it could be the former. But one needs to consider the use of the verb elsewhere and the broader connotations of the term. Aside from the present passage, the verb is found in the New Testament only in the Revelation (7:15; 12:12; 13:6 and 21:3). There the heavenly setting and the obviously metaphorical use of the term combine to call for the idea of permanence.

Looking back into the Old Testament, we conclude that the representation of God as dwelling in the midst of his people in the tabernacle was not intended to convey the idea of a temporary relationship but was rather an adaptation to the nomadic condition of his people at that time. This phase was followed by his dwelling in the temple, the more permanent structure being suitable to the settled condition of Israel in the land. At the time John wrote, the temple had been destroyed, but this only pointed up the fact that the removal of Jesus Christ from the earthly scene did not mean withdrawal of his presence. His body was indestructible, whether considered from the standpoint of his own personal body or his body the church (John 2:19). We should take into account also the teaching of the Lord concerning his abiding with his people by means of the Spirit after his own departure from the world (14:16-20). Wilhelm Michaelis is justified in holding that the statement in John 1:14 "does not refer to the temporary and transitory element in the earthly existence of the λόγος but is designed to show that this is the presence of the Eternal in time."[3]

A casual reading of the text could easily lead to the assumption that "among us" has reference to the same group as the words that follow, "and we beheld." However, the "us" may look backward rather than forward, having its connection with verse 11, "He came to his own inheritance and his own people did not receive him." The λόγος came to his own realm, to Israel. As God had consented to dwell with his covenant nation in the past, he has now granted them a new manifestation of his presence. The writer confesses by the "us" that he himself belongs to Israel. What confirms this as the true interpretation of John's intent is the difficulty encountered in the next statement, "and we beheld his glory," if the "we" is referred to the nation as a whole. A perusal of this Gospel reveals that whenever the glory of Christ is connected with seeing, his followers alone constitute the subject (11:40; 17:24). The only other passage involving the seeing of his glory concerns the vision of Isaiah (12:41).

Cullmann writes, "The difference between the synoptics and John's Gospel is that the synoptic tradition is the collective work of the community of the faithful, while in John's Gospel we are dealing with a more individual and consciously confessional witness."[4] If this is so, it becomes the more unexpected to have a "we" introduced in the Prologue. It appears to be a recognition on the writer's part that despite his individualistic approach he must call others to his side (and is able to do so), lest the impression be created that his presentation lacks the consensus that the apostolic witness is expected to have.

Those who failed to receive Jesus saw him with the physical eye, but his followers saw him not only on this external plane but also on a different level. "It is impossible to make any sense of a saying like 'He that hath seen me hath seen the Father' unless we can assume that the first act of seeing is something much more than mere visual receptivity."[5] The humanity of Jesus veiled the pre-incarnate glory (John 1:1; 17:5) to which only the eye of faith could penetrate to some degree by contact with his person, his words, and his deeds.

If it is inadequate to explain the beholding as a physical act, it is also wide of the mark to maintain that it refers to mystical vision such as was emphasized for initiates into mystery religions. The verb θεάομαι is never used in John with any such association. It is suggestive that in 11:45 it is employed of a beholding that leads to believing. That is its meaning in 1:14. The aorist does not refer to one specific incident, but is summary in its force.

Although λόγος in the personal sense does not appear in the Gospel after the Prologue, there is at least a possibility that the concept underlies John's use of the title Son of Man, with emphasis on the factor of mediation (cf. 1:51). Granted John does not use the word δόξα in 1:51, yet the fact that he introduces the idea of seeing in a trans-physical sense suggests the background of 1:14. Odeberg understands the seeing here as a reference to "a particular subjective faculty of the seer, which enables him to perceive—one might be tempted to add: permanently, and with increasing clearness—the *doxa* of Christ: the union of the celestial with the terrestrial."[6]

The glory (δόξα) of the λόγος is the focal point of the seeing. Before considering the force of the word, it is helpful to glance at its semantic development. In classical Greek it was used with various connotations, principally as expectation, opinion, and reputation. In the LXX the meaning "opinion" does not appear. The word is used most often to render the Hebrew *kabod,* which has the literal meaning of heaviness that occasionally comes through in the New Testament use of δόξα (2 Cor 4:17). One could be weighted down with wealth, honor, praise, authority, etc., so that a carry-over of the meaning "reputation" presented no difficulty. But *kabod* had also a distinctive use as a means of denoting the light-manifestations of the God of Israel. By using δόξα for this purpose, the translators were imparting to it a meaning it had not possessed before. This meaning was carried over into the New Testament in some of the occurrences of δόξα, such as the manifestation of the angelic host at the birth of Jesus (Luke 2:9), the scene on the Mount of Transfiguration (9:31; cf. 9:29), and the representation of God and the Lamb in the eternal city (Rev 21:23). Something of the majesty of God is conveyed by the abnormally brilliant display of light.

In the Old Testament the presence of God as indicated by means of the pillar of fire and cloud is noted for the first time in connection with the exodus (Exod 14:19, 24), and this served to express at once the power of God to safeguard his people and to deal effectively with their enemies. Later, a similar manifestation occurred at Mount Sinai. "Now the appearance of the glory of the Lord was like a devouring fire on the top of the mountain in the sight of the people of Israel" (Exod 24:17). This served to remind the nation of God's power and holiness, his "otherness." He could be approached only by a designated intermediary, the man Moses who had been called to be the deliverer from the land of bondage, although the seventy elders of Israel and representatives of the priesthood were permitted to go partway up the mountain where they "saw" God, including a luminous substance under his feet, "as it were a pavement of sapphire stones, like the very heaven for clearness" (Exod 24:10). Subsequently, Moses is pictured as alone with God and making a twofold petition: to be shown the ways of God (Exod 33:13), and to be shown God's glory (Exod 33:18). In answer to the former request, assurance is given concerning the continuance of the divine presence. With respect to the second request (which MS B of the LXX renders "Show me thyself"), the answer is tentative. God's goodness will be displayed to the leader of Israel. That he is gracious is demonstrated by his willingness to let Moses see his back (v. 20) but not his face, for the reason that no one can see his face and live. Recall the mention of feet in connection with the experience granted to the elders of Israel. The narrative moves from feet to back to face. Moses is treated in a way that sets him apart from the elders, but to see God's face is asking more than the Almighty can grant. This direct contact, this looking into the very mind and heart of God, was the privilege of λόγος before the incarnation (John 1:1). It speaks of communion with God on the basis of knowing him as he is, in the fulness of his being and character. What could not be granted to Israel or the elders or even to Moses is now granted in the fulness of time to believers in the Son of God. "We beheld his glory." Now at length the prayer of Moses, his second prayer, has been answered. The δόξα of God can now be revealed, not simply to one man but to all who long to see it. Great indeed is this mystery—God manifest in flesh. The yoking of two apparently disparate elements, the δόξα and the σάρξ, is accomplished without diluting the δόξα or deifying the σάρξ. The incarnation is a phenomenon remote alike from a demi-god or a superman. It is *sui generis*. It has no predecessor. It will have no successor.

It is morally certain that Paul had the Moses/Christ tension in mind when he wrote, "For it is the God who said, 'Let light shine out of darkness,' who has shone in our hearts to give the light of the knowledge of the glory of God in the face of Christ" (2 Cor 4:6). This conclusion is based on several observations. Paul has been contrasting Moses with Christ in the preceding chapter, laying great emphasis on δόξα. Also, he carries forward the figure of the veil from 3:13, 18 to 4:3. Finally, the emphasis on "face" that stands out in 3:17-18 reappears in 4:6.

Could John be referring in 1:14 to the transfiguration on the holy mount which is described by the synoptists? This is unlikely for the reason that transfiguration means literally "a change in form." John is not thinking in such terms. He is concerned with inner reality ("full of grace and truth"), not with a temporary display of visible glory. As noted above, the aorist in the verb "beheld" is summary and comprehensive. One might say, of course, that John would have been willing to regard the transfiguration as a display of glory and in that sense worthy of being included, but it is clear that he is not writing of a precise event in the career of Jesus as he makes his statement of the incarnation. As a matter of fact, he differs from the synoptists in his total picture of the life of our Lord in this matter of glorification of the Son. Whereas Luke 24:26, for example, presupposes a sharp distinction and even disjunction between the sufferings and the glory (cf. 1 Pet 1:11), John includes the glory in the sufferings (John 12:23-24; 13:31). He appears to have only one specific instance of δόξα with a futuristic frame of reference, and the setting is heavenly (17:24). The point that John is stressing is that in his suffering the Savior is pre-eminently glorifying the Father (17:4). This provides a pattern for his followers, even though their sacrifice is not redemptive (21:19). The Johannine perspective in this matter is a clear instance of realized eschatology. Whereas the synoptists present the transfiguration as an earnest of the future glory to offset the dejection of the disciples over the announcement of Jesus that he must go to Jerusalem to suffer and die, John emphasizes the perspective gained by the disciples through the resurrection: it was the glory of the Son that he was willing to do the Father's will even to the point of dying at the hands of sinful men.

In this connection it is worth noting that whereas both Matthew and Luke include at an early point in their narratives a precise indication of the redemptive mission of the one to be born into the world (Matt 1:21; Luke 2:11), John says nothing of this nature in his Prologue. He allows the redemptive purpose to come out later, especially in the words attributed to Jesus himself (e.g., 6:33, 51). His first concern is to establish the identity of the λόγος. Paul does much the same thing in his letter to the Romans, introducing the person Jesus (1:3-4), but saying nothing about his work, reserving that for a later point in the presentation. One should not give the impression that John says nothing in the Prologue about the contemplated work of the λόγος, but only that the redemptive mission is not explicitly stated. The latter comes out at 1:29, and may even be hinted at in 1:14

where the combination of "dwelt" and "glory" recalls the tabernacle with its accent on the holiness of God and the need of approaching him with appropriate sacrifice.

We should not leave consideration of the concept of δόξα without some word concerning its further use in the fourth Gospel. Not all the occurrences have the same meaning as in 1:14. In the body of the Gospel the word is almost uniformly used in the sense of praise or glorification (5:41, 44; 7:18; 8:50, 54; 9:24; 11:4; 12:43). The element of power is present occasionally (2:11; 11:40; cf. Rom 6:4), answering to the emphasis at the exodus when the pillar of cloud and fire symbolized divine intervention on behalf of God's people and in the interest of his own covenant pledges. The pre-existent glory is noted in 12:41 and 17:5, the future glory in 17:24, and the communication of the glory of the Son to his followers in 17:22. The latter concept is probably the most difficult to grasp, but there seems to be a hint that the disciple may enter into his Master's glory to the extent that his commitment to the will of God is genuine, full, and extending to death for the Lord's sake if need be.

Beyond the use of the word "glory" is the way in which it pervades the structure of the Gospel. John has made 1:14 the seed-plot of all that follows. This can be verified in broad outline, as one compares the structure of the tabernacle with the progression in John's account. Corresponding to the first item confronted in the tabernacle, the brazen altar, is the clarion announcement of the Baptist, "Behold the Lamb of God who takes away the sin of the world" (1:29). For the remaining material through chapter 12 Jesus is pictured as moving about in the outer court, so to speak, active in the service of God. At the beginning of chapter 13 he stops at the laver, washing the disciples' feet. This leads immediately to a description of what occurred in the upper room, a place apart, a holy place, where the people cannot come. The Master's teaching during this period may be said to tally with the objects of furniture in the holy place. Though nothing is said about instituting the Lord's Supper, (its essence has already been indicated in chap. 6), the deeper meaning of the bread of the presence is intimated in terms of the mystic union between the Lord and his own, their life being sustained by him even as he lives by the Father. The emphasis on the Holy Spirit as the Spirit of truth answers significantly to the golden candlestick. He illumines for the disciples the meaning of Jesus' mission and teaching. There is new instruction on prayer (14:13-14), which suggests the altar of incense and its function. Then Jesus enters the holy of holies to intercede for his own (v. 17). Finally, as already noted, John links glory with the death of the Son, so that the δόξα concept pervades the Gospel.

In passing, it should be noted that John is not alone in ascribing δόξα to the Lord Jesus Christ. Some of the more notable passages are 1 Corinthians 2:8, Hebrews 1:3, and James 2:1, each one of which repays careful study.

John is not content to introduce the concept of glory simply by using the word δόξα, for he goes on to amplify the thought by adding two clauses. The first of these reads: δόξαν ὡς μονογενοῦς παρὰ πατρός. Two problems emerge here. One is the meaning of μονογενοῦς (μονογενής in the nominative case). The other is the anarthrous construction of this word and πατρός. Μονογενής is used three times in the Gospel according to Luke: of the son of the widow of Nain (7:12); of the daughter of Jairus (8:42); and of the son of the distraught father who appealed for help to Jesus as the Master came down from the Mount of Transfiguration (9:38). In each the word "only" (child) appears to be an adequate translation. Literally, the word means "the only one of its kind." In the Lukan passages the emphasis falls heavily on "only," since there were no other children. It is doubtful that the Greek term should be translated "only begotten," since the root "to beget" is not present here (it does occur as the final word in the Greek text of John 1:13). The two roots, "to become" and "to beget," have a common base, and one could include the second half of μονογενής. This does not mean, of course, that they are interchangeable.

The history of the translation of μονογενής is of some interest. R. E. Brown writes, "The Old Latin correctly translated it as *unicus,* 'only,' and so did Jerome where it was not applied to Jesus. But to answer the Arian claim that Jesus was not begotten but made, Jerome translated it as *unigenitus,* 'only begotten,' in passages like this one (also 1:18; 3:16, 18). The influence of the Vulgate on the King James made 'only begotten' the standard English rendition."[7] It is significant that Isaac could be spoken of as Abraham's μονογενής (Heb 11:17), when as a matter of fact he was not such in the strict sense, since Ishmael was born before Isaac. But in the light of the promise he was the only one to be considered. It is this uniqueness that must be recognized in John's use of the term in 1:14. R. Schnackenburg points out that since δόξα was a feature common to heavenly beings, the clause beginning with ὡς is designed to indicate what differentiates the incarnate Son from all others.[8]

This observation may serve as an introduction to the second problem. What is the significance of the fact that both μονογενοῦς and πατρός lack the definite article? A number of translations reflect this in their wording: for example, Moffatt, Weymouth, Phillips, Goodspeed, Rieu, and the New Testament in Basic English. These differ somewhat in their precise wording. Rieu has "glory such as comes from father to only son." Phillips has "the splendor as of a father's only son." The assumption is that John is drawing on an earthly, human phenomenon to make meaningful the relationship between God and the λόγος, thus giving it an element of warmth. Barrett resists such efforts at translation, holding that the two words in question are "too characteristic of the Johannine writings, and too theological in use, to permit us to render in general terms, 'the glory as of a father's only son.' "[9]

This may be the "safe" approach. On the other hand, it is only just to observe that the consistent use of the article with Father throughout the Gospel, except when he is addressed in prayer, needs to be taken into consideration as a factor favorable to the other viewpoint. In fact, the article appears in the immediate context (v. 18). In the Johannine Letters, 2 John 3 provides the lone example of πατήρ without the article. A decisive verdict on this problem is difficult indeed, but the adding of articles in translation is questionable.

The concluding statement of 1:14 continues to be occupied with the incarnate λόγος, who reflects the glory of God in full measure because of his unique relationship to him. Here he is described as full of grace and truth (we are assuming that the indeclinable adjective πλήρης refers back to αὐτοῦ rather than to δόξαν, though the latter is a possibility).

Not one of the Gospels records that Jesus spoke of grace in its theological sense. So when John confines mention of it to the Prologue, he is strictly in line with his fellow evangelists. Grace has its Old Testament background in the Hebrew *chesed,* meaning "loving-kindness" (KJV in Ps 103:4, etc.), which is a better rendering than "mercy," as the KJV rendering in Psalm 136, for example. "Steadfast love" is the felicitous rendering of the RSV in the passages just noted. But the question persists as to why grace has a place in the Prologue but not in the remainder of the Gospel of John. What has been said about *chesed* and its translation can serve as a useful pointer. To be explicit, John's use of love (ἀγάπη) in the body of the Gospel seems intended to absorb the element of grace, seeing that the love of Christ as it was exhibited in attitude, word, and deed, as well as in the incarnation itself, was not a response to love shown to him, but was freely offered. It reflected that gracious condescension of God expressed in the δόξα, the glowing presence of God among his people in Old Testament days.

What is the thrust of John's statement that the incarnate Word is full of truth? Since the concept of truth is multifaceted, we can hardly hope to find the answer in a single element, at least in this passage. To begin with, absence of error may be taken for granted, and sincerity of purpose likewise. They are assumed here, but are not the burden of the message conveyed by the word in question.

Scholars have debated whether John's use of truth is Hellenic or Hebraic. If the former, then reality is the key to the concept. If the latter, reliability or trustworthiness is the essential ingredient. Since it can scarcely be doubted that the writer was aware of the currents of thought in his time, there is no antecedent reason why both ideas of truth could not be included. William Manson went so far in his advocacy of the Greek background as to render "truth" in our passage as "likeness."[10] One cannot help wondering, however, whether the word would not in that case have been positioned ahead of grace in the sentence as being a prior consideration and even more fundamental than grace. We propose to move in on the problem by handling first the more obvious and probable aspects. The close conjunction of truth with λόγος suggests that whatever is intended precisely by the word, the λόγος can be counted on to make it known. That will be central to his mission.

Since John couples truth with grace (grace in the sense of loving-kindness) in typical Old Testament fashion (cf. Ps 36:5), the idea of faithfulness in bringing to realization the divine promises should be included in the complex of meanings suggested by ἀλήθεια here. Paul affirms that Christ was sent to show God's truthfulness (ἀλήθεια) so as to confirm the promises given to the patriarchs (Rom 15:8). The apostle could say, in fact, that all the promises of God find their Yes in him (2 Cor 1:20). What remains to be fulfilled of the program of God does not cause anxiety in the believer when he contemplates the incarnation and what has already been achieved thereby.

Some help may be obtained by observing that John has used the adjective "true" (ἀληθινός) in verse 9. The emphasis in this word is not on true as opposed to false (John the Baptist is not being denigrated), but true in the sense of complete or ultimate as opposed to the partial and the preparatory. As a light, the Baptist bore a faithful witness, but over against him and his work stands the true light who is able to illumine the whole spiritual realm. He is the light and life of men. By saying that the incarnate one is full of truth, John is saying more than that he is the revealer of the knowledge of God and his ways. If this one is the λόγος, the effulgence of the Father's glory, then he *is* the truth in its essence and permanence. He has come not only to make the Father known with a fulness impossible before, but to become the one indispensable way to the Father (14:6).

A fact or proposition may be true in the sense that it is free from falsehood or inaccuracy and yet be quite inconsequential. The λόγος came into the world not to deal with trivia or to underscore the commonplace. He came to reveal what matters most in time and in eternity—the nature and purpose of God and how to know him so as to partake of his nature and life. In line with this, the promise of Jesus to his disciples regarding the coming of the Spirit as the one who would support and extend his ministry of teaching is couched not so much in terms of the Spirit's holiness (14:26 is a solitary passage), and not at all in terms of the Spirit's power, but rather in terms of his ability to impart divine truth. Accordingly, he is called the Spirit of truth (14:17; 15:26; 16:13).

In this Gospel Jesus, as the truth, is set over against the devil. Whatever success the devil has in the world is due to deception: there is no truth in him (8:44). Herein lie the seeds of his ultimate ruin. But the kingdom that

Jesus came to establish is necessarily built on truth, pre-eminently the truth of his person and work (18:36-37). It will abide.

Truth profoundly affects worship, the highest service of man. True worship of God is dependent on coming to him in the Spirit and with faith in the Son who came to reveal the Father (4:23-24). In these and other respects the concept of truth, placed in the forefront of the Gospel, permeates what follows.

The conclusion is unavoidable that John is introducing the λόγος as the one who transcends the Torah, for he is God's final Word to men, one who not only declares the truth with authority and finality but who exhibits it in his life. He has come to reveal the Father, not simply to interpret the Torah or to set up a new one.

The pre-existence of the λόγος (1:1) answers to the rabbinic claim that the Torah was one of seven things created before the world was made. "With God" (1:1-2, 18) answers to the rabbinic observation that the Torah was on God's knee or in his bosom. It is sometimes described as the daughter of God. Its creative role is based on Genesis 1:1, where "the beginning" is taken as a term for the Torah and the wording is construed as meaning "through" rather than "in" the beginning. In this way the agency of the Torah in creation is asserted (cf. John 1:3). That the Torah is life and health for those who use it aright is a truism in rabbinic circles and is often affirmed. The case is the same with respect to the concept of light (cf. John 1:4).

Rabbinic assertions identifying truth with the Torah are numerous. The way was prepared for this by the affirmations of the Old Testament. For example, "Thy law (Torah) is truth" (Ps 119:142). It is notable that John goes out of his way to mention Moses and his part in conveying the Torah to Israel, and then sets over against this statement the affirmation that grace and truth (repeated from 1:14) came through Jesus Christ (1:17). The intent here is not to depreciate Moses or the Torah. Rather, John is doing exactly what he has done with the Baptist (1:6-9), recognizing his service and then asserting the superior excellence of the one to whom the forerunner bore witness. In this connection, observe that the writer does not permit himself to exaggerate the difference between Moses and Jesus by introducing verse 17*b* with a "but." In line with this, we find that there is appeal both to the Baptist and his witness (5:33; 10:41) and to the witness of Moses (5:45-46) in the body of the Gospel.

The adulation of the Torah is a well-known feature of late Judaism.[11] It is strikingly evident that John's statements regarding the λόγος are couched in such a way as to point to the extravagant claims of the Jews for the Torah, as though to say that these exaggerated claims should now be laid aside. God has spoken in a Son (cf. Heb 1:1-3).

Notes to Chapter 3

1. C. H. Dodd, *The Bible and the Greeks* (repr.; London: Hodder and Stoughton, 1954) 120.
2. B. F. Westcott, *The Gospel According to Saint John* (repr.; Grand Rapids: Eerdmans, 1950) *s.v.*
3. W. Michaelis, "σκηνή," *TDNT* 7 (1971) 386.
4. O. Cullmann, *Early Christian Worship* (*SBT* 10; London: SCM, 1953) 39.
5. G. L. Phillips, "Faith and Vision in the Fourth Gospel," *Studies in the Fourth Gospel* (ed. F. L. Cross; London: Mowbray, 1954) 83-84.
6. H. Odeberg, *The Fourth Gospel* (Chicago: Argonaut, 1968) 37.
7. R. E. Brown, *The Gospel According to John I-XII* (*AB* 29; New York: Doubleday, 1966) 13.
8. R. Schnackenburg, *The Gospel According to John (HTCNT;* New York: Herder) I, 270.
9. C. K. Barrett, *The Gospel According to John* (London: SPCK, 1955) 139.
10. W. Manson, *The Incarnate Glory* (London: Clarke, 1923) 68.
11. See Strack-Billerbeck, *Kommentar zum Neuen Testament* (6 vols.; Munich: Beck, 1924) II, 361-362.

4: The Jesus of Saint John

LEON MORRIS

"From the historical viewpoint, the Church committed an error when it declared the Gospel to be orthodox."[1] So runs the verdict of Ernst Käsemann on the fourth Gospel. He, of course, sees a wide diversity in the teachings of the various parts of the New Testament. Probably no one in recent years has done more to emphasize the variety of teaching in the New Testament than he. He has argued that "early Catholicism" is to be found in writings like the Gospel of Luke and the Pastoral Epistles, and that this must be set in opposition to the teaching of Paul. He is quite ready to accept the concept of a canon within the canon, accepting Pauline teaching as essential Christianity and rejecting the early Catholicism that he sees as in opposition to it. In Johannine studies he has argued forcefully that John cannot be thought of as in essential agreement with other early Christians, and in the sentence quoted at the head of this study he gives it as his opinion that John's Gospel is not "orthodox." Such views are not uncontested. G. E. Ladd, for example, stresses the unity in the New Testament, though he recognizes that there is diversity there too: "Our thesis is that the unity of New Testament theology is found in the fact that the several strata share a common view of God, who visits man in history to effect the salvation of both man, the world, and history; and that diversity exists in the several interpretations of this one redemptive event."[2]

Käsemann's position opens up many issues. The one with which we will concern ourselves is his view that John has a docetic Christology which is central to his Gospel. Käsemann says things like "John changes the Galilean teacher into the God who goes about on earth."[3] More than once he speaks of John's "naive docetism,"[4] and he can speak of "my key word, unreflected docetism."[5] Several times he repeats the statement that this Christology is of central importance.[6] Obviously this is a key point. Unless it can be established, Käsemann's whole position is vulnerable. It is worth looking into the evidence.

Käsemann has an excellent summary of the kind of thing that impresses him and leads to his verdict of docetism. He says we must ask,

> In what sense is he flesh, who walks on the water and through closed doors, who cannot be captured by his enemies, who at the well of Samaria is tired and

> desires a drink, yet has no need of drink and has food different from that which his disciples seek? He cannot be deceived by men, because he knows their innermost thoughts even before they speak. He debates with them from the vantage point of the infinite difference between heaven and earth. He has need neither of the witness of Moses nor of the Baptist. He dissociates himself from the Jews, as if they were not his own people, and he meets his mother as the one who is her Lord. He permits Lazarus to lie in the grave for four days in order that the miracle of his resurrection may be more impressive. And in the end the Johannine Christ goes victoriously to his death of his own accord. Almost superfluously the Evangelist notes that this Jesus at all times lies on the bosom of the Father and that to him who is one with the Father the angels descend and from him they again ascend. He who has eyes to see and ears to hear can see and hear his glory. Not merely from the prologue and from the mouth of Thomas, but from the whole Gospel he perceives the confession, "My Lord and my God". How does all this agree with the understanding of a realistic incarnation?[7]

Put that way, the answer to the last question must be, "It does not agree at all." But we must ask whether the evidence is quite as Käsemann says it is. He allows that there are some other features.

> I am not interested in completely denying features of the lowliness of the earthly Jesus in the Fourth Gospel. But do they characterize John's christology in such a manner that through them the "true man" of later incarnational theology becomes believable? Or do not those features of his lowliness rather represent the absolute minimum of the costume designed for the one who dwelt for a little while among men, appearing to be one of them, yet without himself being subjected to earthly conditions?[8]

But the question is whether these other features are as unimportant as Käsemann says they are, and whether the evidence for docetism is as weighty as he says it is. He argues as though the evidence is clear and straightforward and that only the reluctance of Christians to face its implications has kept them from seeing that John does depict a docetic Christ. Yet every item on his list is contestable and some are certainly erroneous. The position is complex and we should be on our guard against attempts at oversimplification. Let us look first at the evidence Käsemann adduces for docetism.

He begins by telling us that Jesus "walks on the water." This gives the impression that in the fourth Gospel Jesus habitually engages in the practice. Yet there is only one possible instance in John, and even here there is nothing to match the plain statements of the synoptists (who, Käsemann agrees, picture Jesus as a man). The question concerns the right understanding of the statement that the disciples saw Jesus walking ἐπὶ τῆς θαλάσσης (6:19). In my opinion Käsemann is right in seeing a reference to walking on the water, but he might have noted that this is not beyond all doubt and that there is what Raymond E. Brown calls John's "lack of emphasis on the miraculous."[9] The identical expression is found in John 21:1, where the meaning is "by the sea" and not "on the sea," and some exegetes think that in the present passage John means no more than that the disciples saw Jesus walking on the shore. They point to the statement in the next verse, "immediately the boat was at the land to which they were going."[10] If John's Christ was docetic, would there have been any doubt?

To say that Jesus walks "through closed doors" reads strangely. There is no example of this during the earthly life of Jesus. Presumably Käsemann is referring to the post-resurrection appearances, but the synoptists are just as definite as John that Jesus' resurrection body was not subject to the limitations that characterized the pre-resurrection body. We cannot argue from the one body to the other. Jesus did not walk through closed doors on earth. There is not one example of his doing so during the whole of his earthly life.

Käsemann's next point is that Jesus "cannot be captured by his enemies." Why then does John say that he "walked in Galilee, for he would not walk in Judea, because the Jews were trying to kill him" (7:1;[11] cf. 11:53-54)? These words clearly mean that his enemies could have captured him, and that to avoid this Jesus went to Galilee. It is true that on one occasion John says that a band of men failed to arrest Jesus, but there is no indication in the narrative that this was because Jesus was immune to capture. As John tells it, the arresting posse gave as their reason that they were impressed by Jesus' teaching (7:45-46) and the Pharisees that these officers were "deceived" (7:47). In John's account there is no hint of anything docetic. On other occasions the evangelist tells us that no one laid hands on Jesus "because his hour was not yet come" (7:30; 8:20). But these passages surely do not mean that Jesus was immune from arrest. They simply affirm the operation of God's providence. Jesus would not die before his time. Indeed, John Calvin sees here an illustration of "a general doctrine . . . though we live unto the day, the hour of every man's death has nevertheless been fixed by God . . . we are safe from all dangers until God wishes to call us away."[12] Is John really saying anything more than this?

Jesus "desires a drink, yet has no need of drink." Is there any evidence of this at all? In the context of his request for a drink it is explicitly said that Jesus "wearied (κεκοπιακώς) from his journey" (4:6), which does not read as though it referred to one who had no physical needs and no physical problems. When he hung on the cross Jesus said in set terms, "I am thirsty" (19:28), and he drank some wine when it was brought to his lips (an incident, by the way, which the synoptists do not record). Where does Käsemann get his idea that Jesus "had no need of drink"? Certainly not from the evidence.

Again, Käsemann tells us that Jesus' food is "different from that which his disciples seek." The reference is surely to John 4:32, where Jesus was sustained during his counselling of the Samaritan woman. But is this really so strange? Everett F. Harrison sees the words as meaning that "Christ had lost for the time the desire for food in the consuming joy of pointing a needy soul to the place of forgiveness and rest."[13] Do John's words mean more? And cannot many of us testify to something of the same experience? When we have been actively engaged in doing the Lord's work we have known what it is not to feel hunger. There is no docetism here. Moreover, it should not be overlooked that the disciples lived with Jesus and they did not notice that his food was different from theirs. On this occasion they could think only that someone had given Jesus something to eat (v. 33). This was a misunderstanding, but we should not miss the point that, as John sees it, those who were closest to Jesus took it for granted that the food Jesus would eat would be the ordinary food that sustained them. If there was a docetic Christ they knew nothing about him.

"He cannot be deceived by men, because he knows their innermost thoughts even before they speak." I do not know whether this is true of the Johannine Christ or not, but I suspect it is not.[14] It is a pity that Käsemann cites no evidence. He may be referring to John 2:24-25, but this simply means that Jesus was not deceived by facile protestations of belief. He knew men better than that. There is no reference to men's thoughts. It is, of course, the case that John does ascribe unusual knowledge to Jesus. As I have written elsewhere, "John clearly regards Jesus as possessed of a knowledge that is more than human, but just as clearly he does not regard this as vitiating His real humanity. Jesus' knowledge is derived from His close communion with the Father (8:28, 38; 14:10)."[15] John makes it plain that Jesus had all the knowledge he needed to fulfil his mission, and that this knowledge came from God. But this is not the knowledge of omniscience. It is the outworking of the Father's commission when he sent Jesus. And is there any evidence that Jesus knew men's thoughts before they spoke? I know of none. He had to "find" the man he had cured of blindness (9:35) after he had heard that he had been put out of the synagogue (he also "found" the man he cured of lameness, 5:14). After the feeding of the multitude Jesus "came to know" (γνούς) that the mob wanted to make a king out of him (6:15)—apparently he did not know it intuitively. To avoid this he withdrew into the mountain: he did not perform some miracle. He did not know where the tomb of Lazarus was and asked a question to find out (11:34). Indeed, in this Gospel Jesus constantly asks questions (see 1:50; 3:10, 12; 5:6, 47; 6:5, 67; 7:19, 23; 8:43, 46; 11:34; 16:31; 18:4, 7, 21, 23, 34). Some of these prove nothing, being the kind of questions asked when one knows the answer and is not seeking information. For example, Jesus asked his audience, "Why do you not understand my language?" and answered, "Because you cannot comprehend my thought" (8:43; Rieu's translation). The rhetorical question simply drives the point home. But other questions are different, such as that seeking the whereabouts of the tomb of Lazarus, or the one that Jesus put to Pilate, "Do you say this of yourself, or did others tell you about me?" (18:34). It is plain that in some matters Jesus was ignorant just as in others he had unusual knowledge.[16]

As to Jesus' debating "from the vantage point of the infinite difference between heaven and earth," this appears to be a private opinion of Käsemann's. F. C. Burkitt had a very different estimate with his well-known objection to the authenticity of the teaching John ascribes to Jesus: "It is quite inconceivable that the historical Jesus of the Synoptic Gospels could have argued and quibbled with his opponents, as He is represented to have done in the Fourth Gospel."[17] The measure of truth in what Käsemann says is that John sees Jesus as living closer to the Father than other men, and as speaking out of the enlightenment that that gave him. But in some measure it is true of every great saint that he speaks "from the vantage point of the infinite difference between heaven and earth." That is what distinguishes him from the worldly-minded. John sees this as true in especial measure of Jesus, but he does not depict it as a non-human trait.

"He has need neither of the witness of Moses nor of the Baptist." But what does this mean? Surely that Jesus had the deep-seated conviction that the Father was bearing witness to him in the works he was doing (5:36-37) and that therefore he needed nothing more.[18] Is this not a perfectly human trait? Is it not true of all of us that in the last resort we rely on the conviction that what we are doing is right in the sight of God, not necessarily that it is attested by Moses or the Baptist or Luther or Calvin or whoever? And if Jesus did not rely on Moses or the Baptist, he was clear that both did bear witness that agreed with what he was doing (5:33, 46).

"He dissociates himself from the Jews, as if they were not his own people." What then are we to make of the words, "You worship you know not what; we know what we worship, for salvation is of the Jews" (4:22)? Quite early John assures us that the Baptist saw the manifesting of Jesus "to Israel" as the purpose of his practice of baptizing (1:31). And we should not forget that Jesus' greeting to Nathanael was, "Look, truly an Israelite" (1:47), nor that he was not denigrating Nicodemus when he called him "the teacher of Israel" (3:10). He insisted that Moses, the great lawgiver of the Jews, wrote about him (5:46) and that Abraham, the progenitor of the Jewish nation, rejoiced to see his day (8:56; cf. 8:39-40). He constantly appealed to the Jewish scriptures. John twice records the use of the title "King of Israel" (1:49; 12:13), and he puts some emphasis on the fact that Jesus was crucified as "King of the Jews" (19:19-22).

There is anger against "the Jews" in this Gospel, and there is upbraiding of those who profess to be God's people and are not. But that does not mean that Jesus dissociates himself from the nation. On the contrary. To the very end he remains a faithful Jew, worshipping in the temple and observing the Jewish feasts. Käsemann does not notice that in this Gospel "the Jews" are often a part of the nation only, as when the parents of the man born blind, who were clearly Jews themselves, are differentiated from "the Jews" (9:22). Nor that Jesus' sheep are of the "fold" of the Jews in the first place, even though there will be others "not of this "fold" (10:16). Nils Dahl points out that "the Jews who do not believe because they are 'of the world' have never been true children of Abraham."[19] True Jews belong to Jesus, and this is an important part of the fourth Gospel. Dahl also sees significance in the early disciples' reference to Jesus as "him of whom Moses and the prophets wrote," and their "we have found the Messiah."[20] Such sayings affirm a continuity with Israel, not a separation from it. It should not be overlooked that other ways of understanding "the Jews" have been accepted. Thus some have seen the expression to mean "Judaeans as opposed to Galileans."[21] O. Cullmann holds that "the way in which the Gospel speaks in so many places of 'the Jews' as a collective enemy could derive from the terminology which heterodox communities applied to official Judaism."[22] And there are other possibilities.

That "he meets his mother as the one who is her Lord" does not address the real question, namely, "Was he her Lord?" If he was, there is no problem. If he was not, then not only John but all the other New Testament writers as well have been led astray and John has no special position.

"He permits Lazarus to lie in the grave for four days in order that the miracle of his resurrection may be more impressive." This is obviously wrong. Neither Jesus nor John says that the delay was to make the miracle more impressive. This has to be read into the narrative. As John tells it, Jesus could not have reached Bethany in time to save Lazarus from death. It was a day's journey from that village to the place where he was in trans-Jordan. The four days John mentions will be taken up with one day for the journey of the messengers, two days with Jesus remaining where he was, and one more day for Jesus' journey. Putting all this together, John is saying that Lazarus must have died shortly after the messengers left Bethany. He must have been dead before the messengers reached Jesus. Jesus could not possibly have gotten there in less than two days after the death, and we can only conjecture as to why he waited two more days. The journey undoubtedly involved danger (11:8, 16), and Jesus may have taken time to be sure that it was the right thing to do.[23] If so, the delay was certainly due to a very human reason. Or the delay may be connected with John's picture of Jesus as moving in his own time and not as he is advised by others.[24] Or there may have been some other reason. It is better to admit our ignorance than to assert dogmatically that John depicts Jesus as allowing his friends to suffer the grief of bereavement for four days simply to enhance a miracle. That would be quite out of character,

"And in the end the Johannine Christ goes victoriously to his death of his own accord." I am more in agreement with this than with what Käsemann has said previously. John does depict Jesus as sovereign in the way he went to his death, but this is no more than a matter of emphasis. The synoptists are just as definite that Jesus knew what lay ahead of him, but went forward to meet it. They tell of Gethsemane, which means that Jesus knew what was coming and had time to flee but did not. In the synoptists, too, he went to his death of his own accord. Moreover, it is quite possible for one who is no more than a man to approach death in the manner of a conqueror. Ignatius is an example that springs to mind, and he is all the more important in that he owed this attitude to what Jesus had done for him. If the follower could choose a death he saw as victorious, why could not the leader?

"Almost superfluously the evangelist notes that this Jesus at all times lies on the bosom of the Father and that to him who is one with the Father the angels descend and from him they again ascend." Two sentences later, Käsemann says that the Godhead is seen "not merely from the prologue and from the mouth of Thomas." But where is there a reference to the Father's bosom other than in the Prologue? And Käsemann has heightened even this reference by inserting an "at all times" of his own, and making it "lies on" instead of the simple "is in" (1:18). In his Prologue John is saying that Jesus, from his close communion with the Father, has been able to declare him to men. But it is a far cry from this to the assertion that, in this Gospel, Jesus is "at all times" lying on the Father's bosom. In fact, there are some who deny that the words have any reference to the earthly life of Jesus. Thus Th. C. de Kruijf writes, "this must mean the present situation, the situation of the glorified Christ after the resurrection. It is not a metaphysical statement."[25] It is not necessary to agree with this to see that Käsemann's is not the only possible interpretation of the words.

Again, Käsemann scarcely seems to be dealing fairly with the reference to the angels. He makes it sound as though the heavenly train was constantly waiting on the heavenly visitant to earth in order to serve him and to manifest his glory. But the Jesus of John does not say that "to him who is one with the Father the angels descend. . . ." He says to Nathanael, "You [plural] will see heaven opened and God's angels going up and going down on the Son of man" (1:51). The words are not an abstract statement about the nature of Jesus. They are words of encouragement to a new believer and an assurance that Jesus will bring him (and others) into further knowledge of heavenly realities. "The wide open heaven, and the ascending and descending angels symbolize the whole power and love of God, now available for men, in the Son of man."[26] At the very least, these words of R. H. Strachan are a possible understanding of the words, so that Käsemann's assumption that his is the only view must be rejected. And in my judgment Strachan's interpretation is not only different, it is better. That is surely what Jesus is saying. We should also notice that there is nothing in the text that corresponds to Käsemann's "to him who is one with the Father," and that the reference to angels does not necessarily point to deity, as is seen in the fact that there is a strand of rabbinic interpretation of Genesis 28:12 which sees angels as ascending and descending on Jacob.[27] I do not see this as the right understanding of the Genesis passage, nor do I think that John is saying that Jesus was no more than Jacob. But the existence of that exegesis is a fact, and it shows that Käsemann's claim about the angels is exaggerated.

It is one of Käsemann's contentions that John 1:14 has been misunderstood. People have put their emphasis on "the Word was made flesh," whereas they should have seen that John is emphasizing "we beheld his glory." He finds the rest of the Gospel full of the thought that the glory of God is revealed. But it may be doubted whether Käsemann is doing justice to either half of the statement.

Let us look at the "glory" that matters so much to him. And let me say right away that I agree that there is glory throughout this Gospel. But there is a paradox which Käsemann does not mention, the paradox that real glory is to be seen in lowliness rather than in a display of majesty. There is what Origen long ago called "humble glory."[28] The Johannine Christ does not seek glory for himself but for the Father (8:50; 7:18). The glory he has is not self-derived but given him (8:54). We see something of the complexity of the idea of glory in this Gospel when we look at the raising of Lazarus. That man's sickness was "not with a view to death but for the glory of God, that the Son of God might be glorified through it" (11:4). There is to be no doubt about the glory. The glory of both the Father and the Son is involved, and these two glories are intimately connected. What makes for the glory of the One makes for the glory of the Other. The outcome of the miracle in which the glory is manifested is twofold. First, as a result of the raising of the dead man, many believed (11:45). This is what we immediately recognize as glory. Jesus is seen for the wonderful being he is, and people believe. But John puts little stress on this. He goes on to point out that another result of the miracle was that events were set in train that would lead to the cross (11:50). There is glory there, too. We should overlook neither aspect if we are to understand John's view of glory.

As we have seen, the glory of the Father is closely linked with that of the Son. This is shown in a number of places, but we might profitably notice the prayer Jesus offered with the cross in immediate prospect: "Father, the hour has come; glorify your Son so that the Son may glorify you" (17:1). There can be no question but that he has the cross in mind. That is "the hour" to which everything in this Gospel leads. And in the cross there will be seen, not only the glory of the Son, but that of the Father. The two are not to be separated.

Throughout the fourth Gospel Jesus takes a lowly place, and it is one of John's great paradoxes that the true glory is to be seen in this lowly service, and especially in Jesus' death on the cross (12:23-24; 13:31). Käsemann sees the references to glory, but incredibly he does not see the paradox.[29] Even when the paradox is not stressed, as for example when Jesus' glory is shown in miracles, the glory may be perceived only by a restricted circle. Thus, at the wedding in Cana of Galilee the disciples saw Jesus' glory and believed (2:11). But John says nothing of any effect on the ruler of the feast, or the guests, or even on the servants who knew that what had been taken to the ruler of the feast was water (v. 9). It is quite a different picture in Acts 14:8-18, where the people of Lystra thought themselves the recipients of a divine visitation. They saw glory in the healing of the lame man and immediately hailed Barnabas and Paul as gods. They brought bulls and garlands in order to offer sacrifice to them. That is the kind of thing that may be expected when the gods come to earth. There is no equivalent in John. He is writing about something quite different.

There is an interesting note about glory in John 12:39-43. Here the evangelist quotes a prophecy of Isaiah which explains why many people did not believe in Jesus: their eyes were blinded, their hearts were hardened, etc. Then John adds, "Isaiah said these things because he saw his glory." We might have expected "because he saw his rejection" or the like. But for John there was glory in Jesus' acceptance of the way of rejection and suffering, and it is glory that he links with the prophecy of rejection.

And if Käsemann does not do justice to John's paradoxical view of glory, neither does he give sufficient weight to the evangelist's declaration that "the Word was made flesh."[30] Even if Käsemann were right in seeing the emphasis on the reference to glory (and we have just seen that this is debatable), these other words must be given their due meaning. And it must be recognized that σάρξ is a strong term that puts emphasis on the physical reality of the incarnate Jesus. John does not say, "the Word became man," or even, "the Word took a body." He uses the forceful, almost crude, word "flesh." There should be no denying the physical reality of one of whom this can be said. The word "expresses that which is earth-bound (3:6), transient and perishable (6:63), the typically human mode of being, as it were, in contrast to all that is divine and spiritual."[31] Schnackenburg notes that there was a widespread idea at the time that divine beings might appear on earth.

> But after the affirmation of the Incarnation in 1:14 the Christian teaching on the Son of God made man cannot be reduced to one variety among others: it can only be understood as a protest against all other religions of redemption in Hellenism and Gnosticism. It is a new and profoundly original way of confessing the Saviour who has come "palpably" (1 John 1:1) in history as a unique, personal human being, who has manifested himself in the reality of the "flesh".[32]

The verb ἐγένετο is also significant. It indicates a change (whether we translate "was made" or "became"), and it seems impossible to reconcile the use of this verb with the view that the divine Christ remained as he was, in all his glory. Du Toit maintains that the verb "bridges the enormous distance between the divine Logos and the σάρξ," that it "states the solid, the 'crude' fact of the incarnation," and that it "entirely cuts off the possibility of any docetic misinterpretation."

> The incarnation means, according to verse 14, that the divine Logos substituted his heavenly way of existence for the frail, broken, earthly, human way of existence. This human existence of the Word is not to be understood in a docetic way, a mere being "in the flesh," but as a "becoming flesh," and yet without sacrificing his essential being as Logos.[33]

The combination of the verb ἐγένετο and the noun σάρξ points irresistibly to a genuine incarnation, with all that that means. It conveys the thought that Jesus did not play at becoming man; he really became man and accepted all the limitations and suffering and so on that that involves.

The reality of Jesus' manhood might be deduced also from the repeated references to him as a man; see 4:29; 5:12; 7:46, 51; 8:40; 9:11, 16 *(bis);* 10:33; 11:47, 50; 18:14, 17, 29; 19:5. Of these we might notice particularly 8:40, where Jesus himself says, "you are trying to kill me, a man who has spoken the truth to you," and 10:33, where the Jews say, "We are not stoning you for a good work but for blasphemy and because you, being a man, make yourself God." The former gives Jesus' own claim as John sees it, and in the latter the Jews call Jesus a man at the very same time as they recognize that he claims to be something more. The claim carries no conviction to them because, whatever else he was, he was certainly a man, and that for them had implications. John's repeated use of "man" in reference to Jesus gives food for thought. If he was trying to depict a docetic Christ, why this repeated stress on his real humanity? It makes no sense.[34]

Käsemann seems to undervalue the passion narrative. Convinced as he is that John portrays a docetic Christ, he can make nothing of the narrative of Jesus' death other than a reluctant acceptance of a tradition too firmly held to be dismissed. He sees it as "a mere postscript which had to be included."[35] We are tempted to retort, "Some postscript!" This is a full and absorbing narrative. It cannot be said that John has skimped on this part of his story; his inclusion of details found nowhere else indicates an interest in the subject. R. T. Fortna has another objection when he says that "all the themes pervading the gospel and coming to a climax in the crucifixion—most notably, Jesus' 'hour,' his 'glorification,' and the completion *(telein)* of his work—are plainly Johannine insertions into the older narrative material."[36] I do not accept this myself, but at least it is a point of view that ought to be considered, and Käsemann does not consider it. Fortna makes a better point when he says, "in the present gospel it is no longer the resurrection as such that carries the greater weight but Jesus' glorification on the cross, by which he draws all men to himself (xii.32)."[37] The whole Gospel emphasizes the cross. "Even before Jesus appears his mission is summarized as tragic

(i. 10f.)."[38] When he comes to the story of the actual death of Jesus, John seems to go out of his way to emphasize its physical aspects. He tells us of Jesus' thirst (19:28). He alone tells of the spear thrust and the water and the blood (19:34-35). There seems to be an opposition to anything docetic in his insistence that there is a witness who can bear testimony to the fact that water and blood flowed from the side of the crucified Jesus. There are mysteries here, but at the very least there is testimony to a dead body. One does not write thus about a docetic being.

As we saw earlier, Käsemann says that he is "not interested in completely denying features of the lowliness of the earthly Jesus in the Fourth Gospel" but holds that these do not picture Jesus as "true man." He asks, "do not those features of his lowliness rather represent the absolute minimum of the costume designed for the one who dwelt for a little while among men, appearing to be one of them, yet without himself being subjected to earthly conditions?"[39] This immediately raises the question of whether Käsemann has really done justice to Jesus' dependence on God. The Johannine Jesus says plainly, "the Father is greater than I" (14:28),[40] and the Gospel is filled with the thought that he cannot act by himself. "The Son can do nothing of himself," Jesus says, "but only what he sees the Father doing" (5:19). This aspect of Johannine teaching was emphasized by J. Ernest Davey, who devoted sixty-seven pages (far and away his longest chapter) to "The Dependence of Christ as presented in *John*."[41] He speaks of Jesus as dependent on the Father for power ("I can do nothing by myself," 5:30), for knowledge ("my judgment is true, because I am not alone, but I and he that sent me," 8:16), for his mission and message ("My food is to do the will of him who sent me and accomplish his work," 4:34), for being, nature, and destiny (the Father "has given to the Son to have life in himself," 5:26; "I live through the Father," 6:57; "the cup which the Father has given me," 18:11), for authority and office ("as thou hast given him authority," 17:2; the Father gave him authority to judge, 5:22, 27, and to lay down his life, 10:18), for love (3:16; 17:24-26), and for glory and honor (God "will immediately glorify him," 13:32; "my glory, which thou hast given me," 17:24; the Father has given all judgment to the Son "so that all may honor the Son," 5:23). Christ is pictured as obedient to the Father (his food is to do the Father's will, 4:34), as dependent on him for his disciples ("all that the Father gives me will come to me," 6:37, and negatively, "no one can come to me unless the Father who sent me draws him," 6:44; "the men whom thou gavest me out of the world," 17:6). He depends on the Father for testimony ("If I bear witness about myself my witness is not true; there is another who bears witness about me"; "the Father who sent me has borne witness about me," 5:31, 37), for the Spirit (who descends on him at baptism, 1:33, and whom the Father gives him without measure, 3:34), for guidance (Davey sees this as the meaning of passages like, "if anyone walks in the day he does not stumble because he sees the light of this world [i.e. God]," 11:9; "Here mystical guidance is clearly expressed"). Jesus' dependence is seen in his relationships with God ("he who sent me is with me, he has not left me alone," 8:29) and men ("you will know that I am in the Father and you in me and I in you," 14:20), and is illustrated by his prayers (chap. 17) and by his titles (there are twenty-two in the Gospel and 1 John and most imply dependence, e.g., "Son" depends on "Father," "Lamb of God" probably points to Christ as "the victim offered by and sent from God," etc.).

Davey agrees that there are aspects of the Johannine presentation which might be taken in a docetic sense.[42] He denies, however, that these give us the typical Johannine view. That is rather dependence. "Few persons who have not studied the Fourth Gospel with care in this regard can have any conception of the extent to which this idea of dependence is emphasized in it as the chief constituent in Christ's experience of God the Father; one might indeed call this dependence the ruling element in John's portrait of Christ."[43]

There is then in John an important stress on Jesus' dependence. But there is more: the whole manner of Jesus' life is human. We might start with the name itself, for John uses the human name "Jesus" 237 times (Matthew uses this name 150 times, Mark 81 times, and Luke 89 times), more than a quarter of the total in the whole New Testament (905). "Jesus Christ" is found twice only, while the title "Christ" occurs nineteen times (in accordance with John's declared aim of showing Jesus to be the Christ [20:31]). This human Jesus seems to have enjoyed normal family relations (2:12). He went to a wedding with his mother (2:11). He had brothers who told him what he ought to do in a manner which anyone who has grown up with brothers will immediately recognize (7:3-5). He was concerned for his mother, even as he hung on the cross (19:26-27). He loved his friends Martha, Mary, and Lazarus (11:5). He was troubled at the prospect of his death and wondered whether he should pray to be delivered from it (12:27). He could be tired and thirsty (4:6, 7); he could be ignorant and ask questions. He could shed tears (11:35) and be troubled in spirit (11:33). John twice uses of Jesus the unusual verb ἐμβριμάομαι (11:33, 38), which is properly applied to the snorting of horses.[44] It is a very down-to-earth word. There is dispute among commentators as to whether we should take it in John 11 to refer to anger or some other deep feeling, but none about the very human quality of the emotion it denotes. He could not prevent some of his followers from falling away from him (6:66), and one of them from betraying him. On one occasion he said, "Now my soul is troubled (ἡ ψυχή μου τετάρακται" (12:27), and John tells us that in the upper room Jesus "was troubled in spirit (ἐταράχθη τῷ πνεύματι)" as he contemplated the betrayal (13:21). All this is part of the evidence and points to a real humanity.[45]

There are also a few passages in which Jesus as simply God on earth seems to be denied. Thus in the Prologue we read that "no one has ever seen God," but that Jesus has set him forth (1:18). This is reinforced when Jesus later says of God, "you have neither heard his voice nor seen his form" (5:37), and again, "Not that anyone has seen the Father" (6:46). In each case the position is somewhat complex. In the Prologue Jesus appears to be called μονογενὴς θεός; in chapter 5 Jesus is claiming that he has intimate knowledge of the Father, and in 6:46 he goes on to differentiate himself from those who have not seen the Father by claiming that he has done just this. I am not arguing that any of these passages is simple, but rather that Käsemann is oversimplifying by not considering the implications of such words. If, as he claims, Jesus was simply "the God who walks on the face of the earth,"[46] then many people had seen God and heard his voice. But that is not what John is saying. His emphatic words to the contrary should not be overlooked.

Again, we should bear in mind that the Gospel of John does not stand alone. It is one of five writings which together make up the Johannine literature. Whether any one author wrote more than one of these books is hotly disputed, but it is undeniable that the Gospel and 1 John, if not from the same pen (though many do hold to unity of authorship), are clearly from the same basic situation. There is no doubt that 1 John opposes teachings of a docetic kind with its stress on handling as well as seeing and hearing the word of life (1 John 1:1), its insistence on confessing that Jesus Christ has come "in the flesh" with its counterpart that to deny this is to manifest the spirit of the antichrist (1 John 4:2-3; cf. 2:22), its stress on seeing Jesus as the Son of God (1 John 4:15) and as the Christ (1 John 5:1), and its stress on the importance of Jesus' coming "not in the water only, but in the water and in the blood" (1 John 5:6). It is not easy to see how and why the Gospel could be setting forth a teaching which the Letter combats so vigorously.[47]

From all this it is clear that Käsemann is oversimplifying. That is my quarrel with his whole book. I have spent many years in the study of the fourth Gospel and have reached the highly unoriginal conclusion that it is a complex and difficult book. I am at a loss to understand why Käsemann makes it all sound so simple. On his view we have nothing more complicated than a picture of "one who dwelt for a little while among men, appearing to be one of them, yet without himself being subjected to earthly conditions."[48] This seems to me to be nothing less than a refusal to face the problems of the fourth Gospel (incidentally a favorite accusation of Käsemann's against the generality of Johannine scholars). It results from a selective reading of the evidence, ignoring or minimizing the force of all that does not fit into the desired picture. For the fact is that the Jesus of the fourth Gospel is at one and the same time both supremely great and very lowly. He is fully God, certainly. Käsemann sees this with crystal clarity. But he is also fully man, and that should not be overlooked.

Others recognize the complexity of the problem. In an essay written to honor G. E. Ladd it is proper to notice that scholar's balanced opinion: "We may conclude that John portrays Jesus in a twofold light without reflection or speculation. He is equal to God; he is indeed God in the flesh; yet he is fully human."[49] That is the conclusion to which the evidence points us. Raymond E. Brown has also looked at the problem, and is unimpressed by the view that this Gospel was written to refute docetists of some kind. He finds features that are anti-docetic, but they are not prominent enough to give us the main motive for writing this Gospel. He sums up with, "An honest judgment would be that an anti-docetic motif is possible and even probable in the Gospel, but it has no great prominence."[50] Brown wrote before Käsemann's book appeared, so he is not directly dealing with his contentions. But his judgment has relevance all the same. A survey of the evidence convinces him that not a docetic thrust but an anti-docetic thrust is probable.

Nils Dahl is another who finds John opposed to docetism. He thinks that a docetic Christology "may have been supported by allegorical interpretations of the Old Testament. Over against such tendencies, John bears witness to the true humanity of Jesus and to the reality of his death (6:41-42, 61; 19:35)."[51]

H. Ridderbos has given attention to the Prologue and surveys a number of views of its composition and significance.[52] Arising out of his study he can say,

> The Gospel, therefore, is not in the first place a witness of the faith, but of that which has been seen and heard and handled with the hands. And, therefore, whoever asserts that the background of the faith of the evangelist is another than that of the events which he narrates, attacks not only the narrative, but also the Kerygma of the evangelist at its very heart.[53]

The genuine humanity of Jesus in this Gospel, his becoming *flesh,* is at the heart of the matter as Ridderbos sees it.

From the evidence, then, it seems that Käsemann is oversimplifying. No one who studies John's Gospel will want to deny that Jesus is there depicted as divine. He is the very Son of God sent to earth to bring about man's salvation. But to say that therefore he is not also very man is to overlook a great proportion of the evidence. There seems no doubt whatever that these scholars are right who see a balance in John between the deity and the humanity. For all its brilliance, there is nothing in Käsemann's study to disturb this conclusion.

Notes to Chapter 4

1. Ernst Käsemann, *The Testament of Jesus* (London: SCM, 1968) 76. He thinks that this Gospel's "acceptance into the Church's canon took place through man's error and God's providence" (ibid., 75).

2. G. E. Ladd, *The Pattern of New Testament Truth* (Grand Rapids: Eerdmans, 1968) 41; see also 108-111. S. Smalley argues similarly with regard to this Gospel, "Diversity and Development in John," *NTS* 17 (1970-71) 276-292.
3. Käsemann, *Testament,* 27.
4. Ibid., 26, 45, 70.
5. Ibid., 66. There are those who object to the use of such designations as "docetism," for example, George T. Montague who says, "to apply to Jn the later categories which developed as a result of isolating and emphasizing certain Johannine tendencies seems to err by reading back into the Gospel a historical situation that is post-Johannine, as one might accuse Mt of Ebionitism or Paul of Marcionism" *(CBQ* 31 [1969] 438).
6. Käsemann, *Testament,* 42, 50, 58, etc. Perhaps we should notice that some see the emphasis otherwise. Thus F. V. Filson holds that the author of this Gospel makes "the theme of life so central that the Gospel is rightly called the Gospel of Life" ("The Gospel of Life, A Study of the Gospel of John," in *Current Issues in New Testament Interpretation: Essays in Honor of Otto Piper* [edd. W. Klassen and G. Snyder; New York: Harper, 1962] 123). We should not miss either R. Schnackenburg's point that John's Christology "is completely orientated towards soteriology" *(The Gospel according to St. John* [*HTCNT;* New York: Herder, 1968] I, 548). But others support Käsemann. Thus W. Nicol writes, "This intense concentration on Jesus alone is the primary characteristic of the Fourth Gospel. The Synoptic Gospels place Jesus in the frame of the Kingdom and Paul of the eschatology, but the fourth Evangelist brings Jesus alone on the stage with all lights on Him" *(Neot* 6 [1972] 17).
7. Käsemann, *Testament,* 9.
8. Ibid., 10.
9. Raymond E. Brown, *The Gospel according to John (AB* 29; New York: Doubleday, 1966) 254.
10. J. H. Bernard, for example, thinks that if we had only John's account "we should have no reason to suppose that he intended to record any 'miracle.' . . . It is probable that he means here that when the boat got into the shallow water near the western shore, the disciples saw Jesus in the uncertain light walking by the lake, and were frightened, not being sure what they saw" *(A Critical and Exegetical Commentary on the Gospel according to St. John* [Edinburgh: T. & T. Clark, 1928] 185). Barclay is another who sees no miracle, and A. M. Hunter holds that "it is far from certain that John 6:16-21 implies a miracle: the crucial phrase *peripatounta epi tes thalasses* would naturally mean 'walking by the sea' " *(According to John* [London: SCM, 1968] 66). Later he says that in this narrative John "appears to 'de-miraculize' the miraculous" (ibid., 71). Bultmann cites B. Weiss as another who finds no miracle here.
11. C. K. Barrett comments, "the Jewish opposition had been fierce. The step taken in v. 10 was therefore both dangerous and decisive" *(The Gospel according to St. John* [London: SPCK, 1955] 256).
12. John Calvin, *The Gospel according to St. John 1-10* (Grand Rapids: Eerdmans, 1959) 193.
13. Everett F. Harrison, *John: The Gospel of Faith* (Chicago: Moody, 1962) 34.
14. J. H. Bernard agrees that knowledge like this is possessed by God and that the Old Testament makes this clear. "But it is also, in its measure, a prerogative of human genius; and (with the possible exception of 1^{48}) it is not clear that Jn. means us to understand that the insight of Jesus into men's motives and characters was different in kind from that exhibited by other great masters of mankind" *(John,* 99).
15. Leon Morris, *The Gospel according to John (NICNT;* Grand Rapids: Eerdmans, 1971) 207 n. 99.
16. The questions asked by the risen Christ (20:15; 21:5, 15, 16, 17, 22) are not relevant to our subject, since on any showing the risen Lord was in some respects significantly different from the earthly Jesus.
17. F. E. Burkitt, *The Gospel History and its Transmission* (Edinburgh: T. & T. Clark, 1907) 228.
18. Cf. C. K. Barrett, "Jesus, who knows the witness of the 'Other', is independent of human witness" *(John,* 220).
19. Nils Dahl, "The Johannine Church and History," in *Current Issues,* 138.
20. Ibid., 136.
21. G. J. Cuming, *ExpTim,* 60 (1948-49) 292. He thinks that the way John uses the term "strongly suggests that the Evangelist was a Galilean" (ibid.).
22. Oscar Cullmann, *The Johannine Circle* (London: SCM, 1976) 38.

23. Cf. A. Henderson, "It was not that he made up his mind not to go to Bethany for two days; but that for those two days he waited for light, which he was sure would come, as to his Father's will. When it came he set out, doubting and fearing nothing" (quoted by T. E. Pollard, *SE*, VI, 438).
24. Barrett rejects the view that Jesus waited for Lazarus to die "in order that a more glorious miracle might be effected," and thinks it more probable "that John wished to underline the fact that Jesus' movement towards Jerusalem, and so to his death, was entirely self-determined" (*John*, 325).
25. Th. C. de Kruijf, "The Glory of the Only Son," *Studies in John Presented to Prof. Dr. J. N. Sevenster on the Occasion of his Seventieth Birthday* (Leiden: Brill, 1970) 121. Bernard sees the words as expressing "the intimate relationship of love between the Son and the Father" (*John*, 32).
26. R. H. Strachan, *The Fourth Gospel* (London: SCM, 1955) 11.
27. The relevant passage is quoted in H. Odeberg, *The Fourth Gospel* (Chicago: Argonaut, 1968) 33-34. See also the notes in the commentaries of Bernard and Barrett.
28. Cited in M. F. Wiles, *The Spiritual Gospel* (Cambridge: Cambridge University, 1960) 82.
29. As C. K. Barrett, for example, does: "the story of Jesus can be told in terms of glory—he has laid aside but will resume the glory he had with the Father before creation; he seeks not his own glory but the glory of the Father, yet in his voluntary humiliation and obedience, and pre-eminently in the disgrace of the cross, he is glorified, and manifests his glory. . . . There is a characteristic Johannine paradox here" ("The Theological Vocabulary of the Fourth Gospel and of the Gospel of Truth," *Current Issues*, 211-212). Vincent Taylor could write, "There could be no vainer controversy than the dispute whether in these passages (i.e. John 3:14; 8:28; 12:32) the crucifixion or the exaltation is meant. The death *is* the exaltation" (*The Atonement in New Testament Teaching* [London: Epworth, 1946] 147).
30. S. Smalley holds that "It is possible to expound" this expression "in the manner of either Bultmann or Käsemann only if violence is done to the balance between humanity and divinity, humiliation and glory, that are an inescapable part of the Johannine perspective" (*SE*, VI, 498).
31. R. Schnackenburg, *John*, I, 267. He goes on to notice that what Bultmann calls "the language of mythology" "takes the utmost pains to avoid the term σάρξ and it never speaks of 'becoming flesh' " (ibid., 268). A. B. Du Toit sees σάρξ as pointing to "the typical human mode of existence in all its frailty, brokenness and defectiveness in contrast to the heavenly, divine mode of existence" (*Neot* 2 [1968] 15). R. Bultmann sees σάρξ as referring in John "to the sphere of the human and the worldly as opposed to the divine, i.e. the sphere of the πνεῦμα, 3:6; 6:63 . . . but whereas σκότος refers to the worldly sphere in its enmity towards God, σάρξ stresses its transitoriness, helplessness and vanity (3:6; 6:63)." He holds that "the Revealer is nothing but a man" and that "the *offence* of the gospel is brought out as strongly as possible by ὁ λόγος σὰρξ ἐγένετο" (*The Gospel of John: A Commentary* [Oxford: Blackwell, 1971] 62, 63).
32. Ibid., 268.
33. Du Toit, *Neot* 15-16, 18.
34. Cf. the essay by G. Sevenster, "Remarks on the Humanity of Jesus in the Gospel and Letters of John," in *Studies in John*, 185-193. He gives particular attention to John 19:5.
35. Käsemann, *Testament*, 7.
36. R. T. Fortna, "Christology in the Fourth Gospel: Redaction-Critical Perspectives," *NTS* 21 (1974-75) 497. Barnabas Lindars holds that Käsemann "relies almost exclusively on the later strands of the gospel from the point of view of literary criticism (the Prologue, the Supper Discourses, the Prayer), which represent the mature reflection of the evangelist rather than his original impetus; and that the exegesis is so heavily worked into the categories of contemporary German thought that it constitutes a creative theology rather than an exposition" (*Theology* 72 [1969] 157).
37. Fortna, "Christology," 497.
38. Ibid., 502.
39. Käsemann, *Testament*, 10.
40. C. K. Barrett has a thought-provoking article in the Schnackenburg *Festschrift* entitled, " 'The Father is greater than I' (Jo 14, 28): Subordinationist Christology in the New Testament." He argues that John has an important strand of teaching in which he depicts the Christ as subordinate to the Father. There is an element of paradox here: "It is natural, and not in the

end wrong, to describe the result in the language of paradox: one speaks of majesty veiled in humility" *(Neues Testament und Kirche* [ed. J. Gnilka; Freiburg-Basel-Wien: Herder, 1974] 158; Barrett refers to Hoskyns and Davey). There is a problem and Barrett does not claim to have solved it. But we do not get rid of it by denying one element in the paradox. John has something more in mind than God walking on earth.

41. J. Ernest Davey, *The Jesus of St. John* (London: Lutterworth, 1958) 90-157. Italics mine.

42. Ibid., 12, 85, 133, 186.

43. Ibid., 77. He goes on to refer to the view that John portrays a Christ "who is omniscient, omnipotent, self-determining and independent" as "a myth." He thinks that theologically the synoptists emphasize the deity of Christ and the fourth Gospel the humanity, though, of course, both elements are found in all four Gospels (ibid., 170). A. M. Hunter accepts Davey's argument *(According to John,* 115).

44. Cf. the definition in G. Abbott-Smith, *A Manual Greek Lexicon of the New Testament* (Edinburgh: T. & T. Clark, 1954) *s.v. "to snort in* (of horses, Aesch.), hence, to speak or act with deep feeling" (here he sees the meaning, "to be moved with anger").

45. Franz Mussner points out that in this Gospel "The believer in the act of knowing sees, of course, just as 'the world' does, Jesus in his sheer humanity," and goes on to maintain that this "sheer humanity" does not become "transfigured even for the believer and knower but is radically maintained" *(The Historical Jesus in the Gospel of St. John* [New York: Herder, 1967] 28).

46. Käsemann, *Testament,* 66.

47. C. F. D. Moule criticizes Käsemann for "detaching the Gospel from the First Epistle in an unjustifiable way" *(Studies in John,* 158). Hoskyns paid a good deal of attention to 1 John in setting forth his view that the fourth Gospel opposes docetism (E. Hoskyns, *The Fourth Gospel* [London: Faber, 1950] 48-57).

48. Käsemann, *Testament,* 10.

49. G. E. Ladd, *A Theology of the New Testament* (Grand Rapids: Eerdmans, 1974) 252.

50. Brown, *John,* lxxvi-vii.

51. Dahl, "The Johannine Church," *Current Issues,* 142. In the same volume Markus Barth, writing on Hebrews, says, "No other book of the New Testament (except the Fourth Gospel) puts the real deity and true humanity of Jesus Christ so clearly side by side" ("The Old Testament in Hebrews, An Essay in Biblical Hermeneutics," 58). O. Cullmann more than once says that in this Gospel there is at least an implicit opposition to docetism *(The Johannine Circle,* 17, 58, 61). See also R. H. Strachan, *John,* 44-45; T. W. Manson, *On Paul and John* (London: SCM, 1963) 156-157, etc.

52. H. Ridderbos, "The Structure and Scope of the Prologue to the Gospel of John," *NovT* 8 (1966) 180-201.

53. Ibid., 200.

5: The Book of Acts and History

W. WARD GASQUE

Recent scholarly research on the Acts of the Apostles has focussed primarily on its theology.[1] Ever since the pioneering work of Martin Dibelius (1883-1947),[2] who, though he considered the author of Luke-Acts to be a historian, argued that the question of historical reliability was of little importance, scholars, particularly in Germany, have emphasized the work of Luke as a creative theologian.

Insofar as this has led to a fresh appreciation of the work of the author of Luke-Acts as an author and theologian in his own right to be placed alongside Paul, Mark, John, and the other writers of the New Testament, this new look in Lukan studies has been salutary and has added an essentially positive dimension to our understanding of the third Gospel and the Acts of the Apostles. The author does have a theology that is distinctively his, at least in certain features; and in his interpretation of both the work and words of Jesus and the events of the first three decades of the church's existence he has not simply chronicled history and transcribed traditions which have been handed down to him by others. There is no retreating from these firm conclusions. We may speak therefore of "the theology of Luke" and seek to trace its features and to compare it with the other theologies of the New Testament. And when we speak of him as a historian, we must not fail to recognize that, as the one to whom this *Festschrift* is dedicated has observed, he "is not a critical historian in the modern sense of the word."[3] However, this does not by any means justify the assumption that the author has little concern for historical reality or that the narrative he has written is unreliable from a historical point of view, nor does it excuse contemporary scholars for their neglect of the positive conclusions of an earlier generation of scholarship concerning the trustworthiness of Acts.

I

THE NARRATIVE OF ACTS AND THE DATA OF HISTORICAL RESEARCH

The real test of the historical reliability of Acts is the hard data of historical research, and it is a study of these that leads, I believe, to a positive conclusion concerning the subject. The following examples are offered as illustrations of the ways the narrative of Acts is confirmed when tested by the usual canons of historical research.

One of the best-known examples of the careful accuracy of the author of the Acts of the Apostles is his use of technical terms when referring to the various important personalities who appear on the pages of his narrative. In contrast to the modern writer, who has access to research tools in libraries to give him accurate information concerning the historical details of an age or a geographical region other than his own, the historian in antiquity did not have such resources at his disposal; rather, if he was to be accurate in the portrayal of a historical situation other than his own he had to have direct access to firsthand information, either by way of written or oral sources or through personal experience. He had no way to check his information as the modern historical novelist does.[4] There was no such thing in antiquity as "historical imagination" in the modern sense; if a historian proved to be accurate, it was because he had access to (and used!) accurate information. Thus it is very impressive indeed when one observes that the author of Acts is invariably accurate in his use of the proper titles of a large variety of people spread over a large geographical area in the Eastern Roman Empire during a limited period of the first century A.D.

For example, when Paul and Barnabas arrive in Cyprus about A.D. 47, they have an encounter with the *proconsul* (ἀνθύπατος), Sergius Paulus (Acts 13:7). This is precisely the correct title for the Roman governor at this particular time (the situation was different at both an earlier and later date), since Cyprus was a senatorial province. The same is true in the case of the provinces of Achaia and Asia, which were also senatorial. Thus Acts refers to Gallio as the proconsul of Achaia (18:12). It is noteworthy that here the author of Acts, who normally prefers to use the ethnic or popular names for various countries (cf. 20:2, where he calls Achaia by its more ordinary name Greece), departs from his custom and uses the governor's official title. It is of further interest that an inscription was discovered at Delphi which not only indicates the accuracy of the author of Acts in his use of the correct title but also gives Gallio's name and indicates a date which fits the narrative of Acts perfectly. In Acts 19:38 the town clerk of Ephesus refers to "proconsuls," using the plural. It is just possible to interpret this as a "generalizing plural" (but why not: "There is the proconsul"?), but a study of the chronological evidence shows that only a few months prior to the time represented by the narrative of Acts 19 there had been an assassination of the proconsul of Asia, Junius Silanus, by agents of Agrippina, the mother of Nero, who had just become emperor. A successor had not yet arrived, and the murderers of Silanus, Helius and Celer by name, were in charge of the emperor's affairs in Asia. Thus the plural may have been used because these two men were acting as proconsuls, or simply because there was no official proconsul resident in Asia at the time. In either case the use of the plural is significant.

Luke also refers to the town clerk (γραμματεύς) and the asiarchs at Ephesus (19:35, 31). The former was an official native to Ephesus who acted as the link between the city government and the Roman administration. The asiarchs were the representatives of the province who presided over the provincial cult of "Rome and the Emperor." It may be that they were in Ephesus for the local festival of Artemisia, where they would represent the Emperor. In Thessalonica the chief magistrates are given the title "politarchs" (πολιτάρχαι, 17:6, 9), a title not found in classical literature but abundantly attested by inscriptions as a title of magistrates in Macedonian towns, including Thessalonica. On Malta the chief official is called "the first man of the island" (28:7), a title which has been found in both Greek and Latin inscriptions as the designation of the governor of Malta. Correct terms are also used in referring to the Roman soldiers mentioned: two centurions (Cornelius and Julius) with the names of their cohorts (Italian and Augustan) and one tribune (χιλιάρχος), Claudius Lysias by name (21:31, 33, 37; 22:24; 23:10, 17, 19, 26). Furthermore, the author of Acts seems to display detailed knowledge of the unique division of the province of Macedonia into four administratively separate parts (16:12). And so the examples could be multiplied.

The narrative of Acts is, in fact, full of historical details incidentally mentioned by the author which suggest that he must have been writing on the basis of a careful knowledge of the events included. For example, the author has Paul encountering the high priest Ananias a short time before he meets the procurator Felix (23:2, 33; 24:2, 3); he indicates that Felix was married to Drusilla at the time (24:24); he further notes that Felix was superseded by Festus shortly thereafter and that Festus, just after his arrival in Palestine, gave Paul a hearing in the presence of King Agrippa II, who was living with his sister Bernice at the time (25:1-27). As R. P. C. Hanson[5] comments, "This is a very remarkable piece of synchronization on the part of the author."

> It would have taken a very considerable amount of research for a later historian to discover that Ananias must have been the high priest contemporary with Paul at that point, that this took place in the period when Felix was married to Drusilla (who had been born in 38 and had had one husband already before Felix), and that not long afterwards Bernice (who had already had two husbands) was living for a period (a limited period) with her brother, during the procuratorship of Festus.[6]

Concerning this same small section of the narrative of Acts, the Roman historian A. N. Sherwin-White[7] notes a further minor but important sign of the author's careful accuracy. In his question to Paul, Felix asks him concerning the province he comes from and then decides to hear his case when he hears that he came from Cilicia (23:34-35). Ordinarily one would expect Paul to be sent back to his home province for trial. But Cilicia—at this particular time and *only* at this time—was merely a part of the larger province of Syria, and the legate of Syria would not wish to be bothered with a relatively minor case from an outlying part of his territory. The situation was entirely different during the Flavian period (A.D. 69-96), when Cilicia was a province in its own right. Earlier in the same section of Acts (21:38), the Roman tribune refers to the Egyptian who recently stirred up a revolt and led the four thousand "men of the Sicarii" into the wilderness as if it were a recent occurrence. Josephus mentions the same minor event as taking place during the procuratorship of Felix (though he exaggerates the number of participants to 30,000)—another highly unlikely piece of historical accuracy on the part of a writer who is alleged to have had very limited access to the actual facts of the age he recounts. Again, there is Claudius Lysias' statement (22:28) that he obtained his Roman citizenship by the payment of a large sum of money (i.e., by a bribe), a practice which was common under Claudius but which was discovered and effectively ended in the time of Nero; thus both this incidental statement and his name fit the facts perfectly.[8] Finally, there is the accurate designation of the two Roman centurions mentioned in Acts (Cornelius in 10:1 and Julius in 21:1) by their Gentile *nomina* only. This was an old-fashioned type of name which was found only in the Roman army by the middle of the first century. That the author of Acts uses this type of Latin name for only two people, both soldiers, at the precise time in history when only soldiers are likely to be still using it, is surely no mere historical accident.[9]

In more general terms, Sherwin-White takes a look at the legal, administrative, and municipal background of the activities of Paul as portrayed in Acts. At some length he demonstrates that detail of the account of Paul's various experiences as narrated in Acts fits the historical conditions prevailing at the time of the dramatic date of the events (the middle of the first century A.D.) exactly. He argues, further, that various legal practices, the meaning of Roman citizenship, etc. began to change toward the end of the century, and that the situation was very different in many important respects at a later date. In his careful examination of Acts 16-28 he finds that the account of the preliminary trials before Felix and Festus, the details regarding the legal privileges and organization of the government of the various cities visited by Paul, the references to Roman legal problems, the use of the names of Roman citizens and the meaning of Roman citizenship,[10] and, above all, the details concerning Paul's Roman citizenship and his appeal to Caesar[11]—all correspond to what we know of the historical situation which existed during the last half of the first century, rather than at a later date (i.e., the time when many who deny its historicity suggest Acts was written). Sherwin-White concludes his examination of the historical data with the observation that the essential historicity of that part of Acts which pertains to the life and ministry of Paul, when tested by the ordinary canons of historical criticism, is demonstrated beyond any serious doubt. This makes the suggestion that Acts was written by an author who was not very closely connected to the events which he narrates, or who lived at a time much later than the time about which he writes, extremely implausible. It is historically improbable, if not impossible, for an author who lived at a much later time than the time about which he writes to have been so minutely accurate concerning the actual historical context of the story he is narrating. A later writer would certainly have been guilty of anachronisms of which the author of Acts is never guilty.[12] Much more could be said on the subject if space allowed, but enough has been said to indicate that there are very good reasons for accepting the Book of Acts as a historically trustworthy document.[13]

Two questions remain, however, among those which have been raised by modern scholarship, and these deserve to be answered. These questions concern (1) the use of speeches in Acts and (2) the alleged contradiction between "the Paul of the Acts" and "the Paul of the Epistles."

II

THE SPEECHES IN THE ACTS OF THE APOSTLES

According to many recent interpreters, the speeches of Acts, which play an important role in the development of the narrative (comprising approximately three hundred out of a total of a thousand verses), are the free literary creations of the author.[14] Not only are they not verbatim reports of what was said on any given occasion, neither are they abbreviated summaries of what was said by the speakers upon whose lips they are placed. Nor do they represent traditional materials which the author has incorporated into his narrative. In short, they are not intended to give an impression of what Peter or Paul or Stephen or James said on such and such an occasion, but rather what the author intends them to say to the church of his day, or, at most, what the author conceived to be the sort of thing that these early Christian leaders would have been likely to say. They are of historical value primarily as representatives of the ideas and theology of the author of Acts—and perhaps also of the church of his day—rather than as sources for the ideas and theology of the original speakers or the primitive Christian community.

There are a number of reasons put forward in support of this negative judgment. It is argued (1) that it was the generally accepted pattern for Graeco-Roman historians to freely invent speeches and to introduce them into their narratives for dramatic effect, for the impression that they will make on the reader. By the use of speeches, the point is made, the historian in antiquity may attempt to sum up the significance of the occasion, offer an insight into the meaning of the event which transcends the facts of history, portray the authentic character of the speaker, or develop the ideas which he is attempting to promote by means of his historical writing. On occasion, he may simply be attempting to further the action of the story in order to maintain a high degree of interest among his readers. Various proof-texts are quoted from ancient historians to demonstrate the point (e.g., the famous passage in Thucydides, *History of the Peloponnesian War* 1.22.1) as well as the obvious example of some writers (e.g., Josephus).

It is further argued (2) that there would have been no existing records of any of the speeches for the author of Acts to make use of even if he were inclined to do so; (3) that the literary style of the speeches are all the same, regardless of who is speaking; (4) that there is a theological unity to the speeches which ignores the historical differences which existed between, e.g., Peter and Paul; (5) that similar literary techniques are used in several of the speeches (e.g., the sudden interruption of Acts 2:47; 7:54; and 22:22); and (6) that a common outline provides the basic pattern for each of the speeches.

Again, space will not allow an attempt to demonstrate that some of the above assumptions are highly questionable indeed. This will have to be left to another time and place.[15] However, it must be noted that there are some very good reasons to doubt the suggestion that the author of Acts has freely invented the speeches he has included in his narrative.

First, it is not entirely clear that it was the accepted practice for ancient historians to compose speeches freely and to introduce them into their narrative as expressions of their own ideas. Certainly, some historians did just this. Josephus is a notable example, and he no doubt was following the pattern of many second-rate historians. The question is, however, whether this was the universal practice, whether *all* historians freely invented speeches which had no basis in fact and put these into the mouths of the leading characters of their narratives, and whether this was a generally accepted custom.

There is evidence that some ancient historians were more responsible in their use of speeches than this theory would suggest. In fact, a few of the references alleged to illustrate the acceptability of the custom of inventing speeches among ancient historians[16] actually point in the opposite direction.

The celebrated passage from Thucydides, for example, if taken at its face value, contradicts this thesis. In the section of his history where he spells out his historical methodology (1.22), he has this to say about his handling of the speeches contained in his narrative:

> With reference to the speeches in this history, some were delivered before the war began, others while it was going on; it was hard to record the exact words

> spoken, both in cases where I was myself present, and where I used the reports of others. But I have used language in accordance with what I thought the speakers in each case would have been most likely to say, adhering as closely as possible to the general sense of what was actually spoken.

This passage is interpreted by Martin Dibelius and others as an attempted justification by Thucydides of the practice of composing speeches with little or no regard for what actually may have been said. In point of fact, Thucydides makes the exact opposite claim, namely, that he did *not* invent speeches! "For some of the speeches," he says (to paraphrase), "I was present and heard what was actually spoken. For others I am dependent on the report of other people who heard them. It has been, of course, difficult to recall verbatim what was said on each occasion; therefore, I have made the speeches say what I thought was appropriate to the occasion, *keeping as closely as possible to the general idea of what was actually spoken.*" Some scholars, it is true, have questioned whether Thucydides really lived up to the high standard which he claims. Others, however, have given a good case for the view that he did.[17] At any rate, it is clear that Thucydides did not consider the invention of speeches an acceptable historiographical method—at least, in principle.

Polybius (*ca.* 201-120 B.C.), the second great Greek historian after Thucydides, time and again explicitly condemns the custom of the free invention of speeches by historians. In one passage (12.25.1) he roundly condemns a historian for inventing a speech and makes the point that the historian, in his synopsis of a speech, must be true to the actual words of the original. Elsewhere he accuses another writer of trying to imagine the probable utterances of his characters instead of "simply recording what was said, however commonplace" (2.56.10). In his view there is a place for literary embellishment in the speeches, calling attention to important stages of development in the narrative; but even here the speeches must be true to τὰ κατ' ἀλήθειαν λεχθέντα ("the words actually spoken").[18] Again, it is perhaps debatable whether Polybius always lived up to the high standard he set for himself and his fellow historians. However, there seems to be evidence that he often did—or that he, at least, made the attempt to do so.[19]

In his celebrated essay on the speeches in Acts and ancient historiography, Martin Dibelius argued that the ancient historian felt under no obligation to reproduce the text of a speech even if he had access to it. As proof of this he pointed to a well-known speech of Claudius concerning the conferring of the *jus honorum* upon the people of Gaul, which is preserved in an inscription[20] but is found in a different form in Tacitus' *Annals* (11.24); the speeches which Josephus in the *Antiquities* puts into the mouths of the patriarchs; and the fact that Josephus reproduces a speech of Herod in two different forms. Few will be prepared to defend Josephus; however, the example to which Dibelius points in Tacitus not only does not support the point he is attempting to make but contradicts it. A careful comparison of the surviving fragments of the published inscription of the speech alongside the version in Tacitus[21] makes it clear that Tacitus has not freely created the version which appears in the *Annals* but rather has freely abridged and paraphrased the original speech by Claudius. The classicist Furneaux comments:

> On the whole, the substance of the existing portions [of the inscribed speech] may be said to have been given [by Tacitus], and the fact that they are represented by but a few sentences would go to prove that the whole speech (as indeed the fragments themselves suggest) was long and discursive, and could only be brought into a space proportionate to the narrative of the *Annals* by much omission and abridgement.[22]

In short, the style and expression of the speech as found in the *Annals* belong (with the exception of a few verbal parallels) to Tacitus, but its contents belong to Claudius. The matter of the speech has been condensed, rearranged, and adapted; but the ancient historian has remained true to the essential ideas of the original.

Thus some of the examples cited by Dibelius and others in an attempt to demonstrate the general acceptability on the part of Graeco-Roman historians of the custom of inventing speeches actually go to prove the opposite, except in the case of Josephus. To this could be added other examples,[23] though it must be admitted that an imposing number of counter-examples could also be adduced. Enough has been said, however, to make it clear that the free invention of speeches was not a *universally* accepted practice among historians in the Graeco-Roman world. It may have been the general practice; it was certainly a widespread practice. But Thucydides and Polybius were in principle opposed to the practice, as were other men of letters (e.g., Lucian); and it is probable that there were many who attempted to be just as responsible in their handling of speeches.

But what about the author of Acts? Are there evidences that he is not freely inventing the speeches he includes in his narrative? I believe there are. First, there is the very evident contrast between the speeches of Acts and the obviously composed speeches of the inferior Greek historians. Josephus (*Ant.* 1.13.3), for example, puts a lengthy speech into the mouth of Abraham as he is about to sacrifice Isaac. Elsewhere he substitutes "several hundred words of dreary rhetoric, highly polished and unbearably insipid, whose frigidity is matched only by that of the answering speech" for the brief and moving words of Judah in Genesis 44.[24] By contrast, the speeches in Acts do not give obvious evidence of being simply the rhetorical compositions of the author. They are generally very brief, fitting to the occasion, and not by any means the most literary part of the author's work. Furthermore, as A. Ehrhardt has pointed out,[25] if the author has invented speeches, he has missed a number of very good occasions on which a speech would be expected (for example, following 5:21 and 28:16). The best explanation of such omissions is that he knew of no speech on these occasions.

Secondly, those who believe that the author of Acts invented speeches tend to dismiss the speeches of the third Gospel (where the author can be checked) as evidence for the author's methodology in the speeches of the Book of Acts (where the author cannot be checked). In spite of assertions to the contrary—based on the twin assumptions that the early Christians had no interest in their own history and that they would have been interested in remembering only the words of Jesus and not anything that the apostles had said[26]—the fact that Luke does not invent speeches in the Gospel cannot be arbitrarily set aside when inquiring into the author's historical methodology in the second volume of his work. Where we can compare Luke with Mark, presumably one of his sources for the Gospel, we find that he has rearranged and reworded the sayings and speeches to some degree (in the authentic tradition of the Greek historical writers);[27] but he has not been unfaithful in his reproduction of their essential meaning. Therefore, the dictum of F. F. Bruce: "If this is the verdict on Luke in places where his fidelity to his source can be controlled, we should not without good reason suppose that he was not equally faithful where his sources are no longer available for comparison."[28] Luke's handling of the speech material in the Gospel is not *proof* that he must have used the same technique in the Book of Acts, but it would seem to demand a serious consideration of this possibility.

A third factor which goes against the hypothesis that the author of Acts freely composed his speeches is the diversity—both linguistically and theologically—which characterizes them (again, in spite of an assertion to the contrary). No one, as far as I know, denies that the *language* of all the speeches is, generally speaking, Luke's. This is true in the Gospel, even though the content stems from his sources. The real question is whether there is evidence to support the view that the author may have been dependent on sources of some kind, written or oral, for the *content* of the speeches.

In spite of the *similarities* which exist among the speeches, the *differences* are also great. The layman who hears the suggestion that the speeches of Peter in the early chapters of Acts, the speech of Stephen, the Areopagus address of Paul at Athens, and Paul's farewell address to the Ephesian elders at Miletus are all the literary creations of a single mind may be tempted to scoff at the absurdity of the suggestion. This is not the impression which one has when one compares them. Although there is a basic unity of language and even of theology (as one would expect, if the picture the writer of Acts gives of the essential agreement of the early church on basic issues[29] is accurate), there are also striking differences. For example, as C. F.

D. Moule has demonstrated,[30] the Christology of the speeches in Acts is not uniform. If the older generation of scholars, both conservative and radical, were agreed on anything, it was the primitive nature of the theology of the speeches of the early chapters of Acts. Furthermore, Stephen's speech has no real parallels in the rest of the Book of Acts.[31] Again, J. W. Doeve[32] has pointed out the different use of the same passage of scripture (Ps 16:10) in the speech attributed to Peter in Acts 2 and in the one ascribed to Paul in Acts 13. Both the structure and the argument in the two instances are different, the influence of Aramaic idiom being evident in the development of the argument of the former and the argument of a schooled rabbi being perceptible in that of the latter. Doeve's conclusion is this:

> If the author of Acts composed the discourse in chap. XIII himself, then he must have had an excellent command of hermeneutics as practised in rabbinic Judaism. If one assumes that he also composed the discourse in Acts II, this implies that he was capable of imitating different styles of exegesis.[33]

The author of Acts, it should be remembered, is recognized by the vast majority of scholars as a Gentile Christian; and those who regard the speeches of Acts as his own composition assign him to a time in history when contacts between church and synagogue are all but non-existent. And this same author is considered to be responsible for the speeches of the latter part of Acts as well. To fulfill the requirements of a role like this the author must have been a remarkable *litterateur* indeed!

Further evidence which tends to go against the view that the speeches of Acts are Lukan compositions is the presence of many small phrases contained in the speeches, often semitic,[34] which do not seem to be due to the author's own hand, presumably features which he has failed to edit out. If Luke had simply invented the speeches for rhetorical and theological purposes, one would expect them to represent the high point of his literary achievement. But with the possible exception of the Areopagus speech of Acts 17, this is definitely not the case. In fact, the speeches of the early chapters are often extremely awkward in style. To suggest that this awkwardness is due to (or even evidence for!) Luke's literary ability, that he is deliberately patterning his style after that of the Septuagint to give an archaic flavor to the early part of his narrative, is scarcely plausible. Though it is theoretically possible that the author possessed the literary genius necessary to create speeches as different as Peter's Pentecostal address and Paul's speech before the Areopagus, to compose speeches in the style of the Greek Old Testament in the early chapters and in a semi-classical style in the latter, and to vary his theology according to speaker, there would seem to be a higher degree of historical probability in favor of the view that some kind of source (written or oral) lies behind the speeches. Therefore, upon taking a closer look, there seems to be a good prima facie case against the view that Luke freely invented the speeches contained in Acts.

III

"THE PAUL OF ACTS" AND "THE PAUL OF THE EPISTLES"

Now to the second remaining question. In an introductory section on "Luke and Paul" in his great commentary,[35] Haenchen lists three items which he considers to be proof that the author of Acts could not have been "ein Paulus Gefährte." First, the author solves the problem of the Gentile mission and the controversy concerning the law in a totally un-Pauline fashion. Secondly, the portrait of Paul in Acts contradicts the letters in that Paul is made to be a miracle worker, a forceful speaker, and not an apostle of equal standing with the Twelve. And, thirdly, he contradicts the Pauline letters in his portrayal of Jewish and Gentile relations. But the classic recent exposition of this point of view is an essay by Philipp Vielhauer on the "Paulinism" of Acts.[36]

In his essay Vielhauer contrasts the theologies of the "Lukan Paul" (the Paul of Acts) and the "historical Paul" (the Paul of Romans, Galatians, and the Corinthian letters) on four points: natural theology, the law, Christology, and eschatology. In his discussion of the "natural theology" of the Lukan Paul, Vielhauer argues (in dependence on Dibelius)[37] that the ideas of the speech are essentially Hellenistic (based on Stoic philosophy), that the emphasis of the speech is on man's natural kinship with the divine, and that the thought expressed betrays a positive and definitely un-Pauline attitude toward pagan religion. By contrast, the "natural theology" of the real Paul (in Romans 1, for example) was connected with an emphasis on man's sin and God's wrath; it was the foundation for his scorching condemnation of the sinner. Moreover, the Areopagus address has no concept of "sin and grace"—and, above all, no "word of the cross." In both his positive emphasis and in his omissions the Paul of the Areopagus address is as far removed from Paul as he is near to the second-century apologists.

According to Vielhauer, the historical Paul waged an anti-Jewish polemic against the law, but the Lukan Paul is utterly loyal to the law. The Paul of Acts differs from other Jews *only* in the fact that he "believes in Jesus as the Messiah in contrast to the Jews," who have rejected him as such; he is the representative of the authentic Israel in contrast to the representatives of official Judaism. Although Vielhauer admits that it is a theoretical possibility that Paul could have kept some of the outward forms of Judaism merely as "an accommodation of practical attitude," he finds two points of the narrative of Acts impossible to believe.

The first of these impossibilities is Paul's participation, on the advice of James, in a Nazirite vow to disprove the accusations of the Jews and the Jewish Christians that he was teaching the Jews of the Dispersion to apostatize from the law of Moses (21:18-28). In Vielhauer's opinion participation in such a vow would have been rank hypocrisy on the part of Paul, who did in fact teach Jews to forsake the law! For Paul to have taken part in such a ceremony with the end in view attributed to him by the author of Acts would have meant a denial of "his actual practice and his gospel, . . . a denial that the cross of Christ alone was of saving significance for Gentiles *and* Jews." The second impossibility concerns the account of the circumcision of Timothy (16:3). The Paul who wrote in Galatians 5:2, "If you receive circumcision, Christ will be of no advantage to you," could never have caused Timothy to be circumcised. Thus Vielhauer comments: "The statement about the circumcision of Timothy stands in direct contradiction to the theology of Paul, but it fits Luke's view that the Law retains its full validity for Jewish Christians and that Paul acknowledged this in a conciliatory concession to the Jews."

A further contrast between the Lukan Paul and the historical Paul is found in Acts 13:38-39, the only reference to "justification" in any of Paul's speeches. Here, according to Vielhauer, justification is equated with the forgiveness of sins and thus is conceived entirely negatively, which Paul never does. Furthermore, the reference to "forgiveness of sins" does not occur in the major Pauline letters, but only in Colossians and Ephesians; on the other hand, it *does* occur in the speeches of Peter in Acts (2:38; 3:19; 5:31; 10:43). In addition, the forgiveness of sins is tied to the Messiahship of Jesus, which is based on the resurrection; as Franz Overbeck had commented, "nothing is said . . . about the particular significance of his death." Finally, Luke, a Gentile Christian belonging to a later generation, never experienced the law as a way of salvation and therefore was able to understand neither the antithesis between the law and Christ in the thought of Paul nor the essential nature of the conflict over the law in the early church. Thus he "speaks of the inadequacy of the law, whereas Paul speaks of the end of the law, which is Christ (Rom. 10.4)." In the theology of the author of Acts, "the 'word of the cross' has no place because in Acts it would make no sense."

Thirdly, there is nothing at all of Paul's Christology in Acts. The Christology of the speeches is simply that of the undeveloped theology of the early church (so Dibelius). There is no reference to the pre-existence of Christ, which was so important for Paul. And there is not the slightest trace of the distinctively Pauline soteriology. Salvation rests solely on the resurrection of Jesus: the cross is not central in the preaching of the Lukan Paul, and it has no soteriological significance. "According to Acts . . . the crucifixion of Jesus is an error of justice and a sin of the Jews, Who despite knowledge of holy Scripture did not recognize Jesus' messiahship."

Finally, Acts has no eschatology—at least, eschatology has little importance for the author. "Eschatology has been removed from the center of Pauline faith to the end and has become a 'section on the last things'." Here Luke distinguishes himself "not only from Paul but also from the earliest

Church, which expected the return of Christ, the resurrection of the dead, and the end of the world in the immediate future. . . ." Paul lived in the expectation of the imminent parousia; this fact motivated his mission and determined his relationship to the world. Luke, by contrast, has a theology of history. His conception of history is that of "a continuous redemptive historical process." The parousia has been delayed and relegated to a place in the distant future; meanwhile, the church digs its roots into history and prepares for a long period of existence and expansion.

This emphasis on redemptive history (in contrast to the eschatological emphasis of Paul and the earliest Christians) is seen by Vielhauer and other critics as being the fundamental feature of Lukan theology. "The fact of Acts" is considered to be a demonstration of the difference between the perspective of Luke and the first generation of Christians (including Paul). As long as the early Christians believed that the end of the world was at hand, they had no interest in writing about their own history!

In this way Vielhauer states the problem in the sharpest way possible. One simply must choose between the real Paul and the Lukan Paul, between "the Paul of the Epistles" and "the Paul of Acts." However, both his conception of the main features of Pauline theology and his treatment of the Acts material are open to serious criticism. For a start, his understanding of Paul's Areopagus speech is dependent on the interpretation offered by Dibelius and has been demonstrated by B. Gärtner to be essentially erroneous.[38] Then, his understanding of Paul's relation to the law and Judaism is based more on his rigorous Lutheran understanding of the antithesis of law and gospel in Paul than on a careful exegesis of the letters of Paul.[39] There is not a shred of evidence in the Pauline letters that Paul ever taught Jewish Christians to forsake the law of Moses. Paul was not anti-law (in the sense of Old Testament ceremonies and Jewish practices) but anti-legalism (i.e., the law as a means of salvation). Vielhauer's conception of Paul's attitude fails to understand the practical problem of Paul's missionary career. If Paul was to engage in any evangelistic ministry among Jews—and the letters bear witness to the fact that he did—it would have been essential for him to have done the sort of thing which Acts says he did. And, Vielhauer notwithstanding, no good reason has yet been brought forward to prove that he should not have so acted.

Perhaps the basic criticisms to be leveled at Vielhauer are in the area of critical methodology. First, he is obviously concerned to defend a thesis, not primarily to understand a historical situation. He is as "apologetic" in his approach to the text of the New Testament as any of the older "apologists" were; it is just that he is concerned to defend a particular critical understanding of "Luke," rather than Luke himself. Secondly, his approach to the speeches is wrong, regardless of the view one takes concerning the nature of the speeches in Acts. Vielhauer's method is to take the teaching of the speeches of Paul in Acts *as a whole* and to compare this with the teaching of the letters *as a whole.* This approach overlooks the fact that one should not expect to find a full-blown and well-rounded theology of Paul in either the speeches of Acts or the letters. It is not good criticism to expect a few representative sermons, even if they do represent the authentic thought of the speaker, and an accidental collection of four occasional letters to provide anything approaching an adequate account of Paul's theology. What sort of picture would one have of the theology of Augustine or of Luther or of Calvin or even of Karl Barth if all that remained from the pen of each were four controversial letters and a half-dozen brief synopses of their sermons? No student of the history of thought will doubt for a moment that our understanding of them all would be quite different if this were all that remained of their thought, nor would he be surprised if it proved difficult to correlate the thought expressed in the sermons with that of the letters. (It is difficult enough as it is to harmonize the seemingly inconsistent strands in the theologies of these men, even when one limits oneself to their strictly theological writings!) But, narrowed by the limited perspective of concentration on a very small body of literature, the type of New Testament criticism represented by Vielhauer seems to have lost touch with the true nature of the documents with which it is working.

A few examples will be sufficient to illustrate the weakness of Vielhauer's method. Let us imagine that we had only Galatians from the pen of Paul. What then would we know of Paul's eschatology, which Vielhauer describes as "the center" of his faith? Nothing! One can conceive of scholars writing learned essays and monographs on Paul, arguing that eschatology had as little place in the theology of the historical Paul as in that of Vielhauer's Luke. But the fact is that Galatians gives us only a few of Paul's thoughts, which were written with haste in the white heat of ecclesiastical controversy: it is by no means a reasoned theological treatise or a formal confession of faith in the later sense of the term. Again, if Paul had not written 1 Corinthians, or if this letter had been among those which were lost to subsequent generations, we would not know that Paul ever heard of the eucharist. Nor would one know that the resurrection of Christ played a very significant role in his theology. Without the two Corithian letters (and assuming, as Vielhauer seems to do, that 1 Thessalonians is either inauthentic or unimportant), we would know very little about Paul's ideas concerning the final resurrection. One would have thought that it was a self-evident fact that *all* the letters of Paul (i.e., the ones the critic considers to be authentic) as a group give only an indication of *some* of the aspects of the theology of Paul, rather than the whole spectrum of his thinking on the themes of Christian faith and practice. But Vielhauer's approach fails to give due recognition to this fact.

To ascertain whether the thought of the speeches in Acts is really compatible with the thought of the Paul of the letters, the proper critical approach would be to see whether there are traces in the letters of *any* of the ideas of the speeches. One should not expect to find *detailed* correspondences between the speeches and the letters. And there is certainly no obvious reason why a former associate of Paul should be expected to parrot Paul's theology in all its peculiarities outside of the speeches attributed to Paul. On the other hand, assuming the independency of Acts and the letters of Paul, the fact of incidental agreements between the ideas expressed in the letters and in the speeches of Acts would at least indicate the possibility that the speeches could represent authentically Pauline thought, if not his actual words. When the problem is approached from this point of view, the impression is quite different from that given by Vielhauer's essay. There are, in fact, many "undesigned coincidences" between the speeches and the letters. These are especially evident in Paul's speech before the Ephesian elders at Miletus (Acts 20:18-35), which contains the most detailed correspondences to the letters; but the same is also true of the Areopagus address (though to a lesser degree), as Gärtner has shown.[40] Thus when one frees the speeches from the critical straitjacket which requires them to contain a full-blown Pauline theology—and, it may be added, a theology which many would regard as a less than adequate representation of the theology of the historical Paul—they give some evidence of possible authenticity.

So much for the limitations of Vielhauer's approach. But there is much more to be said on the positive side concerning the concurrence rather than conflict between "the Paul of Acts" and "the Paul of the Epistles." While recognizing the independence of Acts and the letters and giving all due credit to Luke's special emphases and concerns, which may not always coincide with those of Paul, there are an impressive number of agreements and "undesigned coincidences" between our two chief sources for a knowledge of Paul's life and thought. What follows is a mere sample of these.[41]

Paul in his letters tells us that he is from the tribe of Benjamin (Rom 11:1; Phil 3:5); Acts tells us that his Jewish name was Saul (Acts 7:58-8:3; 9:1, 4, 8, 11, 17, 22, 24; 13:9; etc.), the most prominent member of that tribe in the history of Israel. Paul speaks of himself as "a Hebrew born of Hebrews" (Phil 3:6; cf. 2 Cor 11:22), which probably implies that the language spoken in his home was Hebrew (i.e., Aramaic). This is the language in which he is addressed by the risen Lord in his Damascus road vision (26:14) and which he uses in a public speech in Jerusalem (21:40; 22:2). In both Acts and the letters Paul claims to be a Pharisee (Phil 3:5; Acts 23:6; 26:5). In Acts Paul claims to have been educated in the school of Gamaliel, the leading Pharisaic teacher of his generation (22:3); in Galatians (1:14) he makes the more general claim to have ". . . advanced in Judaism beyond many of my own age among my people, so extremely zealous was I for the traditions of my fathers." His role as a persecutor of the infant

Christian community is attested in similar language in both Acts and the letters (Acts 8:3; 9:1; cf. Gal 1:13; 1 Cor 15:9; Phil 3:6).

It is possible to go through the outline of the life of Paul subsequent to his conversion provided by the narrative of Acts and find detailed correspondence with the letters in the vast majority of details.[42] There are difficulties in relating the two, to be sure; but these are no more than what would be expected in attempting to collate incidental details culled from a small collection of occasional letters with an independent narrative account of a man's life written by the pen of another. The difficulties do not, in fact, impress anyone but a small cadre of New Testament scholars as being anything other than what would be expected under the circumstances. These "difficulties" of harmonization are part of the stock-in-trade of scholars who work with ordinary "secular" historical materials.

But in addition to the biographical data contained in both Acts and the letters which can be related to one another, there are also an impressive number of parallels concerning the details of Paul's life-style and missionary strategy. For example, both Acts and the letters agree that it was Paul's custom to provide for his own financial support by his own work rather than to allow himself to be a burden to his friends and converts (Acts 18:3; 20:34; 1 Thess 2:9; 2 Thess 3:7-8; 1 Cor 9:18). In the beginning of his letter to the church at Rome he stresses that the order of evangelization is "to the Jew first and also to the Greek" (Rom 1:16; 2:9-10); in Acts he visits the synagogues first in city after city (cf. Acts 13:46). Acts indicates that the leaders of the Jewish communities opposed Paul in his mission time and time again, which explains both his "great sorrow and unceasing anguish" for his fellow-Jews expressed in Romans 9:2-3 and his description of his Jewish opponents as those who "displease God and oppose men by hindering us from speaking to the Gentiles that they may be saved" (1 Thess 2:15-16; cf. Acts 17:5-9). An incidental confirmation of the situation portrayed in Acts is Paul's reference in 2 Corinthians to the fact that he had been sentenced to be beaten by Jewish authorities on five different occasions (2 Cor 11:24; cf. Deut 25:3).

Those who have attempted to set the Paul of Acts over against the Paul of the letters have tended to minimize his important words in 1 Corinthians 9:19-23,[43] where Paul underlines his adaptation of his life-style at various times to the various groups to whom he ministered. "To the Jews I became as a Jew . . .; to those under the law I became as one under the law. . . . To those outside the law I became as one outside of the law . . .; to the weak, I became weak. . . . I have become all things to all men that I might by all means save some." Is not this exactly what we have in Acts!

It is quite possible to be very selective in one's use of the data of Acts and the letters and thus to emphasize the differences between the two. However, such an approach is unfair both to the author of Acts and to Paul.

Paul did not himself write an autobiography, nor did Luke intend to write a biography of his friend and hero. Paul wrote letters to specific churches in response to specific problems arising in their individual historical situations, rather than a collection of literary epistles which were intended for publication; and it is in this context that he provides contemporary New Testament scholars with data which are valuable for the reconstruction of the details of his life and thought. But it must be remembered that these data are really quite limited and that the resulting reconstructions must always remain tentative. Luke also offers biographical data for a life of Paul, but he also has an interest in the Jerusalem church and in his own theological problems, which were quite different from the issues which concerned Paul. Perhaps Luke's concern to give equal justice to the contribution made to Christian faith and life in the second generation of the church's existence by both Jerusalem and Paul leads him to stress the essential unity between them (which Paul also affirms, e.g., in 1 Corinthians 15 and Galatians 2) and to "throw a veil of silence over" (M. Schneckenberger) the tensions between the two which Paul's letters indicate actually existed for a time.[44] The real Paul, insofar as *we* can know him, is the Paul of Acts *and* the letters. A view of Paul reconstructed on the basis of the exclusive use of either of our sources would be decidedly one-sided and therefore unhistorical.

Notes to Chapter 5

1. See W. C. Robinson, Jr., "Acts of the Apostles," *IDB Sup* (edd. Keith Crim et al.; Nashville: Abingdon, 1976) 7-9, with bibliography.
2. On Dibelius, see W. W. Gasque, *A History of the Criticism of the Acts of the Apostles* (*BGBE;* Tübingen: Mohr, 1975) 201-235.
3. G. E. Ladd, *A Theology of the New Testament* (Grand Rapids: Eerdmans, 1974) 314.
4. In commenting on my *History of the Criticism of the Acts of the Apostles,* Hans Conzelmann (*Erasmus* 28/3-4 [1976] cols. 65-68) suggests that arguments applied to defend the historicity of Acts on the basis of its correspondence to the details of local custom and history could be used to prove that the novels of Karl May, the German writer, are historical! This naive illustration misses the point which I have just made—a point which I also made in my book.
5. R. P. C. Hanson, *The Acts* (Oxford: Clarendon, 1967) 8.
6. Ibid.
7. *Roman Society and Roman Law in the New Testament* (Oxford: Clarendon, 1963) 55-56.
8. Ibid., 154-156.
9. Ibid., 160-161.
10. Roman citizenship was still very rare in the eastern provinces during the middle decades of the first century. The situation changed rapidly in the final decades of the century and the beginning of the next, when Roman citizenship was conferred upon more and more political subjects and as a result lost much of its value.
11. Cf. also A. H. M. Jones, "I appeal unto Caesar," in his *Studies in Roman Government and Law* (Oxford: Blackwell, 1960), who makes the same point.
12. It is important to note that Sherwin-White is not a Christian apologist but rather a classical historian, indeed, the leading authority on several of the subjects upon which he comments.
13. See esp. A. Wikenhauser, *Die Apostelgeschichte und ihre Geschichtswert* (*NA* 8,3-5; Münster: Aschendorff, 1921).

14. Cf. M. Dibelius, *Aufsätze zur Apostelgeschichte* (Göttingen: Vandenhoeck und Ruprecht, 4th ed. 1961); E. Haenchen, *Die Apostelgeschichte* (MeyerK; Göttingen und Ruprecht, 14th ed. 1965); and H. Conzelmann, *Die Apostelgeschichte* (*HNT;* Tübingen: Mohr, 1963).
15. I have dealt with this subject at greater length in "The Speeches of Acts: Dibelius Reconsidered," in *New Dimensions in New Testament Study* (edd. R. N. Longenecker and M. C. Tenney; Grand Rapids: Eerdmans, 1974) 232-250. See also F. F. Bruce, *The Speeches in the Acts of the Apostles* (London: Tyndale, 1943); and "The Speeches in Acts—Thirty Years After," in *Reconciliation and Hope* (ed. R. Banks; Grand Rapids: Eerdmans, 1974) 53-68.
16. Cf. Gasque, "The Speeches of Acts."
17. See A. W. Gomme, "The Speeches in Thucydides," in his *Essays in Greek History and Literature* (Oxford: Blackwell, 1937) 156-189; *A Historical Commentary on Thucydides* (4 vols.; Oxford: Clarendon, 1945) I, 139-148; and T. F. Glasson, "The Speeches in Acts and Thucydides," *ExpTim* 76 (1964/65) 165.
18. Cf. F. W. Walbank, *A Historical Commentary on Polybius* (2 vols.; Oxford: Clarendon, 1957-67) I, 13-14; II, 397-399.
19. Walbank, *A Historical Commentary,* I, 14, suggests: "Any failure," for Polybius to live up to the high standards he set for himself, "is due to practical shortcomings rather than a deliberate betrayal of principle."
20. *Corpus Inscriptionum Latinarum* 13 (1668).
21. Cf. *Cornelii Taciti Analium,* edd. H. Furneaux, H. F. Pelham, and C. D. Fisher (2 vols.; Oxford University Press, 1906-07) II, 54-60.
22. Ibid., 54-55.
23. Cf. Gasque, "The Speeches of Acts," 244-246.
24. Bruce, *The Speeches in the Acts of the Apostles,* 7.
25. A. Ehrhardt, *The Framework of the New Testament Stories* (Manchester: University Press, 1964) 88.
26. Haenchen, *Die Apostelgeschichte,* 73.
27. See H. J. Cadbury, *The Making of Luke-Acts* (New York: Macmillan, 1927) esp. 76-98, 157.
28. Bruce, *The Acts of the Apostles,* 19.
29. Paul himself emphasizes his basic agreement with the other apostles concerning the gospel (e.g., 1 Cor 15:3-11; Galatians 2).
30. C. F. D. Moule, "The Christology of Acts," in *Studies in Luke-Acts* (edd. L. E. Keck and J. L. Martyn; Nashville: Abingdon, 1966) 159-185; cf. Bruce, "The Speeches in Acts—Thirty Years Later."
31. Cf. M. E. Scharlemann, *Stephen: A Singular Saint* (Rome: Pontifical Biblical Institute, 1968).
32. *Jewish Hermeneutics in the Synoptic Gospels and Acts* (Assen: Van Gorcum, 1953) 168-176.
33. Ibid., 175.
34. In addition to those works referred to in my essay, "The Speeches of Acts," 248-249, n. 95, see also (more recently) M. Wilcox, "A Foreword to the Study of the Speeches in Acts," in *Christianity, Judaism and Other Greco-Roman Cults* (ed. J. Neusner; 1976) I, 206-225.
35. Haenchen, *Die Apostelgeschichte,* 99-103.
36. "Zum 'Paulinismus' der Apostelgeschichte," *EvT* 10 (1950/51) 1-15.
37. M. Dibelius, *Paulus auf dem Areopag* (Heidelberg: Winter, 1939); contained in his *Aufsätze,* 29-70.
38. B. Gärtner, *The Areopagus Speech and Natural Revelation* (Uppsala: Gleerup, 1955); cf. Gasque, *History,* 213-214.
39. The same could be said in regard to Haenchen. This simplistic understanding of Paul's relation to the law, and therefore to Judaism, fails to take into consideration the many passages where Paul has a positive view of the law, e.g., Rom 3:31; 7:12; chaps. 9-11; etc. It is sufficient to point out that one may consult any of the numerous works on the theology of Paul written outside of German Protestant circles and find a more balanced statement of the subject. Cf., e.g., the most recent work by K. Stendahl, *Paul Among Jews and Gentiles* (Philadelphia: Fortress, 1976).
40. Gärtner, *The Areopagus Speech,* 248-252.
41. For greater detail, see F. F. Bruce, "Is the Paul of Acts the Real Paul?" *BJRL* 58 (Spring

1976) 282-395. Cf. also A. J. Mattill, Jr., "A Spectrum of Opinion on the Value of Acts as a Source for the Reconstruction of the Life and Thought of Paul," *Society of Biblical Literature: Seminar Papers* (Missoula: Scholars Press, 1974) II, 63-83; W. F. Orr and J. A. Walther, "A Study of the Life of Paul," *1 Corinthians* (*AB* 32; New York: Doubleday, 1976) 1-118.
42. Bruce, *BJRL* 58 (Spring 1976) 286-293.
43. Cf. G. Bornkamm, "The Missionary Stance of Paul in 1 Corinthians 9 and in Acts," in *Studies in Luke-Acts,* 194-207.
44. Bruce, *BJRL* 58 (Spring 1976) 305.

6: The One, New Man

WILLIAM BARCLAY*

The Letter to the Ephesians may fitly be called the Letter of the Church. E. F. Scott in *The Literature of the New Testament*[1] outlines the basic thought of Ephesians. The main purpose of Jesus Christ is to unite all things in heaven and all things on earth (1:10). In this world we see nothing but disunity. There is disunity between man and man. There is disunity within our own nature. There is disunity in nature itself, for nature is red in tooth and claw. So God's aim is to do away with all the discord and unite all things with one harmony in Jesus Christ. God's aim is to produce harmony out of discord, and Jesus Christ is his agent in so doing. But Jesus Christ is no longer here in the flesh. He has returned to his glory, and the church is his agent in his work of universal reconciliation. So we can say that Jesus Christ is the agent of God and the church is the agent of Jesus Christ, and Ephesians tells us how the church can best work out its purpose as the agent of Jesus Christ.

The passage from which I want to work is Ephesians 2:11-22:

> 11Therefore remember that at one time you Gentiles in the flesh, called
> the uncircumcision by what is called the circumcision, which is made in
> the flesh by hands— 12remember that you were at that time separated
> from Christ, alienated from the commonwealth of Israel, and strangers
> to the covenants of promise, having no hope and without God in the
> world. 13But now in Christ Jesus you who once were far off have been
> brought near in the blood of Christ. 14For he is our peace, who has
> made us both one, and has broken down the dividing wall of hostility,
> 15by abolishing in his flesh the law of commandments and ordinances,
> that he might create in himself one new man in place of the two, so
> making peace, 16and might reconcile us both to God in one body
> through the cross, thereby bringing the hostility to an end. 17And he
> came and preached peace to you who were far off and peace to those
> who were near; 18for through him we both have access in one Spirit to
> the Father. 19So then you are no longer strangers and sojourners, but

*William Barclay, noted Bible scholar and author of more than 60 books, passed away January 14, 1978.

you are fellow citizens with the saints and members of the household of God, [20]built upon the foundation of the apostles and prophets, Christ Jesus himself being the corner-stone, [21]in whom the whole structure is joined together and grows into a holy temple in the Lord; [22]in whom you also are built into it for a dwelling place of God in the Spirit.

In this passage Paul states how Jew and Gentile were brought together. He is writing to Gentiles, and he reminds them of what they were before they came into contact with Christ. They were uncircumcised. They had not the badge of the chosen people and the holy community. They were separated from Christ. That phrase "separated from Christ" may well mean "without a Messiah." That is to say, without the hope, the ideal, the end and aim in life the possession of a Messiah brings. They were alienated from the commonwealth of Israel. They were strangers to the covenants of promise. They had no hope and they were without God in the world. But now in Christ Jesus they have been brought near in the blood of Christ. He is our peace, that is to say, he has been responsible for the introduction of right relationships between man and man. He has broken down the middle wall of hostility. That phrase may well come from the temple in Jerusalem. The temple was composed of a series of courts, and the outermost court was called the Court of the Gentiles. Into it alone Gentiles could go. It was 750 feet square.[2] It was the place where the money-changers' tables were, and the place where lambs and pigeons for the sacrifice were sold. At the inner end of the court there was a marble screen 4½ feet high, beautifully ornamented, bearing at intervals inscriptions in Greek and Latin warning the Gentiles not to proceed any further on pain of death.[3] So what Paul is saying is that the dividing wall beyond which the Gentiles could not pass has been destroyed, for Jesus abolished the law with its commandments and its ordinances that he might create in himself one new man in place of the two, so making peace and reconciling us both to God in one body through Christ, thereby bringing hostility to an end. The result is that the Gentiles are no longer strangers and sojourners, but they are fellow citizens with the saints and members of the household of God.

This at first sounds as if the Gentiles were being brought into the same position as the Jews, but it does not really mean that. It means far more than that. Paul says in verse 15 that Jesus is creating one new man in place of the two, and the word that is used for "new," καινός, is a special word. There are two Greek words for "new." There is the word νέος and the word καινός. Νέος is simply new in point of time. Suppose there is a machine for turning out lead pencils. The millionth lead pencil is new in the νέος sense, although it is precisely the same as the 999,999 which went before. On the other hand, καινός means new in quality, new in character, unfamiliar, fresh, introducing something which has not been there before and which could not even have been there before.

I

1. First of all, in Classical Greek καινός can mean unfamiliar. Xenophon in the Cyropaedia (3.1.30) tells how Tigranes was pleading for the *status quo* in Armenia, and Tigranes asks: "Consider whether you think the country would be more tranquil under the beginning of a new administration rather than if the one to which we are accustomed should continue." The new is καινός. A new and unfamiliar constitution is obviously going to cause trouble.

Sophocles in the *Oedipus Tyrannios* (916) says about a certain person that "he will not use his past experience like a man of sense to judge our present need." "Our present need" is τα καινά. The present situation is unfamiliar. Man does not have the sense to judge it by the things with which he is familiar. Sophocles' *Trachiniae* (613) tells how Deianeira is about to send to Hercules a garment impregnated with a magic powder which will keep him forever faithful to her, and she says she is sending this garment to display him to the gods. A new sacrificer in a new robe, that is to say, an unfamiliar robe, one for a special case.

2. Καινός can mean new and fresh. In Xenophon's *Memorabilia* (4.4.6) there is a conversation between Socrates and Hippias. Hippias says to Socrates: "Still the same old sentiments, Socrates, that I heard from you so long ago." Socrates answers: "Yes, Hippias, always we say the same, and what is more astonishing, on the same topics too. You are so learned that I dare say you never say the same thing on the same subjects." Hippias answers: "I certainly try to say something fresh every time." "Something fresh" is καινόν. So Hippias tries for novelty, for newness of expression and subject matter.

Isocrates in his speech to Philip (584) says that he has said so much in his *Panegyricus* that it has left him impoverished because "I am not willing to repeat what I have written in that speech, nor can I at my age, cast about for new things." The "new things" are καινά—fresh, novel.

3. Καινός means new and strange. In the *Euthyphro* (3B) Socrates is accused because "I make new gods"—new and strange gods. In the *Apology* (24B) the charge is that Socrates is a wrongdoer because he corrupts the youth and does not believe in the gods the state believes in but in other new divinities, καινὰ δαιμονία—new and strange. There is a certain critical sense in this. It means new and strange and different from the conventional usages and beliefs.

4. Καινός can even mean startling. Lucian in the *Nigrinus* (22) says: "Some, would you believe it, have not time even to be ill," and "would you believe it" is το καινότατον. As we might say, it is a very odd fact that some people haven't the time to be ill.

Enough has been said to show that in Classical Greek καινός has the meaning of something new, fresh, strange, unconventional. Let us now look at καινός in the New Testament itself.

1. First of all, it means unused. They put new wine into new skins (Matt 9:17), and so they preserve both. The new wine is νέον οἶνον and the new skins are ἀσκοὺς καινούς, skins which have not been used before so that they have not lost their elasticity. It is the same with a patch on a garment. You do not patch an old coat with a new piece of unshrunk cloth. If you do, the new will tear away from the old and the rent will become worse (Luke 5:36-38). The tomb in which Jesus was laid is called καινός because it had never been used before (John 19:41).

2. Καινός can mean unfamiliar. So, for instance, in Matthew 13:52 it is said that a scribe who becomes a Christian is like a householder who brings out of his treasure-house things new and old. He brings out familiar things, and he brings out unfamiliar things as well. In John 13:34, Jesus says: "A new commandment give I unto you, that you love one another . . . ," and the new commandment is καινός—unfamiliar. It is said of the citizens in Athens that they spend their time in doing nothing else than speaking about or listening to something new, something which is unfamiliar. In Athens the people ask Paul: "May we know what this new teaching is which you present?" The teaching is unfamiliar, and they want to hear more about it (Acts 17:19, 20).

3. Καινός can mean startling. When Jesus healed the demoniac in the synagogue, the reaction of the people was: "What is this? A new teaching! With authority he commands even unclean spirits and they obey him" (Mark 1:27).

4. Καινός means something new, in the sense of something not obviously existing or even possible before. In Luke 22:20, Jesus says to the disciples: "This cup is the new covenant in my blood . . . ," that is to say, it stands for a new relationship with God, a relationship not existing before and not possible before (cf. 1 Cor 11:25 and 2 Cor 3:6). In 2 Corinthians 5:17, Paul declares: "If a man is in Christ he is a new creation," that is to say, he is something new and different (cf. Gal 6:15). Hebrews 8:8 quotes Jeremiah as follows: "The days will come, says the Lord, when I will establish a new covenant with the House of Israel and with the House of Judah." The covenant is new and unfamiliar, and Hebrews goes on to say in 8:13: "In that he called it new, he has rendered the old obsolete."

5. Καινός may be said to be an eschatological word. It describes things in the new age. Second Peter 3:13 states: "According to his promise, we wait for new heavens and a new earth in which righteousness dwells." The Revelation speaks of the new Jerusalem (3:12; 21:2), a new song (14:3), a new heaven and a new earth (21:1), and God says: "I will make all things new." This is all eschatological, and this newness is the character of things in the age which is to come.

Let us now turn to the works of the Apostolic Fathers, and let us show how καινός is used there.

1. First of all, it is used of that which is new and different. The Letter of Barnabas 2:6 says: "These things he abolished in order that the new law of our Lord Jesus Christ which is without the yoke of necessity might have its oblation not made by man." The law of the Lord is new and different and unfamiliar. The Letter to Diognetus 11:4 says of Jesus: "He was from the beginning and appeared new, and was proved to be old, and is ever new as he is born in the hearts of the hearers." He is old and appears new and unfamiliar and different when he emerges on earth. In the Shepherd of Hermas, the Similitudes 9:12, the shepherd sees the rock and the door, and asks what the rock and the door are. He is told that they stand for the Son of God. He then asks why the rock is ancient and the door is new, and he is told the rock is ancient because the Son of God dates back before the beginning of the world. The door is new because it was in those last days that he came to earth to make the door for man to God. Here, new is fresh, fresh and different. In the Letter to Diognetus 1:1, the writer sets out to answer the question of Diognetus, why this new race and practice have come into being now and not before. Obviously Christianity is being looked at as something new and fresh and unfamiliar. Ignatius, toward the end of his Letter to the Ephesians (20:1), says: "If Jesus Christ permit me through your prayers, and if he will, in the second book which I propose to write to you, I will show you concerning the dispensation of the new man Jesus Christ which I have before begun to discuss, dealing with his faith and with his love, his suffering and his resurrection." For Ignatius, Jesus Christ is the new man, the man who is different. In his Letter to the Magnesians 9:1, Ignatius speaks of how those who walked in ancient custom have come to a new hope, a new, fresh hope which contrasted with the ancient custom. When Clement is discussing bishops and deacons (1 Clem 42:5) he says that they are nothing new, as they are talked about in Isaiah 60:17. There is nothing new and unfamiliar about them. So, in the first place, in the Apostolic Fathers the word καινός means new and unfamiliar.

2. Καινός in the Apostolic Fathers is used to describe the converted people, the people of Christ. It is so used in Barnabas 5:7. Christ came to fulfill the promise made by the fathers and himself, to prepare a new people, which is a different kind of person, practically equal to the converted people. In the Letter to Diognetus 2:1, Diognetus urges the person to whom he writes: "Then cleanse yourself of all the prejudice that occupies your mind and throw aside the custom which deceives you, and become, as it were, a new man from the beginning, and as one of you yourself admit, who is about to listen to a new story." He is pleading with him to become a converted man, a new man. Barnabas 7:5 speaks about Christ offering his flesh for "my new people," and in Barnabas 5:7 he speaks of Christ preparing for himself a "new people"—the body of converted Christians contrasted with the people of the world. In Barnabas 16:8, we find Barnabas

saying: "When we received the remission of sins and put our hope in the name, we became new, being created again from the beginning."

3. The eschatological use of καινός, describing a new kind of life, a new kind of age, is also in the Apostolic Fathers. Barnabas 15:7 speaks of the time when we enjoy true rest, when we shall be able to do so because we are being made ourselves and have received the promise, when there is no more sin and all things have been made new by the Lord. The state of things made new is the eschatological state.

4. Finally, καινός means new and startling. It is used of the star at the birth of Christ, in Ignatius' Letter to the Ephesians 19:2: "The star shone in heaven beyond all stars, and its light was unspeakable and its newness caused astonishment, and all the other stars and the sun and moon gathered in chorus round this star, and it far exceeded them all in its light, and there was perplexity regarding this new star so unlike the others." The star was startlingly new and startlingly bright. It was not just a new star, it was a special star with special brightness. So we can see that in the Apostolic Fathers, the main usages of καινός still exist. Καινός means something new in the sense of unfamiliar, fresh, wonderful, causing astonishment.

II

Since we have looked in some detail at the word καινός in Classical Greek, in New Testament Greek, and in the Greek of the Apostolic Fathers, it will only be fair to look quickly at the other word for new, the word νέος.

1. In Classical Greek, νέος means young, youthful, used particularly of children and youths. "The young will be young" is the Greek for "boys will be boys" (Libanius, *Epistulae* 910:3). Ἐκ νέου means from youth upwards. Τὸ νέον ἅπαν means very young creature.

2. Νέος means what can be ascribed to a youth, youthful. So Pindar speaks of youthful games (Pindar, *Olympians* 2.43). Aeschylus speaks of youthful courage in the *Persae* 744. Euripides in *Iphigenia Aulidensis* 489 speaks of someone being young and foolish. Plato in the *Gorgias* 413E speaks of someone being young and quick tempered.

3. Νέος means new and fresh. It is used, for instance, of the new moon or the first day of the month.

4. It is used of events, often with the idea of strange and untoward allied to it.

Such is a summary of the use of νέος in Classical Greek.

We now look at it in the New Testament.

1. It is said in Matthew 9:17 (cf. Mark 2:22; Luke 5:37) that no one puts new wine (νέος) into old skins, but new wine must be put into new skins (καινός). Here, the difference between the two words is seen. The

wine is new, that is, newly made. The skins are fresh, that is, they have not been used before and so retain their elasticity to cope with the gases issuing from the fermenting wine.

2. Occasionally, νέος means new and different. In 1 Corinthians 5:7 Paul speaks of cleansing out the old leaven, that "you may be a new lump." Here new is νέος, and yet it seems to have some of the meaning of καινός—new, fresh, unfamiliar. Hebrews 12:24 speaks of Jesus as the mediator of the New Covenant. Here it is νέος when we might have expected καινός.

3. In the vast majority of cases, νέος has to do with age. It is used of the younger son in the parable of the prodigal son (Luke 15:12, 13). It is used in the saying in Luke 22:26: "He who is older amongst you must be as the younger, and he who is a leader must be as he who serves." It is used by Jesus of Peter in John 21:18, when Jesus says: "When you were young, you girded yourself and walked where you wished." It is used in Acts 5:6, where the young men are said to come in and bind up the body and carry it out and bury it after the blasphemy of Ananias and Sapphira. It is frequently used in the Pastorals in advice to young men (1 Tim 5:1, 2, 11, 14; Titus 2:6), and it is similarly used in 1 Peter 5:5: "Likewise you that are younger be subject to the elders." So, broadly speaking, in the New Testament the meaning and use of νέος is to speak of a man's age, although it can also mean unused, fresh, unfamiliar.

Now let us look briefly at νέος in the Apostolic Fathers.

1. It can mean new and unfamiliar, much as καινός does. Ignatius, writing to the Magnesians (10:2), says: "Put aside the evil leaven which has grown old and sour and turn to the new leaven which is Jesus Christ."

2. But, as in the New Testament and in Classical Greek, the main usage of νέος in the Apostolic Fathers has to do with a man's age. When Clement writes to the church at Corinth on their misconduct (1 Clem 3:3), he says: "Those who were worthless rose up against those who were in honour, those of no reputation against the renowned, the foolish against the prudent and the young against the old." In Hermas, in the Visions 3.13.4, it is promised: "They, therefore, who have repented shall completely recover their youth and be well founded because they have repented with their hearts." In 1 Clement 1:3 the young are commended with these words: "to you enjoined temperate and seemly thoughts." First Clement 21:6 says: "Let us honour the aged. Let us train the youth in the discipline and the fear of God." In 1 Clement 63:3, Clement writes to the people of Corinth: "We have sent you men who are faithful and wise and who have lived blamelessly amongst us from their youth upwards." Barnabas 19:5 and Didache 4:9 both quote the saying: "You will not remove your hand from your son or from your daughter, but you will teach them the fear of God from their youth upwards."

On the whole, in the Apostolic Fathers there is no difference in the use of νέος. In Classical Greek and in the New Testament and in the Apostolic Fathers, the word describes those who are young in age and can describe that which is newly made and that which is fresh and unfamiliar. So, it can be seen from an examination of Classical Greek, New Testament Greek, and the Apostolic Fathers that the difference between καινός and νέος was maintained, and that καινός means new, strange, unfamiliar, startling, while νέος simply means new in the sense of age or of time.[4]

III

We are now in a position to see more clearly what Paul meant when he spoke of Jesus creating in himself one new man in place of the two, so making peace and reconciling them both to God in one body through the cross, thereby bringing the hostility to an end. What Christ does is to create one new man, and we have seen that this word "new" means of a different quality, of a different kind, not just another man but a different kind of man. He does not try to turn the Jew into a Gentile, nor the Gentile into a Jew, but out of the two he makes one new man.

In this saying a great deal of light is shed on the problem of ecumenicity. In our ecumenical labors our tendency is to try to turn one man into another. For instance, to try to make a Presbyterian out of an Episcopalian, or to make an Episcopalian out of a Presbyterian. But our aim should be not to do that, but to produce one new man who is different from both. It means that we should no longer approach the ecumenical problems of the church either defensively in our own case, making certain that we at least will not change, or aggressively in the case of others with a view to making them the same as ourselves. In point of fact, we should not in our ecumenical deliberations be looking back so much as we should be looking forward. We should not be trying to reproduce one set of circumstances already existing, but we should be trying to produce something new. It is not a question of Presbyterians having bishops or Episcopalians having elders, it is a question of something new emerging which is newer and better than either. It means that we should sit down before the situation without prejudice and see what the situation demands—and the situation, it must be remembered, is not only the situation within the church, it is the situation with regard to the church and the outsider as well. The ecumenical movement should not be a series of competitions between this and that church, nor should it be a series of amalgamations in which one church is swallowed up in the other. It should be the begetting of a new situation with a new kind of man formed out of the two. Chrysostom said that it was as if someone flung into a furnace a statue of silver and a statue of lead, and lo and behold, there came out one of gold. The silver was not turned into lead or the lead into silver, but both were turned into something new, into the statue of gold.

Obviously, to do this we need the spirit of humility and we need the spirit of adventure, the forward-looking spirit. We need to avoid taking up fixed positions. We need to be ready to be always on the march and on the move. The ecumenical movement will never move until it stops trying to turn one church into another, and takes the New Testament method of aiming at a new creation which is different from and better than that which exists at present.

Notes to Chapter 6

1. E. F. Scott, *Literature of the New Testament* (New York: Columbia University, 1932) 180-184.
2. A. W. Edersheim, *The Temple, its Ministry and Services as they were in the Time of Jesus Christ* (London: Religious Tract Society, n.d.) 45-46.
3. Josephus, *Antiquities* 15.11.5.
4. For the material on καινός and νέος the following works were consulted: W. I. Arndt and F. W. Gingrich, *A Greek-English Lexicon of the New Testament* (Chicago: Chicago University, 1957); J. Behm, "καινός," *TDNT* 3 (1965) 447-450; J. Behm, "νέος," *TDNT* 4 (1967) 896-901; E. J. Goodspeed, *Index Patristicus* (Naperville: Allenson, repr. 1960); R. C. Trench, *Synonyms of the New Testament* (London: Macmillan, 1871); and H. G. Liddell and Robert Scott, *A Greek-English Lexicon* (Oxford: Clarendon, 1948).

7: "All Things to All Men": Diversity in Unity and Other Pauline Tensions

F. F. BRUCE

INTRODUCTION

A few years ago a graduate student of mine, John W. Drane, submitted to the University of Manchester a Ph.D. dissertation entitled "Paul and the Gnostics," with the subtitle: "Some Aspects of Pauline Teaching and the Infiltration of Gnosticism into the Early Church." This work was later revised and published in book form with the title: *Paul: Libertine or Legalist?*[1] The answer to the question posed by this title was "Neither"; but the question was asked because in some places Paul allegedly gives the impression of being a legalist, anxious to confine his converts to the straight and narrow path, while elsewhere he asserts the freedom of Christian men and women to a point where some even of his sympathizers might have felt that he was encouraging libertinism.

Certainly in the decades following Paul's death his public image in the church was remarkably transformed, so that the apostle who was widely criticized for antinomianism in his lifetime came to be revered a century later (as is shown in the *Acts of Paul*) as a noble example of asceticism. Whatever degree of unity may be discerned in Paul's policy and teaching (and there is an essential overarching and underlying unity), many in his own day and later have been more impressed by his diversity, not to say inconsistency.

Dr. Drane's exposition starts with the Letter to the Galatians, where Paul denounces the attempt to impose a measure of law-keeping on his Gentile converts and urges them to stand fast in the freedom for which Christ has liberated them. This emphasis, he thinks, was avidly taken up by another group of Paul's converts—those in the permissive city of Corinth—and pushed by them to a degree which made him cry "Halt!" and try to regulate their lives more strictly. In 2 Corinthians, and then in Romans, Dr. Drane discerned a more balanced approach, in which Paul endeavored to do simultaneous justice to the claims both of Christian liberty and of Christian responsibility. The distinctive emphases of Galatians and 1 Corinthians, when pressed to extremes, led respectively to gnosticism and early Catholicism.

Dr. Drane was not, I am sure, influenced by the Hegelian philosophy of history, but a Hegelian-like pattern of thesis, antithesis, and synthesis certainly emerges from his exposition. (If a Hegelian-like pattern was not sometimes discernible in the historical process, Hegel would not have recognized and universalized it.)

The course of Dr. Drane's argument depends to a large extent on his early dating of Galatians. With this early dating I am disposed to agree, but it is too debatable to provide an acceptable basis for a hypothesis. In any case he would not argue that the Corinthians actually had access to a copy of the Letter to the Galatians, but that they were aware of the law-free emphasis in Paul's teaching which finds such eloquent expression in that letter. It is certain that, when we look for examples of diversity and tension in Pauline thought and action, we find them readily in a comparison of Galatians and 1 Corinthians. Our first example comes from another area than that investigated by Dr. Drane: it concerns the tension between revelation and tradition.[2]

I

REVELATION AND TRADITION

In terms which seem to be as absolute as terms can well be, Paul denies in Galatians 1:12 that he "received" his gospel from any human source: it came to him solely "by revelation of Jesus Christ." In the context, this "revelation of Jesus Christ" must have been granted at the moment when, as Paul says, "God . . . was pleased to reveal his Son in me" (Gal 1:16). With the revelation of God's Son came simultaneously the impartation of the gospel which Paul was to proclaim among the Gentiles. The verb rendered "receive" (παραλαμβάνειν) is frequently used, even by Paul himself, in the sense of receiving by tradition, from one's predecessors or teachers; but that sense is excluded here. "I did not receive it from man," he says, "nor was I taught it." Those who were apostles before him contributed nothing to him in this respect, neither did any of the other Jerusalem Christians who had been personally acquainted with Jesus before his death.

The same verb "receive" appears in 1 Corinthians 15:3 in connection with receiving the gospel, and here it is accompanied by the correlative verb "deliver" (παραδιδόναι), meaning to hand on to others a tradition which was earlier received by oneself. Here also it is the gospel that Paul has received, but this time he has received it in common with the other apostles, and part at least of what he has received was apparently delivered to him by some of them—as he in turn delivered it to his converts (with one material contribution supplied by himself). "I delivered to you as of first importance," he reminds his Corinthian friends, "what I myself had received—that Christ died for our sins in accordance with the scriptures, that he was buried, and that he was raised the third day in accordance with the scriptures . . ." (1 Cor 15:3-4). These events, with the interpretation implicit in his recounting of them, were basic to the gospel which he preached, as they were basic to the gospel preached by the other apostles. They were basic to the gospel which he received on the Damascus road "by revelation of Jesus Christ," but here he does not claim to have received them by revelation. And what he next mentions as part of the tradition must have been received by him as information, not as revelation: the message went on to tell, he adds, how the risen Christ "appeared to Cephas, then to the twelve, then to more than 500 brethren at once [of whom the majority, he notes, were still alive a quarter of a century later]; then he appeared to James, then to all the apostles" (1 Cor 15:5-7). Factual data of this kind are not the subject-matter of revelation; Paul knew of them, directly or indirectly, from those who had experienced these manifestations of the risen Christ.

The very passage in Galatians 1:11-20 where Paul is so careful to maintain his independence of the leaders of the Jerusalem church throws light on the circumstances in which he received the information summarized in 1 Corinthians 15:5-7. It is more than a mere coincidence that the two men mentioned by name in the list of those to whom Christ appeared in resurrection are the two apostolic figures that he met in Jerusalem when he paid his first post-conversion visit to that city. In asserting his independence of the Jerusalem leaders and the fact that he was not indebted to them for the gospel, he tells the Galatians that it was not until three years after his conversion that he went up to Jerusalem—after he had already begun to preach the gospel which he had received on the Damascus road, in discharge of the commission entrusted to him then. When I did at last go up to Jerusalem, he says, it was to make the acquaintance of Cephas, with whom I spent fifteen days: as God is my witness, I saw no other apostle except James the Lord's brother.

What concerns us at the moment is his statement that he met Cephas (Peter) and James on that occasion: what more likely than that, as he told them how he had seen the risen Christ on the Damascus road, each of them told him of his own personal experience of the same kind two or three years before? Indeed, that such information was not only received by Paul but actually sought by him during that visit is implied in the stated purpose of the visit: he went up to Jerusalem, he says, ἱστορῆσαι Κηφᾶν (Gal 1:18) not only to make Peter's acquaintance but to make inquiry of him. That Peter in particular could tell Paul much of interest about the words and deeds of Jesus before his passion as well as after his resurrection is the most natural of possibilities—and it betrays a very unrealistic conception of Paul to suppose that he would not have drunk it all in eagerly. What he learned in this way from Peter (and others) he incorporated in his proclamation of the gospel, adding to that tradition his own contribution, which he also delivered to his hearers: "Last of all he appeared also to me" (1 Cor 15:8). Apart from this last clause, which refers to the Damascus-road "revelation of Jesus Christ," there is no hint in 1 Corinthians 15:1-11 that it was by unmediated divine revelation that he received the tradition there outlined, any more than such unmediated revelation was required for him to "receive from the Lord" the account of the institution of the Lord's Supper which also, according to 1 Corinthians 11:23-26, he delivered to the church at Corinth.

By saying that this account was "received from the Lord," Paul indicates that he is substituting a new and authoritative tradition for that to which he had been devoted in his earlier life. The ancestral tradition which stemmed from Moses on Sinai had now given way to the tradition of Christ (cf. Col 2:6). No matter who the intermediaries were through whom it was transmitted, its source was the once crucified and now risen Lord, and from him it derived its authority.

Thus, alongside his emphatic, and indeed passionate, assertion to the Galatians that he received his gospel by revelation, without any human intermediary, we have his matter-of-fact reminder to the Corinthians of his delivering to them the account which had first been delivered to him—an account which was common to himself and the other apostles: "whether then it was I or they, so we preach and so you believed" (1 Cor 15:11). How in fact did the gospel come to him—by revelation or by tradition? By both; but the exigencies of varying situations made him emphasize now the one and now the other in quite exclusive terms (especially when his receiving it by revelation is in question).

Paul no doubt knew, before his conversion, something of the early believers' testimony to Jesus. That Jesus had died by crucifixion was common knowledge, but Paul and the primitive church drew different conclusions from the fact and manner of his death. That Jesus had been raised from the dead and appeared to some of his followers was affirmed by the early believers, but Paul did not entertain their testimony for a moment. To him such a claim, with its implication that the crucified Jesus was Lord and Messiah, was a blasphemous absurdity. But what he had refused to entertain seriously when they asserted it became a matter of compelling certainty when the risen Lord appeared to him on the Damascus road and called him into his service. No human intermediary was involved either in the conversion or in the commission.

If, as Paul implies, he began immediately to preach the gospel, as he had been called to do, what could the substance of his preaching have been? "Jesus the crucified one is the risen Lord"—that much he now knew to be true and could proclaim to others, or, as Luke tells us, he was able on the basis of his conversion experience alone to preach Jesus, saying, "He is the Son of God" (Acts 9:20). That Jesus was the Son of God was implicit in the

Damascus-road revelation: "it pleased God," says Paul, "to reveal his Son in me" (Gal 1:16).[3]

The core of the gospel, then, came to Paul by unmediated revelation. But many of the details of the gospel story were such that he could know of them only from those who had witnessed them: thus, to the gospel as revelation was added the gospel as tradition. That Paul's two accounts of the matter, at first sight so irreconcilable, should be understood in this way is plain and reasonable when we relate them thus. Our difficulty arises from the absoluteness with which he stresses the former. It is not to be wondered at that Galatians should be our main witness for the former as 1 Corinthians is our main witness for the latter; and some of our Lutheran colleagues, for whom Galatians (with Romans) is the norm of Pauline teaching, find it difficult at times to accept the statements in 1 Corinthians equally *au pied de la lettre* with those in Galatians.

This may warn us not to quote passages from the undisputed Pauline letters out of context and say, "*This* is what Paul taught," in such a way as to exclude from Paul's authentic teaching counterbalancing passages from the same group of letters. The authentic Paul must be found, not by splitting the difference between the two extremes (Paul's recommended "moderation in all things" has little in common with Aristotle's golden mean), but in taking both together. Even in Galatians, alongside his solemn warning to his Gentile converts not to submit to circumcision, he makes it plain that what he objects to is not circumcision *per se* but circumcision accepted as a legal and religious obligation. Circumcision in itself is neither here nor there: twice over in this letter he says that "circumcision is nothing and uncircumcision is nothing"—what matters is something much more important: "faith working through love" (5:6); "a new creation" (6:15).

That "circumcision is nothing and uncircumcision is nothing" is a statement which Paul repeats in 1 Corinthians, but there the more important thing is said to be "keeping the commandments of God" (7:19)—something which, in Dr. Drane's eyes, would have been incompatible with the argument of Galatians but is in line with the more disciplinarian note struck in 1 Corinthians.[4]

II

JEWISH LAW AND CHRISTIAN GUIDELINES

Before his conversion, Paul had relied on his devotion to the law of Israel as the ground of his acceptance with God. To keep the letter of the law as interpreted by the tradition of the elders was no easy task but, given infinite painstaking, it was not impossible, and Paul achieved it. Such was his own assessment as a Christian of his pre-Christian accomplishment: "as regards the righteousness which is based on law, I was blameless" (Phil 3:6). The particular tradition of the elders by which Paul had learned to interpret and apply the law was a strict one: he applied Deuteronomy 27:26 ("Cursed is every one who does not continue in all things that are written in the book of the law, to do them") to mean that the breach of one commandment was a breach of the law as such (Gal 3:10). Similarly, his Galatian converts are warned that if they submit to circumcision as a legal obligation, it will be useless, on the principle of legal righteousness, unless it is followed by obedience to the whole law, in all its parts. (This, incidentally, sets a serious question-mark against the tradition that Paul, or indeed his master Gamaliel, belonged to the school of Hillel.[5])

The Damascus-road experience shattered Paul's confidence in the law. When he learned that the crucified Jesus, whose followers he had been trying to extirpate, was indeed (as those followers averred) Lord and Messiah, he was persuaded in a flash of the inadequacy of the law. It was his devotion to the law that had made him such a zealous persecutor of the disciples; now he realized that his persecuting activity had been in fact directed against the Son of God. The law had not been able to preserve him from committing this sin of sins; on the contrary, the law had actually led him into sin. Reliance on the law was a broken reed: for Paul, being under law meant being under sin.

But how? He could find no fault with the law in itself: it was God's law, holy and righteous and good. The fault must lie, then, with the fallible human material on which the law had to operate. The law declared the will of God; the law condemned those who disobeyed that will; but the law could neither supply the power to do the will of God nor prevent one from disobeying it. The hope that acceptance with God could be attained through keeping the law was a vain hope: "by deeds of the law no human being will be justified in his sight, for through the law comes knowledge of sin" (Rom 3:20)—not only external recognition of sin but inward consciousness of sin. Unless a new way to be justified before God was available, the human condition was hopeless indeed. But a new way *was* available: "what the law could not do, because the 'flesh' [our unregenerate nature] rendered it incapable, God accomplished: he sent his own Son in the likeness of sinful flesh to be an offering for sin, and so condemned sin in the flesh [in that very realm of human nature which it had hitherto dominated]; consequently, the law's righteous requirement may be fulfilled in us who lead our lives according to the Spirit, and no longer according to the flesh" (Rom 8:3-4).

The Christ who, from Paul's conversion onward, replaced the law as the center of his life and thought, has also replaced the law as the basis of men and women's acceptance with God: "Christ is the end of the law, so that every one who believes may be justified" (Rom 10:4). Faith in Christ, not conformity to the law, procures the acceptance which divine grace provides, and with this acceptance comes the new power, implanted by the Spirit, to do the will of God. Paul knew himself to have exchanged the bondage of the law for the freedom of the Spirit, and any tendency to revert to law as the basis of winning divine approval was in his eyes a subversion of the gospel and a practical denial that Jesus was the Savior that the gospel proclaimed him to be.

The reader of the Pauline letters may naturally feel some confusion when Paul, after thus firmly putting the law in its place, uses the word with a more positive connotation. But the context usually makes this positive connotation clear. "Bear one another's burdens," he tells the Galatians, "and so fulfil the law of Christ" (Gal 6:2). If the law and Christ are antithetical, what is meant by the law of Christ? It is the law of love, exemplified by the bearing of burdens for those who find them too heavy to bear themselves. Indeed, love, the primary fruit of the Spirit, is said to be the fulfilling of the law; the whole law is summed up in the commandment to love one's neighbor (Gal 5:14). But when law is used in this sense, it means something quite different. The law which could never bring justification before God is viewed as an external code with penal sanctions, like the repeated "Thou shalt not . . ." on the two tablets of stone. The law which is fulfilled in love is an inward principle, "the law of the Spirit of life in Christ Jesus," which breaks the shackles of the other law, "the law of sin and death" (Rom 8:2).

Rules and regulations cannot coexist peacefully with the liberty of the Spirit. But if this was the message for the Galatians, who were being urged to take some elements of legalism into their system, was it the message for those members of the church of Corinth whose slogan was "All things are lawful—anything goes"?

There were not lacking Christian friends of Paul who assured him that, whatever the Galatian situation might require, a good stiff dose of law was precisely what the Corinthians needed. Gifted as the church of Corinth was, it was volatile and undisciplined; what better discipline could be imposed on it than the discipline of law?

The imperative mood is not wanting in Paul's Corinthian letters, whether in the second or third person. A good part of 1 Corinthians is devoted to answering questions posed to Paul in a letter from the church, and when they ask, "What shall we do in this or that situation?" Paul naturally replies, "Do this"—not so much laying down the law as providing guidelines for their conduct, especially (but not exclusively) in matters of church procedure. But there are some matters on which he is quite peremptory. Behavior inconsistent with the gospel, or likely to bring the Christian cause into public disrepute, is not to be tolerated. Even here, however, Paul does not say, "Obey the law," but "Live as befits Christians."

The Corinthian Christians had no thought of worshipping any deity but the living and true God; nevertheless, some of them were accustomed to participate in social activities which involved a certain countenancing of idolatry. Paul might have dealt with this by imposing the ruling of the Jerusalem Council which forbade the eating of food that had been offered to pagan divinities or other "pollutions of idols" (Acts 15:20); instead, he reasons with them, appeals to first principles, and says, "I speak as to wise men; judge for yourselves what I say" (1 Cor 10:15).

Where the besetting vice of Corinth was concerned, he took a firm line. His earliest letter to the church there enjoined dissociation from fornicators and others of like character—dissociation, as he explained later, from people who made a profession of Christian faith and acted in those ways. But again, he does not impose what might appear to be an arbitrary rule but argues in terms of respect for human personality and personal relationships. To be sure, he is completely peremptory in prescribing the disciplinary action to be taken with the man who was cohabiting with his father's wife, but this was not simply because he found this relationship profoundly shocking but even more because it was liable to scandalize the extremely permissive pagans of Corinth and because some members of the church were taking pride in what seemed to them to be such a fine assertion of Christian liberty.

Where he turns to questions of marriage, he is far from trying to make his own celibate preference the rule for his converts' lives. However congenial he might find the ascetic slogan, "It is well for a man not to touch a woman" (1 Cor 7:1), he will not countenance any move to impose it as a general rule, or even as a counsel of perfection. For the majority of Christians, as for other men and women, marriage is recognized as the normal way of life. The only unconditional ruling which he makes is not his own, but the Lord's: between a Christian husband and wife divorce is out of the question. Where no "commandment of the Lord" is available, he expresses his judgment, since he has been asked for it; but his correspondents are free to dissent from it and do as they think best. Even to the ban on divorce there might be an exception: his missionary experience had taught him the unwisdom of insisting that, where a husband or a wife became a Christian, the bond with the non-Christian spouse must be preserved at all costs. If the non-Christian spouse was prepared to go on living with the Christian, well and good; if he or she walked out, it was best to accept the situation: in such a case the marriage tie was no longer binding.

Indeed, some of the most stringent requirements voiced by Paul in his Corinthian correspondence relate to matters which cannot well be subjects of legal regulation, enforced by penal sanctions. More than anything else he insists on the supremacy of brotherly love. No Christian should allow his liberty to be subject to another's dictation, but every Christian should be willing to limit his own liberty in the interests of brotherly love. Legal or ceremonial food-restrictions had no place in Paul's scheme of things, but voluntary food-restrictions out of consideration for the scruples of a weaker brother were most worthy of the Christian name, and Paul was foremost in forgoing his freedom for such a cause: "if food is a cause of my brother's falling, I will never eat meat, lest I cause my brother to fall. . . . I try to please all men in everything I do, not seeking my own advantage, but that of the many, that they may be saved. Be imitators of me, as I am of Christ" (1 Cor 8:13; 10:33-11:1).

Some of the severest language in 1 Corinthians is directed against abuses at the Lord's Supper—abuses which consist in violation not of ritual propriety but of brotherly love. To take the holy supper while in practice of flouting the charity which should be shown to a fellow-Christian was an outrage—an outrage which was too common at meetings of the Corinthian church. This is what is meant by eating and drinking unworthily and so incurring judgment for failure to "discern the body"; "this," says Paul, "is why many among you are weak and sickly, while several have even fallen asleep" (1 Cor 11:29-30). The causal connection between fatal illness and uncharitable conduct at the holy communion may be difficult for us to perceive, but we are left in no doubt about the seriousness with which Paul views breaches of the law of love.

It is a mistake, therefore, to suppose that Paul, having gone almost to the brink of antinomianism in his zeal to warn the Galatians against any tendency to seek justification by deeds of the law, redresses the balance with the Corinthian libertines by imposing a measure of legalism on them. He does lay down guidelines to direct them along the Christian way—"guidelines" is a better term than *Einzelgebote,* "particular commandments."[6] But what he presses on them above all, by precept and example alike, is brotherly love and other manifestations of that fruit of the Spirit which he equally recommended to the Galatians: "against such," he adds (perhaps adapting an Aristotelian remark),[7] "there is no law" (Gal 5:22-23). Law in the sense of rules and regulations has nothing to say to qualities such as these or to the people who are characterized by them.

III

JUSTIFICATION AND JUDGMENT

To be justified by faith, for Paul, was to have one's pardon already pronounced, to be set in the clear here and now in the eyes of divine justice, instead of having to wait anxiously for the last judgment to know for sure what the verdict would be. No one appreciated more than he that peace with God which follows the assurance of having been justified by his grace, and he encouraged his fellow-believers to enjoy this peace as he himself did.

Nevertheless, a time of divine judgment had to be faced. Warning his readers not to sit in judgment one on another and so usurp the divine prerogative, he says, "we shall all stand before the tribunal of God" (Rom 14:10). The same tribunal is called "the tribunal of Christ" in 2 Corinthians 5:10, where Paul similarly states that "we must all appear before the tribunal of Christ." In the latter instance he goes on to say that the purpose of our appearing there is "that each one may receive good or evil, according to what he has done in the body." He is speaking to men and women who have been "washed, . . . sanctified, . . . justified in the name of the Lord Jesus Christ and in the Spirit of our God" (1 Cor 6:11); evidently, however, the justification which they have already received does not exempt them from appearing before the divine tribunal to receive reward or retribution in accordance with their actions in earthly life. Paul himself, assured as he was of his justification by faith in Christ, expected to appear before this tribunal and treated the prospect seriously. He was unconcerned about the assessment passed on him by any human court: "it is the Lord who judges me. Therefore [he adds] do not pronounce judgment before the time, before the Lord comes. He will bring to light the things hidden in darkness and will disclose the purposes of the heart; then every one will receive due commendation from God" (1 Cor 4:4-5).

More particularly, it was Paul's apostolic service that would then be passed in review, and he was eager to win the approval of the Lord who commissioned him. "I do not run aimlessly, I do not box as one beating the air; but I pommel my body and subdue it, lest after preaching to others I myself should be disqualified" (1 Cor 9:26-27). Above all, he longed that his converts should prove to be of such sterling worth that, when he was called upon to give an account of his stewardship, he would need do no more than point to them and invite the Lord to judge his service by the quality of their Christian lives. He could then rejoice in the day of Christ that he had neither run nor labored in vain (Phil 2:16).

Here we may see how one already justified may yet expect to be judged and to receive commendation or disapproval: Paul had no doubt of his own ultimate salvation, but his work as a servant of Christ must come under scrutiny, and the knowledge of this provided him with an incentive to "press on toward the goal for the prize of the upward call of God in Christ Jesus" (Phil 3:14). So, speaking of the one sound foundation that had been laid, he added a warning that anyone who built on it with inferior materials would see his work go up in smoke when the day of fiery testing came: instead of receiving a reward for good and durable workmanship, such a person would "suffer loss, though he himself will be saved, but only as through fire" (1 Cor 3:15).

Here and at other points, however, a question arises: in our attempts to resolve the tensions which we find in his writings, may we not be imposing on Paul a consistency foreign to his nature—that "foolish consistency" which R. W. Emerson described as "the virtue of little minds, beloved of little statesmen and philosophers and divines"?[8] His own converts were aware of these tensions and found them insoluble: when he says that he has made himself "all things to all men" (1 Cor 9:22) he is probably repeating a charge which originated with some of them. He admitted the charge, but asserted that he did it all for the gospel's sake, in order to win men and women of the most diverse kinds. The gospel of free grace was for him the one unchangeable datum; to that, all other considerations were secondary.

IV

ONE GOD, ONE CHURCH: MANY MEMBERS, DIVERSE FUNCTIONS

"There is one God, the Father," said Paul, "from whom are all things and for whom we exist" (1 Cor 8:6). This had been his creed before his conversion, as it continued to be afterwards. But it made a difference to his conception—not, perhaps, of the unity of God but of the implications of his unity—when he learned to add, ". . . and one Lord, Jesus Christ, through whom are all things and through whom we exist." Before his conversion he knew that the one God was the creator of the world and judge of all the earth, the God of Jews and Gentiles alike—the God, that is to say, whom Jews worshipped and whom Gentiles ought to have worshipped. But it was his new confession of "one Lord, Jesus Christ," that enabled him to confess the oneness of God in less partial terms: "Is God the God of Jews only? Is he not the God of Gentiles also? Yes, of Gentiles also, since God is one; and he will justify the circumcised on the ground of their faith and the uncircumcised through their faith" (Rom 3:29-30).

It was in the light of the "revelation of Jesus Christ" on the Damascus road that Paul saw that, since the God of Jews and Gentiles was one, there was one way of acceptance for Jews and Gentiles alike. It was in the light of that same revelation that he saw that, since God was one, his people must also be one, comprising both Jews and Gentiles. "In one Spirit we were all baptized into one body—Jews or Greeks, slaves or freemen—and were all watered by one Spirit" (1 Cor 12:13). The people of God manifest the utmost diversity, comprehended in an all-encompassing unity.

This is the unity which is expounded at greater length in the Letter to the Ephesians. Whatever be said about the authorship of this letter, its substance is pure Pauline doctrine—"the quintessence of Paulinism," to borrow a phrase from another context.[9] "We who first put our hope in Christ" are united with "you also" who in due course "believed and were sealed with the Holy Spirit of promise" to form God's heritage, which is in its turn the pilot scheme for the accomplishment of his eternal purpose, to be realized in "the fulness of time"—his purpose to unite all things under Christ as their true head (Eph 1:9-14). The "middle wall of partition," the barrier of legal ordinances which once kept Jews and Gentiles apart, has been demolished by Christ our peace, "that in himself he might create from the two one new man . . . and reconcile both to God in one body by means of the cross" (Eph 2:14-16). The long-concealed purpose of God, that the Gentiles should be fellow-heirs and concorporate with Israel, has not only been revealed to Paul but has been translated into an experienced fact through his apostolic ministry. As the one God implies one corporate people of God, so the existence of this one Spirit-baptized corporate people provides visible evidence on earth of the oneness of God. "There is one body and one Spirit, just as you were called [Jews and Gentiles alike] in one hope of your calling; one Lord, one faith, one baptism; one God and Father of all, who is over all and through all and in all" (Eph 4:4-6).

This last passage has some of the features of a credal affirmation: the repeatedly emphasized "one" is specially characteristic of eastern creeds like the Nicene, with its confession of faith in "one God the Father almighty, . . . one Lord Jesus Christ, . . . one catholic and apostolic church, . . . one baptism for the remission of sins." But the oneness which is thus confessed must be manifested in life on earth, that the reconciled community of believers may have credibility as the harbinger of the reconciled universe of the future.

Within this one fellowship there is, nevertheless, room for great diversity. "To each one of us grace has been given according to the allocation of the gift of Christ" (Eph 4:7). And it is in practice within the local fellowship, rather than in the universal church envisaged in Ephesians, that the oneness is best maintained and manifested and the diversity of gifts and functions best exercised, in an atmosphere of harmony, for the health and growth of the body. When Paul expounds this theme for the benefit of the Corinthian church, he says, "you are Christ's body, and severally members of it" (1 Cor 12:27). He does not call them *part* of Christ's body, reserving the term "body" for the sum-total of believers throughout the world, but uses in relation to a particular city church the language which is later used in Ephesians of the universal church. It is not that each local church is thought of as a separate body of Christ; this would spoil the analogy by implying that Christ had several "bodies" throughout the world. Rather, the local church is viewed as a microcosm of the universal church. Thus the eucharistic bread which was shared in practice by members of a local church was shared, ideally, by members of the church worldwide: "we, many as we are, are one body, for we all partake of the one loaf of bread" (1 Cor 10:17). The institutional words, "This is my body," are thus given an extended sense: the eucharistic "body" is not only Christ's "body of flesh," given in sacrifice for his people, but also that body of which all his people are members. That is why sins against brotherly love in the context of the holy supper amount to a failure to "discern the body," as we have noted already; they disrupt the common life in the body of Christ which gives meaning to the communion meal.

V

SLAVE AND FREEMAN: MALE AND FEMALE

The cleavage between Jew and Gentile was not the only one which was bridged in Christ: in him, says Paul, "there is neither Jew nor Greek, there is neither slave nor free, there is no 'male and female' "[10] (Gal 3:28). It is possible that Paul had in mind here the traditional wording in which, to this day, an orthodox Jew thanks God that he was not made a Gentile, a slave, or a woman. In any case, Paul insists that, however real these divisions might be in the cultural, social, or domestic spheres, no discrimination must be based on them "in Christ Jesus"—that is, in the Christian fellowship.

That Paul maintained this principle consistently so far as the distinction between Jew and Gentile was concerned is clear in all his letters: the union of Jew and Gentile in Christ was fundamental to his apostolic commission and ministry. How he dealt with the distinction between slave and freeman is clear from his letter to Philemon: if he sends Onesimus back to Philemon with a letter of introduction—or reintroduction—it is "no longer as a slave but . . . as a dear brother" (v. 16). This is not the restoration of a slave to his master but the reconciliation of two temporarily estranged fellow-Christians.

But did Paul maintain with comparable consistency the principle of nondiscrimination between male and female in Christ? We may leave on one side the authoritarian rulings of 1 Timothy 2:8-15, although even there, alongside the declaration that teaching is a male activity, learning the woman's role, attention should be paid to Chrysostom's understanding that, as the men were to pray with holy hands, so the women were to pray in modest dress[11] (i.e., as in 1 Cor 11:4-5, there is no discrimination between the sexes as regards praying in church). We may also leave on one side the passage in 1 Corinthians 14:34-35 enjoining silence on women at meetings of the church, in view of its textual doubtfulness.[12]

But there is no doubt that 1 Corinthians 11:1-16 is authentically Pauline. For all his insistence that in Christ there must be no discrimination between men and women, Paul invokes a number of other considerations when he is confronted, as at Corinth, with actions and attitudes on the part of Christian women which apparently flouted respectable convention and certainly deviated from the practice of other churches. The idea of Christian women praying or prophesying in church with their hair hanging loose was perhaps reminiscent in his mind of the behavior of pagan prophetesses giving voice to their oracles in disheveled frenzy. But in addition to begging them to behave in a more "seemly" manner, he appeals to the order of creator and creation—God, Christ, man, woman—in which each is the "head" (κεφαλή) or origin of the next named (man being the "head" of woman in the sense of the narrative of Gen 2:21-23, where Adam is the source of Eve's being).[13] Then he moves back and forth between this meaning of "head" and its literal sense: the man, by praying with his head unveiled, pays respect to his "head" who is Christ, while the woman, by praying with her head veiled, pays respect to her "head" who is the man (more particularly, perhaps, her husband). The question suggests itself at once, why Paul should appeal to the order of the old creation when the new creation has now been inaugurated, but Paul does not answer this question—doubtless because no one thought of putting it to him. He might have replied that the ordinances of the first creation retain their validity so long as the present world-order lasts. The new creation has not yet superseded the first creation, although the redemptive work of Christ has already undone the effect of the fall. For this last reason he has no thought of citing as a precedent the underprivileged status to which woman was relegated because of the fall: he is too good a Christian for that. "In Christ"—within the community of faith—any such idea of feminine inferiority has been obliterated. For the rest Paul, confronted with a practical and, as we should say, a cultural issue, responds with an *ad hominem* argument, or rather with a series of such arguments. To the appeal to the order of creation he appends an argument from the presence of angels at meetings of the church (where presumably they are impressed by seeing things done decently and in order), an argument with Stoic affinities from what "nature itself teaches" about propriety in demeanor and (as has been indicated) an argument from the custom of the churches in general—including probably the church of Jerusalem as well as the churches of Paul's mission-field. With this appeal to church practice elsewhere he dismisses the subject: if you insist on being different, then at least recognize that you *are* being different. The matter is not so important that divine sanctions have to be invoked, as in the really serious issue of unbrotherly attitudes at the Lord's Supper, to which he moves on next.

This at least must be noted: when he urges the Christian women at Corinth to cover their heads in acts of worship, he encourages them to regard the head-covering as their "authority"—their authority, especially, to pray and prophesy in meetings of the people of God. Their Jewish sisters might not have their head-attire in synagogue prescribed for them, but neither had they authority to pray or prophesy there. The liberty accorded to Christian women to take such a responsible part in public worship was a substantial step forward in the practical outworking of the principal that in Christ there is neither male nor female.

VI

PAUL AND JERUSALEM

As the diversity between one member and another in the local church was subservient to a higher unity, so was the diversity between one local church and another. The churches of Paul's planting had their varying individual characteristics, although no doubt they had features in common which distinguished them from non-Pauline churches, and pre-eminently from the church of Jerusalem. Paul did not discourage such individuality, provided it did not obstruct the unity of all churches and all believers worldwide. He had a horror of schism both within any local church and within the church universal. This was why, with all his asserted independence of the authority of Jerusalem, he was anxious to maintain fellowship with Jerusalem in his Gentile mission and not to get out of step with the mother-church in that city more than was necessary. His concern for the Jerusalem relief fund arose from his eagerness to promote interdependence among churches, and especially between the Gentile churches and the church of Jerusalem, "that there may be an equality, your superfluity contributing at the present time to make good their deficiency, so that [at another time] their superfluity may supply what you lack" (2 Cor 8:13-14).

More generally, Paul's relations with the Jerusalem church provide an outstanding instance of the tensions which appear to have been inseparable from his apostolic ministry. While he resolutely affirms his independence of that church and its leaders, he nonetheless makes it plain that he could not discharge his ministry effectively except in fellowship with them. In the letter in which he most categorically denies that his commission was in any way derived from the Jerusalem leaders, he tells how he visited them with Barnabas on one occasion and laid before them the gospel which he was preaching among the Gentiles "lest somehow I should be running, or should prove to have run, in vain" (Gal 2:2). This implies that, if his Gentile mission had to be conducted without the fellowship of the mother-church, his efforts would be fruitless. No wonder, then, that he did his best to preserve good relations with Jerusalem, even when he suspected that Jerusalem was not equally careful about preserving good relations with him. Perhaps the unsparing severity with which he excoriates his opponents in 2 Corinthians 11:13—"false apostles, workers of iniquity, masquerading as apostles of Christ"—is in some degree a compensation for his refusal to criticize the "superlative apostles" whose authority those opponents invoked.

As the late Arnold Ehrhardt pointed out,[14] Paul was a greater asset to Jerusalem than Jerusalem gave him credit for: repeatedly he brought deviant forms of Christianity into conformity with the Jerusalem precedent. When he looks askance at his own converts' tendency to go their way in disregard of the custom of other churches, he has the church of Jerusalem principally in mind. When he asks the Corinthian Christians ironically, "Did the word of God go forth from you, and are you the only ones it has reached?" (1 Cor 14:36), the former part of the question implies that it was not from Corinth but from Jerusalem that the word of God went forth: in his view, the gospel provided the fulfillment of the prophecy of Isaiah 2:3, "out of Zion shall go forth the law, and the word of the Lord from Jerusalem."

The importance which Paul attached to the Jerusalem relief fund—his positive response to the request in Galatians 2:10 that he should "remember the poor"—is patent in every reference he makes to it, and especially so in Romans 15:25-29. Not only did he hope that it would strengthen the bonds of affection and sense of interdependence between his Gentile converts and the Jerusalem believers; the way in which he looked forward to its presentation in Jerusalem reveals the place which Jerusalem occupied in his thinking—not only as the place where the mother-church was located but as the place where the gospel began and the place, too, where it would experience its glorious climax. Indeed, when he tells the Roman Christians of the extent of his own apostolic service to date, he speaks of having fulfilled the gospel of Christ "from Jerusalem and as far round as Illyricum" (Rom 15:19). Actually, he had begun his gospel preaching in Damascus and Arabia, before ever he paid his first visit to Jerusalem as a Christian, but Jerusalem was, for him as for Luke, the proper starting-place of the gospel; and when his ministry in the Aegean world was completed, Jerusalem was the proper place for him to render to the Lord an account of that phase of his stewardship. Perhaps, indeed, he hoped at a later date, when his projected mission to Spain had also been completed, to visit Jerusalem once more and give an account of yet another phase of his stewardship. We know that this was not to be, but what we know from our perspective was naturally unknown to Paul at the time when he planned what was to be his last visit to Jerusalem. True, he was not over-optimistic about the prospects of that visit: he was aware of the hostility of his Jewish opponents in Jerusalem and of the doubtful attitude of some members of the mother-church, but he hoped that all would go well, that the Gentiles' offering would be acceptable, and that he would be able soon to visit Rome on his way to Spain.

One thing stands out clearly in the account he gives the Romans of his apostolic service: he saw it, as he saw himself, as an instrument for the accomplishment of God's saving purpose in the world. That purpose was that God's "way might be known on the earth, and his saving health among all nations" (Ps 67:2). This had been foreseen by psalmist and prophet in earlier days; what had not been foreseen was the sequence in which all nations would come to know the divine salvation—first the Gentiles and then the Jews. The first believers in Jesus, indeed, had been Jews, and they constituted a "remnant"[15] in which the hope of their people's future was embodied; but the Jews as a nation had not believed in him. Gentiles, on the other hand, had turned to him in large numbers in the last decade and a half. The work of Gentile evangelization was being pressed ahead, by none more energetically than by Paul himself, until the "fulness of the Gentiles"[16] had been gathered in. This ingathering would be the signal for the salvation of all Israel, stimulated to jealousy by the spectacle of so many Gentiles enjoying the gospel blessings which were the fulfillment of God's promise to Abraham: so the kingdom of God would be consummated in the parousia of Christ.

Paul might well magnify his office as apostle to the Gentiles, not only because of its direct fruit in the salvation of Gentiles, but also because of its indirect fruit in the salvation of his own kith and kin. In his own eyes he was in truth a figure of eschatological significance, all unworthy as he acknowledged himself to be. But when the consummation took place, where would it be manifested? In Jerusalem, it appears, for Paul modifies in this sense the wording of the *testimonia* which he quotes, associating the consummation of God's saving work on earth with the occasion when "the Deliverer will come from Zion; he will banish ungodliness from Jacob" (Rom 11:26).[17] From Zion the word of the Lord in the gospel first went forth; from Zion its crowning glory would be revealed.

* * * * *

It is a pleasure and an honor to dedicate these thoughts to a scholar whose worth as a friend and colleague I have appreciated for a quarter of a century. *In multos annos!*

Notes to Chapter 7

1. J. W. Drane, *Paul: Libertine or Legalist?* (London: SPCK, 1975).
2. It is a joy to refer to Dr. G. E. Ladd's treatment of this topic in *A Theology of the New Testament* (Grand Rapids: Eerdmans, 1974) 386-394, the more so as this section of his work was originally contributed by him to a symposium published as a gift to the present writer some years ago.
3. Cf. M. Hengel, *The Son of God: The Origin of Christology and the History of Jewish-Hellenistic Religion* (Philadelphia: Fortress, 1976).
4. Drane, *Paul: Libertine or Legalist?*, 65.
5. Cf. J. Neusner, *The Rabbinic Traditions about the Pharisees before 70* (Leiden: Brill, 1971) I, 341-376.
6. Cf. W. Schrage, *Die konkreten Einzelgebote in der paulinischen Paränese* (Gütersloh: Mohn, 1961).
7. Cf. Aristotle, *Politics* 3.8.2, 1284a: men of outstanding excellence, he says, constitute a law in themselves; it would be absurd to set up a law to regulate them.
8. R. W. Emerson, "Essay on Self-Reliance," in *Essays, Lectures and Orations* (London: Orr, 1848) 30.

9. Cf. A. S. Peake, "The Quintessence of Paulinism," *BJRL* 4 (1917-18) 285-311, reprinted in *Arthur Samuel Peake: Essays in Commemoration* (ed. J. T. Wilkinson; London: Epworth, 1958) 116-142.
10. Paul changes the construction in the third clause, possibly echoing Genesis 1:27, "male and female he created them."
11. Chrysostom, *Homilies on Timothy:* Homily 8.
12. Cf. G. Zuntz, *The Text of the Epistles* (London: Oxford University Press, 1953) 17.
13. Cf. S. Bedale, "The Meaning of κεφαλή in the Pauline Epistles," *JTS,* n.s. 5 (1954) 211-215.
14. Cf. A. A. T. Ehrhardt, *The Framework of the New Testament Stories* (Manchester: University Press, 1964) 94.
15. Galatians 2:10.
16. Romans 11:5.
17. In Romans 11:26-27 Paul conflates Isaiah 59:20-21 and 27:9 with Psalm 14:7 (= 53:6) and Jeremiah 31:34.

8: Paul's Diverse Imageries of the Human Situation and His Unifying Theme of Freedom*

ELDON J. EPP

Beneath the apparent unity of Paul's soteriological views lies a rich diversity of redemptive and salvific motifs. This essay will attempt to show (1) that this diversity is not only actual but more pronounced than is sometimes recognized, and (2) that there is at the same time a distinctive unity that emerges from and through the diversity of motifs or images. Actually, the thesis of this essay is a simple one, that Paul has a single, unitary, and overriding theme in his understanding of what God has done in the Christ-event—God has set his people free, has moved them from bondage into freedom; in making this one, central point, however, Paul's restless and richly faceted mind moves rapidly and easily from one thought-world to another, from one imagery to another, driving home his point in a variety of ways. In this fashion the diversity of his redemptive thought is brought to the support of a unified view of the redemptive acts of God in history, and yet the unity of his soteriology has an underlying diversity of separate conceptions that in themselves are not easily harmonized or conjoined.

It will be obvious that no new data have been brought to bear on the subject of this essay and that few new exegetical formulations result; rather, the essay relies entirely on the common body of well-known data and mostly on the common stock of recognized exegetical conclusions in the field.[1] What is intended to be fresh is, first, the overall formulation in which several truly diverse or distinct imageries in Paul are found to be utilized by him in making his one paramount point that God, through Christ, has brought freedom to humankind, and, secondly, the highlighting of certain implications that flow from this unity amid diversity.

*My debt to George Eldon Ladd is a large one, reaching back twenty-five years when he introduced me not only to the disciplines of New Testament exegesis and biblical theology, but to modern critical scholarship in these fields. Perhaps more than anyone else, he is responsible for my determination to pursue a career in New Testament scholarship, though this is not to suggest that he is responsible either for the course that my scholarship has taken or for its ideological thrust; those decisions rest with me alone. Yet, it was Professor Ladd's infectious enjoyment of both the grand themes and the intricate components of biblical research, his insistence on philological precision, on thoroughness and objectivity, and on fairness in the evaluation of the work of others, and his sincere interest in those who might be inclined to follow a similar scholarly career that were so keenly felt and are so profoundly appreciated.

The development of this thesis will entail an examination, at the outset, of the diversity in Paul's redemptive thought and then a discussion of the single theme on which it all focuses. The difficult decision as to what "Pauline" letters should be employed as sources for the theology of Paul has been made somewhat arbitrarily by utilizing Romans, 1-2 Corinthians, Galatians, Philippians, 1 Thessalonians, and Philemon as undoubted letters of Paul, but also employing 2 Thessalonians, Ephesians, and Colossians in a supplementary way on the ground that they at least represent a "Pauline" viewpoint even though they may be non-Pauline; in every case, however, Ephesians and Colossians will be used with caution and with attention to their secondary status as sources for Paul's thought. The Pastoral Epistles have been bypassed except for occasional comparative references.

I

DIVERSE IMAGERIES OF THE HUMAN SITUATION AND THEIR CORRESPONDING REMEDIES

One prominent manifestation of diversity in Paul's thought comes in his portrayals of the human situation. That there are several such portrayals will be acknowledged readily by all, but that these several portrayals constitute *diverse* imageries may be resisted by some. Such resistance, however, is likely to be based in a failure to recognize the varied thought-worlds that Paul brought to his newfound faith and is likely to be supported further by a lack of appreciation for the richness that these distinct thought-worlds contributed to his theological formulations. All too often Paul's depictions of human enslavement to sin or to cosmic spirit-forces, or of human subjection to the powers of this age or to fate and mortality are allowed to commingle and blend (almost to the point of disappearing) as if they all constituted a single theological understanding or an undifferentiated assessment of the human predicament by Paul, when in actuality several contexts—each rich in ideological nuance and in theological connotation—are involved and ought to be given their due weight as separate vehicles of theological meaning whenever Paul's thought is analyzed. At least five of these imageries depicting the human situation are readily apparent in Paul, and the present discussion will focus on them.

1. *Enslavement to Sin: A Jewish-Sacrificial Imagery.* It is well known that in Greek thought sin (ἁμαρτία) did not involve guilt in a religious sense, that is, as an act of the will that is offensive to God; rather, sin is a failure to reach a goal because of a mistake. This does not mean that classical Greek thought had no notion of guilt, but guilt was based in ignorance—which is human limitation[2]—rather than being based in rebellion or self-assertiveness. It is equally well known that sin in both the Old Testament and the

New Testament is the human self-assertive rejection of God's claims, which is an offense against God and thereby involves guilt.[3] Furthermore, it is clear that "sin" has two chief usages in the New Testament: sin can refer to a single wrongful act, which is the usual meaning in most of the New Testament writings, except for the fourth Gospel and Paul; in this usage the term usually occurs in the plural. On the other hand, sin can have an abstract meaning, referring to the ingrained human hostility against God, which is the usual meaning in the fourth Gospel and Paul (and is rare in the rest of the New Testament); with this signification the term normally is in the singular.

For Paul, then, sin obviously is a much broader term than simply a designation for a wrong act; rather, it is a way of life that falls short of the true goal of human existence—it is the human determination that "I am the master of my fate; I am the captain of my soul." More than this, sin is a state of active hostility against God, and as such it is an offense against God and incurs guilt and stain. This understanding of the human predicament places Paul in the context of the Jewish-sacrificial system, where sin—as guilt and stain—needs to be expiated, atoned for, paid for, cleansed, or forgiven. Paul, as we shall see, shares this view of sin as stain that must be cleansed, yet there is remarkably little in Paul about "cleansing" from sin; the occurrences of the term actually are very few and not what might be expected. For example, it is striking that he can say in 2 Corinthians 7:1 (the only use of καθαρίζω in the undoubted letters of Paul) that we Christians should *"cleanse ourselves* from every defilement . . ." and in 1 Corinthians 5:7 (the only use of ἐκκαθαίρω in the undoubted letters of Paul) that Christians should "cleanse out the old leaven"! (cf. the same meaning in 2 Tim 2:21). Rather, Paul conceives of sin more as a binding power, something that enslaves and dominates; the whole context of Romans 6, for example, is replete with this motif of bondage to sin (esp. Rom 6:12-14, 16-18, 20, 22; cf. 3:9: "All men . . . are under sin" [RSV: "under the power of sin"]).

In what terms, then, does Paul see the remedy for this enslavement of man by sin and for this human guilt before God? As already indicated, Paul moves in the context and thought-world of the Jewish-sacrificial system when he is concerned with humans as held fast by the bonds of sin and when he treats of sin's guilt and stain; after all, guilt before a holy God is the pivot on which the Jewish-sacrificial system turns. It is natural, therefore, that Paul should find the remedy for this enslavement to and domination by sin within this same context; hence, whenever Paul speaks of the shedding of blood, substitution, death for sins, "expiation" (ἱλαστήριον), "redemption" (ἀπολύτρωσις), reconciliation, and the like, he is addressing himself to the remedy that is to be found in the Christ-event, but in doing so he remains in the Jewish-sacrificial world of discourse. This is obvious, for instance, in a passage like Romans 3:23-25, where several key words are related specifically to this imagery: "Since all have sinned and fall short of the glory of God, they are justified by his grace, through the *redemption* which is in Christ Jesus, whom God put forward as an *expiation* by his *blood. . . .*" This emphasis is frequent elsewhere in Paul: "God shows his love for us in that while we were yet sinners Christ *died for us*. Since, therefore, we are now justified by his *blood,* much more shall we be saved by him from the wrath of God" (Rom 5:8-9); ". . . who was put to death *for our trespasses"* (Rom 4:25); "Christ, our *paschal lamb,* has been *sacrificed"* (1 Cor 5:7); ". . . sending his own Son in the likeness of sinful flesh and for sin [*or* as a sin-offering]" (Rom 8:3); "For our sake he made him to be sin [*or* a sin-offering] *who knew no sin"* (2 Cor 5:21); "Christ Jesus, whom God made our . . . redemption" (1 Cor 1:30); and the numerous instances where Paul refers to Christ dying "for sin" (1 Cor 15:3; cf. Gal 1:4), or "for us" or the like (Rom 5:6, 8; 14:15; 1 Thess 5:10; 2 Cor 5:14-15; cf. Gal 2:20). The deutero-Pauline writings elaborate this theme in a series of remarkable passages; see Ephesians 1:7 ("In him we have redemption through his blood, the forgiveness of our trespasses"; cf. Col 1:14); Ephesians 2:13 (". . . brought near in the blood of Christ"); Ephesians 5:2 ("Christ . . . gave himself up for us, a fragrant offering and sacrifice to God"); Colossians 1:20 (". . . through him to reconcile . . . , making peace by the blood of his cross"); 1:21-22 ("And you, who once were estranged and hostile in mind, doing evil deeds, he has now reconciled in his body of flesh by his death, in order to present you holy and blameless and irreproachable before him"); 2:13-14 ("You who were dead in trespasses . . . , God made alive together with him, having forgiven us all our trespasses, having cancelled the bond which stood against us with its legal demands; this he set aside, nailing it to the cross").

In all of these contexts the imagery is a single one, and one with which Paul was thoroughly familiar: the human situation of sin and guilt countervailed by the divinely prescribed sacrifice that issues in atonement, expiation, and forgiveness (cf. the background in Leviticus 4-7, 16). The sure result, as Paul emphasizes several times, is that the Christian not only is forgiven his sin and has its guilt covered (cf. Rom 3:23-26; 2 Cor 5:19-21), thus reconciling him to God (Rom 5:6-11; 2 Cor 5:18-21) and effecting sanctification and eventually eternal life (Rom 6:22; cf. 1 Thess 5:10), but the binding power of sin also is broken. Romans 6:17-22 makes it clear that to be "in Christ" (v. 22) means that Christians "who were once slaves of sin" (v. 17) now have been "set free from sin" (vv. 18, 22). Moreover, every mark of the context of cultic sacrifice is to be found in these passages: the sacrificial victim (1 Cor 5:7), the unblemished victim (2 Cor 5:21), the representative victim whose death is for trespasses (Rom 4:25), and the resultant expiation through shed blood (Rom 3:25).[4]

Clearly, this imagery of sacrificial cult *is* to be found in Paul; attempts to deny it or to remove it are destined to founder on the rocks of hard data and should be abandoned. The problem is not whether the imagery is there, but what its meaning is and what Paul intends by it. Does Paul think in terms of some objective transaction in heaven of a bookkeeping kind, as if each drop of sacrificial blood blots out a specific act of sin and its guilt—as if some *quid pro quo* demand has been met measure for measure, or does he think in terms of a payment made to Satan for humankind—as in the old "ransom to the devil" theory (emphasizing the λύτρον in ἀπολύτρωσις; cf. 1 Tim 2:6), or in some other objectifying terms? To give an answer within the framework only of this one imagery would be to risk the errors of many past interpretations; rather, other Pauline imageries must be considered prior to an attempt at stating the larger meaning of any of them.

2. *Subjection to the Ruling Powers of This Evil Age: A Jewish-Apocalyptic Imagery.* It is unnecessary to document the basic apocalyptic orientation of Paul's thought, for his letters are replete with references to "this age" or "the present evil age" (Rom 12:2; 1 Cor 1:20; 2:6, 8; 2 Cor 4:4; Gal 1:4; cf. "this world" in 1 Cor 3:19; 7:31; cf. also Eph 2:2; 2 Tim 4:10; Titus 2:12), implying the basic structure of two contrasting ages as in Jewish apocalyptic thought. Paul, however (like Jesus before him), modifies the simple present-future (horizontal) dualism of apocalyptic by conceiving of the two ages as already overlapping—the shift of the ages already has been effected—and by viewing the present age as now standing in a (vertical) relationship of polarity with the age to come. Just as, for Jesus, the (temporally future) kingdom of God of apocalyptic expectation had moved already to an active role in the (still existing) present age, so, for Paul, Christians—including Paul himself—are those "upon whom the *ends* of the *ages* have come" (1 Cor 10:11, both nouns plural as in the Greek text).[5] For him, the two ages of apocalyptic thought have converged, overlapping and overreaching one another, with the age to come already active in some real sense, while this present evil age, though in the process of passing away (1 Cor 7:31; cf. 2:6 and 10:11), is still very much in force. The human predicament, as Paul sees it within this imaginal context of the apocalyptic thought-world of Judaism, is that human beings are subject to the ruling powers of this evil age and that "the god of this age has blinded the minds of the unbelievers to keep them from seeing the light of the gospel" (2 Cor 4:4).

What is the remedy, according to Paul? Once again it is the Christ-event, through which God "delivers (ἐξαιρέω) us from the present evil age" (Gal 1:4) and "delivers (ῥύομαι) us from the wrath to come" (1 Thess 1:10; cf. Col 1:13). Not only is the "present evil age" a distinctly apocalyptic conception, but so also is the "wrath to come"; moreover, deliverance from evil or suffering and the vindication of God's own are characteristic themes of Jewish apocalyptic on the positive side. On the negative side, and equally characteristic, is the destruction of evil itself, and here Paul—in the unmistakably eschatological context of 1 Corinthians 15—is quite explicit about Christ's role in destroying all evil and all his enemies: "Then comes the end, when he delivers the kingdom to God the Father after destroying every rule and every authority and power. For he must reign until he has put all his enemies under his feet" (1 Cor 15:24-25; cf. 2 Thess 1:6-10; 2:8-12). To be sure, there is some mingling of imageries in this statement (see below), but the terms "kingdom," "reign," "destroy," and "enemies" all fall into the apocalyptic category.

It is superfluous, perhaps, to point out that the two imageries discussed so far are distinct and separate conceptions that really have nothing in common, except their sharing of a Jewish matrix and milieu. Stained by the guilt and bound by the power of sin are entities different from the domination by evil in an apocalyptic thought-world. This is not to say that the sin mentioned in the cultic-sacrificial context is wholly discontinuous with the subjection of the present age to Satanic forces referred to in the apocalyptic framework; certainly both descriptions of the human predicament have connections with sin, but it is one thing to be enslaved by the binding power of sin's ingrained hostility against God—essentially something initiated by humans and continuously reinforced by the individual, wrongful acts of human beings, and it is quite another thing to be part of that present structure of things that is dominated and controlled by the evil hierarchy of Satanic powers—essentially an extra-human phenomenon that has been allowed a limited existence and that shortly will have run its course. Moreover, the remedies are distinct: in the Jewish-sacrificial imagery, Christ in his death is represented as the means by which the stain and guilt of sin are covered or removed and its bonds are broken, but in the Jewish-apocalyptic imagery Christ is the one who rescues or snatches his own from the clutches of the present, Satan-dominated age prior to its destruction and who then destroys their Satanic enemies.

3. *Bondage to the Cosmic Spirit-Forces of the Universe: A Christus Victor Imagery.* Another way in which Paul comprehends the human situation is to view humans as enslaved by cosmic spirit-forces in the universe. The clearest statements are found in Galatians 4, where—to be sure—there is controversy about the meaning of the Pauline expression, "elemental spirits of the universe" (Gal 4:3, 9; cf. Col 2:8, 20). That issue cannot be discussed here, but it seems clear to many that Paul is moving there in the sphere of recognized Hellenistic conceptions of the (sometimes neutral, though often negative and antagonistic) cosmic spirit-forces that peopled the universe. Romans 8:38-39 doubtless is a catalogue of such forces, and the reference in 1 Corinthians 15:24 to "principalities and powers," though it occurs in an eschatological context, undoubtedly refers also to such cosmic forces; quite clearly there is such a reference also in the mention of beings "celestial, terrestrial, and subterranean" in Philippians 2:10 (note that

"name" in the preceding verse may refer to spirit-forces, as it clearly does in Eph 1:2). Designations for these spirit-forces occur in greater profusion, of course, in the deutero-Pauline writings, where "principalities and powers" occur in Ephesians 3:10 and Colossians 2:10, 15; and within a larger catalogue of such forces in Ephesians 1:21; 6:12; and Colossians 1:16. There can be no mistake that these passages designate cosmic forces; witness Ephesians 6:12: "For we are not contending against flesh and blood, but against the principalities, against the powers, against the world rulers (κοσμοκράτορες) of this present darkness, against the spiritual hosts of wickedness in the heavenly places." Though sparse, the similar terminology in the undoubted letters of Paul is to be understood in the same way.

The human subjection and bondage to these invisible forces is explicit (among the undoubted Pauline writings) only in Galatians 4:3 and 4:8-9:

> When we were children, we were slaves to the elemental spirits of the universe. . . . Formerly, when you did not know God, you were in bondage to beings that by nature are no gods; but now that you have come to know God . . . , how can you turn back again to the weak and beggarly elemental spirits, whose slaves you want to be once more?

The context of Romans 8:38 (that is, the word "conquerors" in v. 37) does imply, however, such domination of humans, and verse 38 speaks of potential separation from God that can be effected by such powers. Yet, once again, it is Ephesians and Colossians that articulate more extensively the human situation as bondage to these spirit-forces; this appears in the explicit description of human conflict with them in Ephesians 6:12 and in the explicit theme of victory over such powers as found in Ephesians 1:21 and Colossians 2:15—victory showing that the domination had been real.

Some will wish to argue that "elemental spirits" (στοιχεία) in Galatians 4 is a reference to cultic observances and perhaps, at least inclusively, a reference to Torah. This would not be inconsistent with the immediate context in Galatians, where 4:4 speaks of the redemption of those who were "under the law"; however, this mention of "law" in verse 4 is incidental in the context, for it responds and corresponds—as a kind of afterthought—to the equally incidental reference just a few words earlier to Jesus Christ as "born under the law" (notice that the two phrases, "under the law," are separated by only two short words in the Greek text). Thus, the whole passage (Gal 4:1-7) has as its major theme the enslavement of human beings to the spirit-forces of the universe, their release from slavery, and their consequent adoption as "sons" through the sending of the "Son." Actually, therefore, the two occurrences of the phrase, "under the law" (and the related words), could be excised without altering Paul's intent in Galatians 4:1-11. Furthermore, verses 8-10, though highly controversial, also can be understood (and often have been) without specific reference to Jewish law and need not be taken as describing anything other than enslavement to the spirit-forces referred to earlier. Moreover, that "elemental spirits" (in Gal 4:9) designates cosmic forces is clear from the closely associated idea of bondage to non-gods (v. 8); and the further association with days, months, seasons, and years (v. 10) is not against this understanding (as has sometimes been argued; see, e.g., *The Oxford Annotated Bible),* but rather can be supportive of the spirit-forces interpretation when it is recognized that Hellenistic astrological views saw higher powers behind all such designations for time.

When we turn to Paul's remedy for this human predicament, it is obvious from Galatians 4 that the Christ-event (vv. 4-5: "God sent forth his Son . . . to redeem . . .") constitutes that remedy, and—from the human standpoint—it is clear that the remedy is appropriated by coming "to know God, or rather to be known by God" (4:9; to love God is to be known by God, according to 1 Cor 8:3). The victory motif is intimated in the context of the catalogue of spirit-forces in Romans 8:37-39 inasmuch as the passage is introduced by the affirmation that "in all these things we are more than conquerors [*or* completely victorious] through him who loved us," and this introduction is linked to the catalogue of "principalities and powers" by the conjunction "for." Moreover, this triumph of Christ over the spirit-forces is to be found also in 1 Corinthians 15:24: "Then comes the end, when he delivers the kingdom to God the Father after destroying every rule and every authority and power" (on this text, see further below). Philippians 2:7-10 appears to be another instance of the triumph theme in Paul, if it is granted (as was suggested earlier) that "name" and beings "celestial, terrestrial, and subterranean" in verses 9-10 indicate a spirit-forces context; in that case, the bowing of every knee before the name (namely, Jesus) that is above every "name," and the confession by every tongue that he is "Lord" shows his triumph and victory over those forces, a victory that is effected through the incarnation and the "death of a cross" (vv. 7-8). Additionally, it is not inconceivable that when Paul describes Christ's assumption of human form as "taking the form of a slave" (δοῦλος, v. 7), he is alluding to the fact that Christ thereby assumed the position of all humankind—"slaves of the elemental spirits of the universe," as Paul in Galatians 4:3-9 puts it (notice δουλόω in vv. 3 and 9; and δοῦλος in v. 7); yet this Christ, who humbled himself and became a slave of the spirit-forces, triumphed over them in the cross and has been exalted above them all.

There is still another dimension to the imagery of human enslavement to cosmic spirit-forces, and it carries with it something akin to a triumph motif. The victory wrought through the Christ-event, both in the Galatians 4:1-11 passage and in the larger context of Romans 8:37-39, issues in adoption as sons. Paul's conception is that when the triumph over the slaveholder had been accomplished and the bonds of slavery had been shattered, the slave—unexpectedly—was adopted as a son and heir: "So you are no longer a slave but a son, and if a son then an heir" (Gal 4:7). What irony and what a put-down for the former slaveholder! This same interplay between slavery and sonship is found in Romans 8:15, and the notion of sonship is carried through the context of Romans 8 from verses 14-17 to verse 23, to verse 29, and is concealed perhaps under the expressions in verses 35 and 39 that imply the impossibility of "separating us from the love of God." Incidentally, only here (in Rom 8:15) and in Galatians 4:6 does the phrase "Abba! Father!" occur in Paul.

Admittedly, though, the *Christus victor* theme is not explicit in any closely knit spirit-forces context in the undoubted Pauline writings. That is not to say that a Christ-as-Conqueror theme is not to be found in these letters; certainly it is: Christ is the power of God (1 Cor 1:24); the cross is the power of God (1 Cor 1:18); the gospel is the power of God (Rom 1:16); and there is power in the resurrection of Christ (Phil 3:10); also, "God . . . gives us the victory through our Lord Jesus Christ" (1 Cor 15:57). Once again, however, it is in the deutero-Pauline letters that the theme of victory over the cosmic forces is most clearly developed. Ephesians 1:19-22*a* is a full and clear statement of this triumph, extolling "the immeasurable greatness of [God's] power in us who believe, according to the working of his great might which he accomplished in Christ when he raised him from the dead and made him sit at his right hand in heavenly places, far above all rule and authority and power and dominion." Colossians 2:15 is even more explicit: through the Christ-event, God "disarmed the principalities and powers and made a public example of them, triumphing over them in him [Christ]/it [the cross]."

Upon reflection, it will be recognized again that the imagery of enslavement to and triumph over the cosmic spirit-forces involves a different and distinct thought-world from that relating to the Jewish cultic-sacrifice motif—with its concern for the removal of the guilt of sin—or from that of the Jewish apocalyptic conception—with its themes of the control of this present evil age by Satanic powers, of the breaking of that power, and of deliverance from the apocalyptic wrath to come.

4. *Confinement under the Law: An Exodus Imagery.* Another aspect of the human situation, according to Paul, is confinement under Torah: "Before faith came, we were confined under [*or* held in custody by] the law, kept under restraint until faith should be revealed. So that the law was our custodian until Christ came . . ." (Gal 3:23-24). Earlier, Paul affirms that "all who rely on works of the law are under a curse" (3:10), and elsewhere he speaks of the law as "that which held us captive" (Rom 7:6) and which leads to or at least occasions death (2 Cor 3:6-7; cf. Rom 7:5, 9-11).

Paul finds the remedy for confinement under law in "being released" (καταργέομαι, Rom 7:6) from the law or in "dying" to the law (Rom 7:4, 6) "which held us captive," and this release or deliverance has been accomplished through Christ (Rom 7:4) and leads to serving God "in a newness of the Spirit" (Rom 7:6). Notice the striking counterpoint in Paul (Gal 5:4): Those who would be justified by law have been "released" (καταργέομαι) from Christ! Elsewhere Paul states that "Christ redeemed [*or* delivered, ἐξαγοράζω] us from the curse of the law" (Gal 3:13), that he is the "end of the law" (Rom 10:4, with τέλος as termination, though perhaps also as fulfillment or goal; cf. Eph 2:14-16), and, in a larger Torah context (Gal 4:21-5:18), that "for freedom Christ has set us free; stand fast therefore, and do not submit again to a yoke of slavery" (Gal 5:1).

The emphasis in most of these passages on release or deliverance from captivity prompts us to label the imagery here as an "Exodus" motif (even if somewhat anachronistically with respect to the original relationship of Exodus and Torah), for the law is conceived of by Paul as a captor (like Egypt over Israel), and Christ is portrayed as the liberator (like the divine deliverance in the Exodus). What may confirm this as the imagery Paul had in mind is the interesting formulation in Galatians 5:18: "If you are led by the Spirit, you are not under the law," which at once recalls the leading of Israel by the pillar of cloud and the pillar of fire (Exod 13:21-22)—symbols of God's presence and guidance, which are also the essential functions of the Holy Spirit; thus, in Galatians Paul thinks of the Spirit as effecting an Exodus out from under the confinement of the law. (Curiously, the only other Pauline use of the phrase, "led by the Spirit," is in Rom 8:14, where his statement, "For all who are led by the Spirit of God are sons of God," is followed immediately by a reference to slavery [v. 15]: "For you did not receive the spirit of slavery to fall back into fear, but you have received the spirit of sonship.") Observe also that in Romans 7:6 (as indicated earlier) the "release" from the law, "which held us captive," brings the Christian out of servitude (δουλεύω) "under the old written code" to servitude "in the newness of the Spirit." Finally, Paul declares in Romans 8:2 that "the law of the Spirit of life in Christ Jesus has set me free from the law of sin and death."

Once again, this Exodus imagery—though it shares an enslavement theme explicitly with the Jewish-sacrificial and spirit-forces imageries and implicitly with the Jewish-apocalyptic imagery—is a distinct conception of the human situation and one that should not be lost sight of through an unthinking blending with other imageries.

5. *Consignment to Mortality but Yearning for Immortality: A Mystery-Religions Imagery.* A number of passages in Paul are concerned with the Christian's identification with and participation in Christ's death and resurrection or refer to an individual's transformation and personal renewal through the Christ-event. These motifs of sharing in the destinies of a god

or goddess and of new life are common to the major mystery religions of the Greco-Roman world and are exemplified in the theme of life and the promise of a happy immortality that spring from the realm of the dead, as found in the Eleusinian Mysteries; in the foretaste of a blissful afterlife achieved through mystical identification with (omophagy) or possession by (entheos) the immortal Dionysus, as in the Dionysiac Religion; in the identification with the fate of Attis—his death and restoration to life—in the Cult of the Great Mother; in the similar theme with reference to the dying and rising Osiris in the Isis Cult; and in the abundance of life that springs from death, as found in the classic bull-slaying scene in Mithraism, as well as in the possible ordeal of a ritual death by the initiate (if one of the frescoes in the Mithraeum at Capua is thus correctly understood). Though much is obscure about both the ritual procedures and their meaning in these cults, yet most will agree that all of them emphasize life or the acquisition of new life and that most of them have a clearly identifiable theme that out of death comes an abundance of life. Most also will agree that two dominant needs that these mystery religions tried to meet were the desire for assurance of a happy immortality and relief from the blows of fate.

Admittedly, when the Pauline writings are examined to discover whether the human predicament is viewed there in terms of humankind sensing itself to be at the mercy of blind fate, that theme is not apparent; however, the universal human destiny—death—and the human yearning for life everlasting are obvious enough in his letters as a description of the human situation. For example, though found immediately following an apocalyptic context (1 Cor 15:51-52), Paul has this imperative proposition (15:53): "For this perishable nature *must* put on the imperishable, and this mortal nature *must* put on immortality," followed by the affirmation that "when . . . the mortal puts on immortality," death will be "swallowed up in victory" (vv. 54-57). The term "immortality" (ἀθανασία), incidentally, is found nowhere else in the undoubted letters of Paul, and its only other occurrence in the New Testament is in the pointed statement that God "alone has immortality" (1 Tim 6:16). That Paul conceives of human beings as mortal hardly requires documentation; Romans 5-7 provide such statements as "Death spread to all men" (5:12), "Death reigned . . ." (5:17), "The wages of sin is death" (6:23), and "Who will deliver me from this body of death?" (7:24); cf. also "In Adam all die" (1 Cor 15:22).

If Paul seems to share with his pagan contemporaries this imagery of destined human mortality and the accompanying yearning for immortality, it is clearer still that he employs the further imagery of the acquisition of life by the Christian devotee through sharing in Christ's death and resurrection. Paul's conceptions here seem striking in their correspondence with those in the mystery cults, as evidenced in the leading passage of this kind, Romans 6:3-11:

> Do you know that all of us who have been baptized into Christ Jesus were baptized into his death? We were buried therefore with him by baptism into death, so that as Christ was raised from the dead by the glory of the Father, we too might walk in newness of life. For if we have been united with him in a death like his, we shall certainly be united with him in a resurrection like his. We know that our old self was crucified with him so that the sinful body might be destroyed, and we might no longer be enslaved to sin. . . . But if we have died with Christ, we believe that we shall also live with him. For we know that Christ being raised from the dead will never die again; death no longer has dominion over him. . . . So you also must consider yourselves dead to sin and alive to God in Christ Jesus.

The three other passages of this sort in Paul are even better known: "I have been crucified with Christ; it is no longer I who live, but Christ who lives in me" (Gal 2:20); "Far be it from me to glory except in the cross of our Lord Jesus Christ, through whom the world has been crucified to me, and I to the world" (Gal 6:14; cf. 5:24); and ". . . that I may know him and the power of his resurrection, and may share his sufferings, becoming like him in his death, that if possible I might attain the resurrection from the dead" (Phil 3:10-11); cf. also Colossians 2:12-13.

Not only are the identification and participation elements most explicit and strikingly vivid throughout these passages, but the emphases on triumph over death ("death has no dominion over him," Rom 6:9), on life springing from death (Rom 6:4, 8, 10; Phil 3:10-11), and on the acquisition of a new quality of life ("newness of life," Rom 6:4; "new creation," Gal 6:15; cf. 2 Cor 5:17: "If anyone is in Christ, he is a new creation; the old has passed away, behold, the new has come") are also clearly present. As in the mysteries, the mystical transaction effects a present transformation and issues in a present reality; *afterlife* does not begin *after life,* but now—prior to death—life takes on the quality of "immortality" or the blessed hereafter, and this is effected through a sharing in the destinies—the sufferings and triumphs—of the central figure, Christ. What is achieved, then, through this transformation is life, but the resurrection mode of existence (to use a phrase of Albert Schweitzer) carries with it, once again, the notions of freedom from enslavement to sin and from the power of death and also freedom from the tyranny of self and the "world."

It hardly seems necessary to point out that this mystery-religions imagery, even though it issues in essentially the same freedoms stressed in the preceding imageries, entails conceptions quite different and distinct from the others. Here there is no thought of stain and guilt (as in the Jewish-sacrificial imagery), no thought of domination by the Satanic powers of this present evil regime or reference to the wrath to come (as in the Jewish-apocalyptic imagery), no hint of enslavement to cosmic spirit-forces (as in the spirit-forces/*Christus-victor* imagery), no conception of confinement under law (as in the Exodus imagery), but something noncontinuous and discrete: a breaking of the inevitable and destined human mortality by an immortal being who has entered into that mortality but who has overcome it and brought abundant life out of death itself. This, moreover, is accompanied by a conception—found in no other imagery—of the devotee empathetically experiencing that triumph over mortality by participating in the victory won by the immortal operant.

There are, to be sure, points at which these several diverse imageries intersect, but the essential distinctions remain nonetheless. For example, Christ triumphs over the opposition in three of the imageries (the apocalyptic, the cosmic-forces, and the mystery-religions contexts), but this does not mean that the imageries blend into one another indistinguishably or coincide in their other aspects; rather, the triumph in each instance is over an enemy or a force that is not envisioned in the other two. In the apocalyptic imagery, Christ destroys the Satanic ruling powers associated with the dualistic "present age," essentially an act appropriate to the final eschatological complex of events, but effected proleptically by Christ in behalf of his own; in the spirit-forces imagery, Christ triumphs over this different group of forces—pervasive cosmic forces—in his incarnation and cross by breaking their power and effecting the adoption by God of those formerly held captive by these forces; and the mystery-religions imagery envisions a triumph by Christ over human mortality by undergoing death but rising from it to renewed life. Similarly, the apocalyptic and Exodus imageries both entail a rescue, but the deliverance in each case is quite different: one is rescue from evil tyranny and from eschatological wrath, but the other is from bondage to law which (on Paul's view) led to death.

Finally, it is not to be denied that there are, in Paul, some instances of mixed imageries, and these admittedly do not strengthen the case made in this essay. The apparent mixture in Galatians 4:3-7, where the phrase "under the law" occurs in a spirit-forces context, has been treated already. Another example, also referred to earlier, is a Corinthians 15:23-28, which constitutes a clearly eschatological (and, for the most part, a specifically apocalyptic) passage, but into which Paul abruptly introduces the terms for cosmic spirit-forces that are found, for example, in Ephesians 1:21: "rule, authority, and power." The problem in 1 Corinthians 15 becomes more or less difficult depending on one's view of the authorship of Ephesians and Colossians, for if the latter are not Pauline, then the terms in 1 Corinthians 15:24 might be taken as references to Satanic powers (in an apocalyptic sense) rather than to cosmic forces, for "principalities and powers" occurs in the undoubted Pauline writings only in Romans 8:38 (where, however, they certainly designate cosmic forces); if Ephesians and Colossians are Pauline, the "principalities and powers" terminology would be so extensive in

Pauline material that it would be difficult (though not entirely impossible) to assign some special meaning to the occurrences in 1 Corinthians 15. It seems defensible, however, to assign a spirit-forces meaning to the terms in 1 Corinthians 15:24 quite apart from Ephesians and Colossians (since two of the three terms occur in this meaning already in Rom 8:38) and to face, rather, the difficulty of a mixture of imageries in 1 Corinthians 15:23-28; it would appear, further, that the reality of that mixture must be acknowledged. Another interlacing of imageries occurs in the benedictory passage in Galatians 1:3-5, where Christ is referred to as the one "who gave himself for our sins to deliver us from the present evil age"; this admixture may be explained (and thereby perhaps excused) in Paul by accepting the necessity of compressed language in such a benediction, as compared to a more specifically theological discussion. (Col 2:12-15 represents a further instance of intermixed imageries.)

Despite these difficulties, however, the presence and employment of several discrete imageries of the human situation, with statements of their respective solutions, are clear enough in Paul's writings. These distinctive imageries are like prominent threads in the fabric of Paul's theology, which—though occasionally intersecting—are essentially separate from one another and yet all together form a soteriological tapestry that conveys a single impression and makes a unitary impact upon the viewer. It is this overriding and unifying theme that remains to be summarized.

II

THE UNIFYING THEME OF FREEDOM THROUGH THE CHRIST-EVENT

One theme emerges from all of Paul's imageries, and that theme is *freedom*—the freedom divinely won for human beings through the Christ-event. This will be obvious already from the several Pauline statements concerning the divine remedies that apply to the various human predicaments, for every one emphasizes the freedom motif. Under the Jewish-sacrificial imagery, those "who were once slaves of sin" have been "set free from sin" (Rom 6:17-18, 20-22); under the apocalyptic imagery, Christ "delivers us from the present evil age" (Gal 1:4) and "rescues us from the wrath to come" (1 Thess 1:10); under the spirit-forces imagery, "God sent forth his Son . . . to redeem" (or "buy back," ἐξαγοράζω), another freedom term, and to effect the transfer from the status of "slave" to that of "son" (Gal 4:5-7); under the Exodus motif, Christ "redeems" (ἐξαγοράζω, Gal 3:13) or "releases" (καταργέομαι, Rom 7:6) humans from confinement under the law that held them captive; and under the mystery-religions imagery, there once again is a reference to being "no longer enslaved" to sin and no longer under the domination of death (Rom 6:6, 9).

That his diverse imageries really were intended by Paul to emphasize the single point of freedom is indicated, if not confirmed, by the fact that in several cases he can use one of his distinctive theological terms for freedom in more than one of the distinct imageries. For example, Paul twice uses the term ἐξαγοράζω, once in a Torah context with an Exodus theme (Gal 3:13) and again in a spirit-forces context (Gal 4:4-5). A second, similar example is the term ἐλευθερόω, which is used by Paul in a Jewish-sacrificial context (Rom 6:17-18, 22; 8:2-3) and also in a confinement-under-law and Exodus imagery (Gal 5:1-4). These two Greek terms are "freedom" terms, as are ἐξαιρέω ("deliver") and ῥύομαι ("rescue"), which are employed by Paul in his Jewish-apocalyptic imagery (Gal 1:4; 1 Thess 1:10), and καταργέομαι ("being released"), which is used in the Exodus imagery of Romans 7:6.

Paul's writings, therefore, are replete with the freedom theme, and inevitably this theme stands within the context of and over against a slavery or bondage motif; to recite the passages all in one series would be impressive, but would only increase the repetitiousness of the present essay. Two points, however, remain to be stressed. First, Paul highlights the paradox that those who have been freed (under whatever imagery) now—ironically—are "slaves" again: "Now that you have been set free from sin and have become slaves of God . . ." (Rom 6:22; cf. 1 Cor 7:22), a point that Paul reinforces by repeated reference to himself as "a slave of Christ" (Rom 1:1; Gal 1:10; Phil 1:1). Secondly, Paul is careful to indicate the life-direction that freedom implies and, indeed, demands: "For you were called to freedom, brethren; only do not use your freedom as an opportunity for the flesh, but through love be servants (δουλεύω) of one another. For the whole law is fulfilled in one word, 'You shall love your neighbor as yourself' " (Gal 5:13-14), and this imperative is followed by a lengthy statement of what it means to "walk by the Spirit" (5:16-6:10), a conception reminiscent of Romans 7:6, which—under the Exodus imagery—refers to release from the captivity to law "so that we serve (δουλεύω) . . . in the newness of the Spirit."

The implications of this Christian freedom as Paul develops it are vast and far-reaching, but essentially he sees freedom as a reality effected in and through the Christ-event, which has broken the power of sin and neutralized the individual hostility against God; which at the same time has covered the guilt and stain of sin and erased the past; which has crushed all enslavement to self, to religious convention, to the present powers of evil, and to cosmic forces; and which has triumphed over every force that dominates humankind, including human mortality itself. But that is only one side of the Pauline coin—the "freedom *from* what?" side; there is also the significant "freedom *for* what?" side, and this many-faceted emphasis in Paul, though it can be simply stated, is infinitely complex in its outworking: a Christian is now free to obey God in a radical fashion by serving his fellow human beings in selfless love.

Finally, what does this Pauline utilization of several diverse imageries—all focusing on freedom—imply about his conceptions of those separate imageries themselves? Does he view the Christ-event as somehow coadunating within itself a whole series of separate divine operations or transactions, each complete in itself and comprehended in an objectifying fashion and yet conceived in such a way that the imageries together form a single amalgam? Such an understanding is not impossible and certainly is a traditional one; on this view the Christ-event was itself a single action that in turn set in motion a series of separate but concurrent additional actions. To employ a crude analogy, the Christ-event then would be something like the action of turning on an automobile ignition switch that puts into operation several separate systems, such as the fuel and combustion, lubrication, electrical, and cooling systems; though these systems work together for one purpose, each nonetheless is complete in itself and has its own integrity. Does Paul, along such lines, think of each of his imageries in an objectifying fashion and does he then conceive of the Christ-event as effecting concurrently (1) a separate and literal transaction that covers guilt, (2) a separate and literal rescue from present Satanic forces and of their eventual literal destruction, (3) a separate and literal triumph over the cosmic forces in an objective encounter in the past and in a final domination over them in the future, (4) a separate transaction effecting release from the confinement of the law, and finally (5) a separate and literal reversal of human mortality by the power of the resurrection? Possibly so, though any definite proof as to how Paul conceived of these imageries is likely to be evasive.

Another interpretation of Paul's approach, however, may have considerable appeal. Could it be that he, as one who was both struck by the divine force and eloquence resident in the Christ-event itself and who was taken with the liberating effect of that decisive event, felt compelled and was determined to employ every conceivable imagery to see that this message of freedom was not to be missed by any one of his hearers? Was he, perhaps, doing what the rhetorician or the homiletician does when he utilizes every possible figure of speech and every appropriate illustration to make his point, even though the illustrations are not always drawn from factual events or real life and even though the figures of speech are not intended to be taken literally? This interpretation finds support in the fact that Paul can use the same terminology for the remedy or result within the context of two or more imageries of the situation remedied, suggesting that Paul, while he is most emphatic about the freedom that issues from the Christ-event, may not have intended that the imageries employed in emphasizing that resultant freedom be taken as literally as has often been the case. In short, it may not be at all contrary to the intention of Paul for us to deobjectify his diverse imageries in the interest of focusing more attention on the result—freedom through the Christ-event. To go one step farther and to substitute for "imageries" the term "mythologies"—in the proper, history-of-religions sense of that term (as a story about the gods and the relation of humans to the transcendent that conveys *meaning*)—may be offensive to some; on the other hand, it may capture precisely the thrust of Paul's thought, who felt constrained to use any appropriate imagery, to employ any pertinent symbol, and to exploit any relevant context in the interest of the effectual communication of God's momentous act in history on behalf of humankind: "For freedom Christ has set us free; stand fast therefore, and do not submit again to a yoke of slavery" (Gal 5:1).

Notes to Chapter 8

1. This is attested by the lack of footnotes in the present essay (quite in contrast with most of my writings); my debt to many scholars will be obvious to any who know this field. The comprehensive work of George Ladd, *A Theology of the New Testament* (Grand Rapids: Eerdmans, 1974), for example, contains the pertinent data, accompanied by discussions of representative exegetical views. Note that the RSV usually is cited in the present essay.
2. G. Stählin and W. Grundmann, "ἁμαρτάνω," *TDNT* I (1964), 196-301.
3. Ibid., I, 289, 316.
4. At many points I have relied on the data and discussions in J. D. G. Dunn's comprehensive article, "Paul's Understanding of the Death of Jesus," *Reconciliation and Hope: New Testament Essays on Atonement and Eschatology presented to L. L. Morris on his 60th Birthday* (ed. R. Banks; Grand Rapids: Eerdmans, 1974), 125-141. All of the data, with extensive discussion—particularly on the matters alluded to here, can be found in Ladd, *Theology,* esp. 423-456.
5. The relative lack of clear references to the "age to come" in Paul (at least in his undoubted letters) has long been recognized; 1 Corinthians 10:11, often overlooked because inevitably mistranslated, is an important text in this connection. Certainly "kingdom of God" in Paul (1 Cor 6:9-10; 15:50; Gal 5:21; cf. 1 Thess 2:12) is equivalent to the "age to come." The clearest passage, of course, is Ephesians 1:21—the only Pauline or deutero-Pauline passage to use the explicit terminology of the contrasting two ages; cf. also the "coming ages" of Ephesians 2:7. The fairly abundant usage of "this age" must not be minimized, however, nor should the accompanying implication that "this age" has its proper counterpart in an "age to come" be overlooked.

9: The Meaning of "Reconciliation"

I. HOWARD MARSHALL

It is one of the many merits of George E. Ladd's *A Theology of the New Testament* that he devotes a substantial section to a consideration of the Pauline use of the category of reconciliation as a means of expressing the significance of the action of God in Jesus.[1] Of all the concepts used to explain the effects of the cross "reconciliation" is the one which (along with "forgiveness") belongs most clearly to the sphere of personal relationships, although it is also used in the language of diplomacy. Other categories express the significance of the cross more in terms of relations between legal parties (justification) or of commercial dealings (redemption) or of cultic ritual (sacrifice). Reconciliation, however, is a term used in interpersonal relationships. Unless, therefore, we regard the use of the term "person" of God as metaphorical, we must claim that this is the least metaphorical and most concrete of the ways in which the new relationship of God to men is expressed.

In view of the aptness of its usage it is mildly surprising that the word-group is used theologically only by Paul and is not taken up by any other writers,[2] although it is just possible that Paul inherited its use from earlier Christians. The terminology is not taken up by second-century writers[3] and thus remains distinctive of Paul. Its origins remain unexplained; the word-group is not used in a theologically significant manner in the LXX, although it is found in the Apocrypha. One of the words used by Paul, ἀποκαταλλάσσω, appears in fact to be a new coinage. We may compare the way in which Paul also uses a largely non-Septuagintal vocabulary to express the concept of redemption, although he supplements this nonbiblical element with material drawn from the LXX.

These considerations suggest that a brief examination of some features of this concept merits inclusion in a *Festschrift* honoring George Ladd that has as its theme unity and diversity in the New Testament. Here is a distinctively Pauline way of presenting the significance of the cross. At the same time the topic certainly demands further research. It is a remarkable fact that most discussions of the concept have explored the means of reconciliation, the effects of reconciliation, and the question whether men are reconciled to God or vice versa, but little has been said about the actual *meaning* of the words involved. Perhaps some light can be shed on this point and others regarding the significance and source of Paul's language.

I

The Greek verb διαλλάσσω is found once in the New Testament (Matt 5:24).

1. It can be used in the active form to refer to the action of a mediator who persuades two quarrelling groups or persons to abandon their enmity toward one another (Xenophon, *Oeconomicus* 11.23; *Historia Graeca* 1.6.7; Plato, *Phaedo* 60c 2; *Symposium* 213d 4).

2. It can also be used in the active form to refer to the action of a person in persuading his enemy to abandon his enmity and treat him peaceably. Josephus relates how Machaeras killed some partisans of Herod, who retaliated by accusing him to Antony. Machaeras, realizing his errors, pursued the king, and by means of entreaties succeeded in pacifying the king (*Jewish War* 1.16.7 § 320).

3. In the passive form the verb can describe how an offended person gives up his enmity. In 1 Esdras 4:31 we are told of a concubine who could twist the king's little finger: "When she laughed at him he laughed; when she was cross with him he coaxed her to make it up" (NEB), i.e., he coaxed her to stop being cross with him.[4] Josephus speaks of God in this way. He was angry with Israel over their treatment of the Gibeonites, and revealed through prophets that if the Gibeonites were allowed to exact satisfaction for the way in which Saul had massacred them, then he would be reconciled to Israel and would cease to express his anger by afflicting them (*Antiquities* 7.12.1 § 295). Similarly, when David confessed and wept over his sin in the matter of Uriah the Hittite, God took pity on him and was reconciled to him (*Ant.* 7.7.3 § 153). Josephus can describe God as one who is easily reconciled by the repentant (εὐδιάλλακτος, *J. W.* 5.9.4 § 415). The picture is of a God who is angry with men because of their sins, but whom they can persuade to put away his anger and cease afflicting them, i.e., to be reconciled to them.

4. Finally, we have the use in 1 Samuel 29:4 LXX. Here the leaders of the Philistines are unwilling that David, who has deserted Saul and attached himself to Achish, should accompany them to battle against Israel. They fear that David is still an Israelite at heart, and when he sees his former friends he will desert to them. But if he does so, David will need to ingratiate himself with Saul, who is angry with him. "With what will this fellow reconcile himself to his master?" they ask; "Will it not be with the heads of those men?" They recognize that only the heads of some dead Philistines will be an adequate appeasement for David to offer to Saul and thus to

placate him. The significant point is that the verb is used in the passive (i.e., deponently) of David taking the initiative in reconciling Saul to himself. This gives the same meaning as in case 2. above. Here the verb does not refer to David giving up any hard feelings that he had against Saul, but rather to David's persuading Saul to give up his anger. The result will be the establishment of friendly mutual relations, but the verb refers specifically to the persuasion effected on Saul.[5]

It is this same deponent use which confronts us in the one New Testament example of the verb (Matt 5:24). A man who is on his way to make an offering to God remembers that his brother has something against him; the brother is angry with him, although we are not told whether the brother's anger was justified or not. In such a situation the man must first go and "be reconciled" to his brother. The passive form here is clearly in the same sense as the active, namely, of taking the action necessary to induce the brother to give up his anger and so to create friendly relations. There is no suggestion that the man himself was angry with his brother and needed to put away his own hard feelings. But where a state of enmity exists, he must go and take whatever action is needed to bring it to an end.[6]

II

By New Testament times the verb καταλλάσσω was becoming more common than διαλλάσσω,[7] but it has the same range of meanings:

1. It can be used in the active of a mediator persuading two warring sides to give up their enmity and hatred. Herodotus describes how "Periander, son of Cypselus, reconciled the Mityleneans and Athenians, for they referred to him as arbitrator; and he reconciled them on these terms, that each should retain what they had" (Herodotus 5.95).[8] Josephus uses the noun καταλλάκτης of Moses in his role of interceding for the people with God and persuading God to spare them the continued punishment of wandering in the wilderness (*Ant.* 3.15.2 § 315).

2. The verb does not seem to be used in the active form of one person persuading another to give up his anger against him.

3. In the passive, deponent form, the verb can refer to the action of one person in persuading another to give up his anger against him. This appears to be the meaning in a passage in Plato concerning a tyrant who "is reconciled" to some of his enemies and destroys others of them, so that one way or the other peace results (*Republic* 8.566e).[9]

4. The passive can also be used of the offended person who is persuaded to give up his anger.[10] When God rejected Saul as king, Samuel entreated God to be reconciled to Saul and not be wroth with him. "But God would grant no pardon to Saul at the prophet's request, accounting it

not just to condone sins at the intercession of another; for nothing more favoured their growth than laxity on the part of the wronged, who in seeking a reputation for mildness and kindness are unwittingly the begetters of crime" (*Ant.* 6.7.4 § 144). To be reconciled to someone is to be willing to forgive or overlook their offense. In the same way Josephus records how David was petitioned to be reconciled to his son Absalom and let his anger toward him cease (*Ant.* 7.8.4 § 184).[11]

5. The verb can be used with a direct object (or perhaps an accusative of respect) to refer to the offenses concerning which reconciliation needs to be made. Herodotus describes how the factious Greeks determined "that, before all things, they should reconcile all existing enmities and wars with each other" (Hdt. 7.145).[12]

The corresponding noun καταλλαγή can refer to the act of being reconciled (*Ant.* 7.9.1 § 196) or the state of reconciliation (2 Macc 5:20).[13]

A particularly important set of references is to be found in 2 Maccabees. The book opens with a mandate, or official letter, from the Jews in Jerusalem to their compatriots in Egypt. In the opening prayer or expression of good wishes the authors pray: "May he open your hearts to his law and his precepts, and give you peace. May he hear your prayers and be reconciled with you, and not abandon you in time of evil" (2 Macc 1:5 JB). The thought is that God will respond to the prayers of the Jews by overlooking their sins. But of particular interest is the story of the martyrdom of the seven brothers at the hands of Antiochus for their loyalty to their ancestral religion. The brothers interpreted their sufferings as being partly the divine punishment for their own sins (2 Macc 7:18) but also as a means of inducing God to forgive the nation for its sin and apostasy. The seventh brother declares that he is "calling on God to show his kindness to our nation and that soon, and by trials and afflictions to bring you to confess that he alone is God, so that with my brothers and myself there may be an end to the wrath of the Almighty, rightly let loose on our whole nation" (2 Macc 7:37-38). It is against this background that we are to understand the earlier comment of the same young man: "We are suffering for our own sins; and if, to punish and discipline us, our living Lord vents his wrath upon us, he will yet be reconciled with his own servants" (2 Macc 7:32-33).

To complete the picture, two further passages should be considered. The first is in 2 Maccabees 5:11-20 where Antiochus is allowed by God to enter the temple and desecrate it without suffering any harm, in contrast to the fate of Heliodorus, who experienced a supernatural punishment (2 Macc 3:24-28). The writer explains that Antiochus "did not realize that the Lord was angry for the moment at the sins of the inhabitants of the city, hence his unconcern for the Holy Place" (2 Macc 5:17). Afterwards, "the place itself, having shared the disasters that befell the people, in due course also shared their good fortune; forsaken by the Almighty in the time of his anger, it was reinstated in all its glory, once the great Sovereign had been reconciled" (2 Macc 5:20). The other incident takes place after the defeat of Nicanor by Judas Maccabeus, when the victors "joined in public supplication, imploring the merciful Lord to be fully reconciled with his servants" (2 Macc 8:29).

The general picture which emerges is clear and consistent. The view of the writer of 2 Maccabees is that when the people fall into sin and apostasy they arouse the wrath of Yahweh. He proceeds to punish them, and on the completion of the punishment his anger is satisfied and he is reconciled to the people. But the experience of punishment may lead the people to pray to Yahweh to be reconciled to them and to give up his anger, and Yahweh may respond to such prayers. Even more powerful is the action of the martyrs who, while recognizing that their sufferings and death are primarily for their own sins, beseech God to accept their suffering as being on behalf of the nation and to be reconciled to the nation as a whole. In short, God is reconciled, i.e., abandons his anger, as a result of the prayers of the people and their endurance (in themselves or their representatives) of the punishment which he inflicts upon them. Men act in such a way as to induce God to be favorable to them. These ideas are expressed with even greater clarity in 4 Maccabees 7:28-29; 17:22.[14]

III

The verb καταλλάσσω occurs six times in Paul (Rom 5:10 [*bis*]; 1 Cor 7:11; 2 Cor 5:18, 19, 20).[15] The noun καταλλαγή is found four times (Rom 5:11; 11:15; 2 Cor 5:18, 19). Paul also uses the verb ἀποκαταλλάσσω three times (Eph 2:16; Col 1:20, 22). There is one secular example of the usage. This is in 1 Corinthians 7:11, which gives Paul's advice to a wife who has left her husband; she is either to remain unmarried or else be reconciled to her husband. Since the discussion is about a wife who takes the initiative in leaving her husband, it is to be presumed that she feels offended by him and in her indignation separates from him. She is now urged to take the initiative by laying aside her feeling of offense and seeking the restoration of friendly relations and the resumption of the marriage relationship. The passive form is used of the wife no longer being bitter against her husband. But the secondary thought of persuading the husband to lay aside any hard feelings he may have can also be present: "you cannot run off and leave me, and then just come back when you choose," may be his reaction. So the thoughts of the wife's putting aside her own wounded feelings and also of persuading her husband to abandon any such feelings on his part may both be present, and the action is complete only when friendly mutual relations are restored.[16]

It has long been noted that in the two main doctrinal passages in

Romans 5 and 2 Corinthians 5 the passive form of the verb is not used with God as the subject, whether in the passive or the deponent sense. Nor is the active form used with God as the object. This in itself strongly suggests that it is God who takes the initiative in the act of reconciliation. Further, it is generally accepted that God's act of reconciliation takes place prior to, and independently of, any human action: it was while we were still sinners that we were reconciled to God. Paul speaks of "the reconciliation" as something that we have received. All this suggests that the act of reconciliation is primarily something done by God. Nevertheless, the verb is also used in both passages in the passive form with men as the subject, and the question arises whether this is real passive or a deponent usage.

If we start from the earlier passage chronologically, namely, 2 Corinthians 5, we observe that Paul arranges his material in a twofold pattern, with a repetition of the same twofold thought in the second part:

18. All this is from God,
A¹ who through Christ reconciled us to himself
B¹ and gave us the ministry of reconciliation
19. that is,
A² God was in Christ reconciling the world to himself,
not counting their trespasses against them,
B² and entrusting to us the message of reconciliation.

These thoughts are then repeated a third time, in inverse order:

20. B³ So we are ambassadors for Christ,
God making his appeal through us.
We beseech you on behalf of Christ, be reconciled to God.
21. A³ For our sakes he made him to be sin who knew no sin,
so that in him we might become the righteousness of God.

The effect of this structure is to show that for Paul the total act of reconciliation on God's side is in two parts. There is the act of reconciliation in Christ, and there is the ministry of reconciliation which consists in the proclamation of this prior act of God in Christ and the declaration of the message, which is then finally specified as an appeal to men to be reconciled to God on the basis of the prior act of God in Christ. Manifestly the act is completed only when there is a human response to the imperative demand to be reconciled.

We have, then, three statements of the divine act of reconciliation which took place prior to the appeal to men to be reconciled to God and which is proclaimed in the appeal to men. Two of the statements elucidate what this meant. The first declares that God does not count the trespasses of men against them, and the second that God made Christ to be sin for us in order that we might be made righteous. Against the background of thought which we have explored, particularly in 2 Maccabees, it follows irresistibly that the picture is of a God who is offended by the sins of men and acts in wrath and judgment against them. But now because of what Christ has done in identifying himself with their sin God regards them as righteous and no longer holds their sins against them. When Paul says that God has reconciled us to himself, the meaning is thus that God has dealt with the sins which aroused his wrath and that there is no barrier on his side to the establishment of peace and friendly relations.[17] Three important points are made: first, the putting away of God's wrath against human transgressions was achieved by what Christ did; the earlier part of the passage speaks of his dying on behalf of men, and the final verse speaks of his becoming sin for us.[18] It is hard to understand this in any other way than that in dying Christ exhausted the effects of divine wrath against sin. Second, the action which took place "in Christ" was the action of God himself who purposed that action (v. 21) and who himself acted in Christ.[19] Although Christ may be regarded as a "third party" who intervenes between God and man, yet here in 2 Corinthians 5 it is clearly God who is the subject (vv. 18, 19). Third, the object of the action is described both as "the world" and as "us" (vv. 19, 18). The "world" is understood in a personal sense as the totality of mankind; this is shown by the use of "them" in verse 19*b* to refer back to "world." If "world" can have a wider meaning in Paul, this is certainly not consciously in mind here.

"God reconciles the world to himself" thus means: God acts in Christ to overlook the sins of mankind, so that on his side there is no barrier to the restoration of friendly relations. The message of the Christian preacher is a declaration of this fact. It is first and foremost a gospel, a declaration of the good news of what God has done. Hence it can speak of "reconciliation" as an accomplished fact. But at the same time the indicative forms the basis for an imperative. Now people are commanded: "be reconciled to God." In view of what God has already done, this cannot be understood to mean that they must render God amenable to them by appropriate action. Rather God and Christ appeal to them to accept the fact that reconciliation has been accomplished and to complete the action by taking down the barrier on their side—the barrier of pride and disobedience and hatred of God. Let them put away their feelings against God and enter into a new relationship with him. And this is possible because of the fact that God is willing to regard them as righteous despite their sin. The total action of reconciliation is thus incomplete until there has been acceptance of God's grace (2 Cor 6:1) on the human side as men are reconciled to God. It is no doubt significant that the active sense of the verb is not used for this human action, because there is no need to reconcile a God who has reconciled the world to himself. The form "be reconciled" could have a deponent sense, with reference to human putting away of enmity. Possibly, however, the verb is best understood as a passive: put yourself into the position of those whom God has reconciled. There is little to choose between these alternatives.

The second Pauline passage is Romans 5:10-11. The thrust of the section Romans 5:1-11 is to show that Christians who have been justified by faith can have sure and certain hope regarding their future acceptance by God at the day of judgment. Paul makes his point by arguing that if God showed such love to men while they were sinners as to send his Son to die for them, he will all the more save those who are now his friends at the day of judgment. Those who have been justified are now in a state of peace with God (v. 1). Consequently, having been justified by the blood of Christ while they were still sinners (v. 8), they will all the more be saved by Christ from the final wrath of God. This point is then repeated in different terminology. Those who were reconciled to God while they were still his enemies by the death of his Son will all the more be saved by his life. The parallelism between the two statements is very close:

	10. For if
8. while we were yet sinners	while we were enemies
Christ died for us.	we were reconciled to God
	by the death of his Son
9. Since, therefore,	
	much more,
we are now justified	now that we are reconciled,
by his blood,	
much more	
shall we be saved by him	shall we be saved by his life.
from the wrath of God.	

It follows that Paul equates the states of sin and enmity, and also that he identifies the death of Jesus for sinners, by virtue of which they are justified, with the reconciliation of God's enemies by the death of his Son. The death of Christ is the basis for God's act of justification which takes place when men believe in Christ, and it is itself the act of reconciliation which becomes effective for men when it is preached to them and they accept it. The difference is that Paul does not speak of God justifying the world in the death of Jesus, but rather of God justifying individual men now on the basis of the redemption and propitiation which took place in the death of Jesus; but he does speak of God reconciling the world to himself in the death of Jesus, and thereby making it possible for individuals to accept the reconciliation. While he can say to men, "Be reconciled," he cannot say, "Be justified." But these are unimportant differences, and they merely demonstrate that we are dealing with two very similar but not identical ideas. The important point is again that reconciliation is an act of God prior to and independent of any abandonment of enmity to God on our part, accomplished by the One who stands closest to him as his Son. It would seem that the verb is again used in two senses, first in verse 10*a* of God reconciling men to himself (passive, of men),[20] and second in verse 10b of men who have actually entered into the state of reconciliation. The contrast is the same as that between "Christ died for us" and "being now justified." No doubt the slight shift in meaning is awkward, but it is by no means intolerable. It is supported by the use of "we have received the reconciliation" in verse 11, which suggests an existing gift to be received by us. There is certainly nothing here to cause us to modify our understanding of the use of the term derived from 2 Corinthians 5.

Paul uses the noun "reconciliation" once more in Romans (11:15). In Romans 11:11-16 he is discussing whether the Jews have fallen away from Christ permanently. This he denies fervently. It was the falling away of the Jews that led to the extension of salvation to the Gentiles, and the effect of the latter will be to make the Jews envious and so turn to Christ. Then Paul comments rhetorically that if the fall of the Jews had such a glorious result as to enrich the world, how much more will their full turning to Christ produce glorious results. Their rejection led to the reconciliation of the world, and their acceptance will lead to resurrection from the dead. Paul's reference is thus to the act of reconciliation wrought in Christ which is effective for the world of mankind as a whole. He uses the concept of reconciliation, as elsewhere, to indicate the worldwide scope of salvation,[21] and the term itself is used in conscious contrast to the thought of God's rejection of unbelieving Israel. It is God who accepts the sinful world, overlooks its sin, and offers peace to it.

In order to complete the picture we must examine the two further passages where the terminology of reconciliation is used. In both of these passages the verb used is ἀποκαταλλάσσω, an unusual form apparently used here for the first time. It is often argued that Paul is using an existing hymn in Colossians 1:15-20,[22] although it should be carefully observed that the fact that the hymn may be earlier in date than the composition of Colossians does not necessarily mean that it is earlier than the composition of Romans 5 or 2 Corinthians 5. The use of the unusual word may reflect incorporation of a non-Pauline hymn, but it still leaves unanswered the problem as to why the unknown author chose to introduce this unusual word when Greek already possessed an ample vocabulary of reconciliation. The answer may be that the new compound stresses more the thought of the restoration of a previously existing relationship, and that it is formed on the analogy of ἀποκαθίστημι (Mark 3:5; 9:12; Acts 1:6; et al.; cf. ἀποκατάστασις, Acts 3:21).

Paul uses the verb in the context of God's creation of all things by and for his Son. God intended that the Son should have first place in all things, because God in his fulness resolved (1) to dwell in him (hence he is worthy to receive the same honor as God) and (2) to reconcile all things to him through him. It is thus as the agent of reconciliation that Christ is worthy to be first in the universe, but the thought is rather loosely attached and the casual connection is not to be pressed here.

Reconciliation is made possible by the fact that God has made peace by means of the blood of his cross. This symbolical language expresses the sacrificial character of the death of Jesus, and thus indicates again that reconciliation is possible on the basis of the appeasing of God's wrath by means of the sacrifice which he himself has provided in Jesus. The participle may be expressive of action prior to or coincidental with the action of the infinitive, and it should probably be taken in the latter sense. A completed work of reconciliation is in mind, as in the earlier references.

Nothing is said at this point about the circumstances which have produced the need for reconciliation, although the fact of sin is implied by the references to peace and to the sacrificial blood of Jesus. But what was implicit becomes explicit in the following section in which Paul applies the general principle to his readers. They in particular were at one time estranged from God and hostile to him because of their evil deeds. But now they have been the object of an act of reconciliation in the body of Christ's flesh by means of his death. The tremendous emphasis upon the physical character of the death is probably anti-docetic, although it is possible that the reconciled are envisaged as being united with Christ in his death. The fact that they were once enemies indicates that now they are thought of as being in the state of reconciliation, so that "reconcile" here has the sense of the actual restoration of good relations. In verse 20, however, the thought is simply of God's provision of reconciliation for the world. The difference between the two uses of the verb is demanded by the fact that in verse 23 Paul implicitly states the terms on which reconciliation becomes a reality: it depends upon faith and acceptance of the gospel preached by Paul. If the Colossians are urged to continue in faith and hope, the implication is clearly that their reconciliation began with their act of faith and hope.

This point has important consequences for understanding verse 20 with its reference to the reconciliation of "all things." It remains true, as in 2 Corinthians 5, that the realization of reconciliation is dependent on acceptance of the gospel and faith, and therefore it is most improbable that any kind of universal salvation of all creation is taught here. The thought is surely that no powers on earth or in heaven can reconcile men to God, since they all needed to be reconciled themselves because of their rebelliousness and sin.[23] Hence Paul's stress is not so much on the fact of their reconciliation as on their own need for reconciliation which renders them unfit to mediate between man and God; only Christ can act as reconciler, and nobody else. If this suggestion is accepted, we are saved from desperate attempts to give "reconcile" a sense other than it usually bears,[24] and Paul's teaching receives a natural interpretation in the light of the errors or possible errors which menaced his readers. There is no question of the reconciliation of inanimate nature, but rather Paul's thought is of the rulers and powers in verse 16.

The thought in Ephesians 2:16 is basically similar. The cosmic dimension is absent here, and Paul's thoughts are concerned more with the fact that the one act of reconciliation is effective in breaking down the barriers between both Jews and Gentiles and God. The twin thoughts of their reconciliation to one another and of both to God run through the passage as a whole. Paul's concept is of the church as a new Israel; formerly the Gentiles were outside Israel (i.e., the old Israel), but now they have been brought into the new Israel through their faith in Christ and so into unity with those of the old Israel who have likewise put their faith in Christ. In verse 16 the thought is primarily of reconciliation to God, and Paul's point is simply that one act of reconciliation—in the one body of Christ—has reconciled both to God. Thereby human enmity—whether toward God or toward other men—has been "slain." Here again, therefore, the thought is of what was achieved by the cross, and the overcoming enmity is very much to the fore. Nevertheless, the general context with its thought of the new possibility of access to God (v. 18) and of the sacrificial blood of Jesus (v. 13) strongly suggests that "reconcile" here has its normal sense of God's overlooking the sins which otherwise he would have had to judge in view of the cross of Christ.

IV

In the light of this discussion we may now try to draw some conclusions.

1. Our study of the secular Greek usage of the two words meaning "to reconcile" showed that they could be used in four possible ways:

A. X persuades Y and Z to give up their mutual anger (active).

B. X persuades Y to give up Y's anger against X (active).

C. X persuades Y to give up Y's anger against X (passive/deponent).

D. X gives up his own anger against Y (passive).

Sense D is found in 1 Corinthians 7:11, and sense C in Matthew 5:24. Paul's usage, however, does not fit into any of these categories. He uses the active form of the verb to describe how God initiates friendly relations between himself and men by putting away the sin which aroused his own anger against them. The meaning given by the passive in sense D is expressed by the use of the active voice. Paul's use thus forms a new category:

E. X removes the cause of his own anger against Y, namely, Y's sin (active). This use of the verb seems to be unprecedented in Greek usage, although I cannot claim to have made anything like an exhaustive survey of the material. We are bound to ask what led Paul to use the verb in this highly unusual, and apparently unique, manner.

We saw also that Paul uses the passive form of the verb to refer to human acceptance of God's act. This is close to sense D above, but the thought is less of men putting away *their* anger against God at some cost to themselves and rather of their entering into the new relationship which God himself has made possible. God and men are not equal partners in reconciliation, but the initiative is on his side, and it is his attitude to human sin which has to be dealt with before reconciliation is possible.

2. The verb has a broader and a narrower meaning in Paul. The narrow sense is found when "God reconciles men to himself" means that he puts away the wrath which he has toward men and women on account of their sins so that there is no longer any barrier on his side to fellowship with them. The broad sense is found when "God reconciles men to himself" means that God enters into the fellowship with men which the death of Jesus has made possible. There are consequently *three* stages in the process of reconciliation. First, there is the reconciling act of God in the death of Jesus. Second, there is the proclamation of reconciliation by the "servants" of reconciliation. As Bultmann rightly emphasizes, this proclamation is every bit as much a saving act as the death of Christ.[25] The news of what God has done must be proclaimed, and the challenge to respond must be made. Third, there is the acceptance of God's message by men, when they accept his act of reconciliation by faith, putting away any feelings that they hold against God. The process is not complete until all three stages have taken place and people have entered into peace with God. The scope of reconciliation is potentially the world, and this can be "unpacked" in terms of Jews and Gentiles or of men and spiritual powers. Paul uses the verb in the active form five times with God (or Christ)[26] as the subject, and three times in the passive of persons who are the objects of God's reconciling work; when the passive is used in the imperative form, it begins to approach a deponent use, but it refers to accepting God's completed work of reconciliation, not to trying to appease God.

3. Paul uses the concept (a) most fully and thematically in 2 Corinthians 5 where it occurs in an appeal to the members of the Corinthian church not to receive God's grace to no effect by refusing to accept him as God's ambassador of reconciliation; (b) as a means of underlining the fact of assurance of final salvation for those who have been justified by faith (Rom 5); (c) in the context of a proclamation of the supreme place of Christ as the one agent of God in creation and the renewal of creation (Col 1); and (d) in an argument designed to show the oneness of Jews and Gentiles in the church of God (Eph 2).

The use of the language is perhaps most surprising in 2 Corinthians.

Here Paul is primarily urging the church to receive him as its pastor and to abandon its hostile attitude to him personally. In effect he is making the point that to reject him is to reject the God whom he serves in the gospel. To accept the gospel of reconciliation involves acceptance of the designated servant of reconciliation. But the language which Paul is using sounds much more like a description of the gospel message proclaimed to the non-Christian. Paul is here making use of the language of evangelism in order to call members of the church to welcome him back personally as their spiritual father. If so, the original use of the language of reconciliation is to be found in the proclamation of the kerygma, and what Paul is describing is the gospel of the cross which he preached. This is confirmed by the usage in Colossians and Ephesians which is also descriptive of Christian conversion. Paul is thus putting the language of the kerygma to a secondary use, and it seems likely that the specialized application in both Colossians and Ephesians is secondary and represents a development of the original use. If so, it would follow that the original source of the language is not the "pre-Pauline" hymn in Colossians 1, but rather this represents a development of the ideas already present in 2 Corinthians 5 which in turn spring from the preaching of Paul.

This raises considerable doubts regarding the thesis of E. Käsemann that the language is drawn from a hymnic tradition, reflected in the citations in 2 Corinthians 5, and that the language was originally cosmological, the application to the individual being secondary.[27] Rather, the language is that of a credal or kerygmatic formula, and the individual application is there from the beginning.

It is uncertain whether Paul is quoting pre-Pauline kerygmatic tradition in 2 Corinthians 5 or is citing his own preaching. The virtual absence of the terminology elsewhere in the New Testament is an argument from silence that the language is Paul's own,[28] and this is confirmed by the way in which it has been so thoroughly assimilated into his argument and made to express the essential Pauline doctrine of justification by grace through faith.

4. In looking for a background to Paul's teaching, we are struck by the fact that Paul always makes God the subject of reconciliation and that he interprets the verb in terms of God's laying aside of his wrath and judgment against mankind. This stands in marked contrast to the teaching of 2 Maccabees where men urged God to be reconciled to them and made an offering for their own sins to him and for the sins of the nation. It is tempting to suppose that Paul's teaching was formulated in conscious contrast to this Jewish attitude.[29] The evidence for Paul's use of 2 Maccabees is admittedly very thin,[30] but there is a good case that Paul was familiar with the martyr tradition which is expressed in 2 and 4 Maccabees and that he made use of it in his interpretation of the death of Jesus as an atoning sacrifice.[31] It would be very like Paul to develop the thought that atonement rests not on the act

of men but of God, that God does not need to be appeased by men because he himself has provided an atonement for sin and so reconciled them to himself, and that this action avails not merely for the Jewish race but for all mankind through the work of the second Adam. The point is beyond proof, but there is a high degree of probability that the Jewish martyr tradition, which surfaces in this particular form in 2 Maccabees, has provided the catalyst to the development of Paul's use of the category of reconciliation.[32]

5. The concept of reconciliation has assumed a far more central place in Christian theology than might have been expected from its limited use in the New Testament. Paul's use of the term was sufficiently creative to produce a concept which has come to the forefront in theological thinking. By his new use of the terminology he made it clear that reconciliation is a term for what God as subject has done in relation to the world as object. But whereas in popular usage "to reconcile Y to oneself" means "to remove Y's grounds for being offended," Paul uses the phrase to mean "to remove Y's offense." The offense in question is the sin of mankind which arouses the wrath of God and prevents him from entering into friendly relations with them; when the sin is removed or cancelled the reconciliation is achieved.

We can now see how those theologians who speak of God *being* reconciled have some justification for their language. They rightly recognize that a change has taken place on God's side. Formerly the world was the object of his wrath because of its sin. Now it is the object of his love. It is not, however, that God has changed his feelings, as if he had somehow to swallow his wrath. Rather in the love which he has always had for the world he has given his Son to bear the consequences of the world's sin and so to remove the barrier caused by sin. God has thus dealt with the sin of the world, and in so doing has rendered his wrath inoperative against those who accept his act of reconciliation. Since the act involved the removal of sin and hence of God's wrath against sinners, it is perhaps permissible to speak loosely of God being reconciled. Nevertheless, it must be clearly recognized that this is not the New Testament usage of the term, and therefore it must not be used without due care. For Paul "to reconcile the world to himself" means "to remove the barrier caused by human sin which prevents him from entering into friendly relations with the world."[33]

We can, therefore, understand what Charles Wesley meant and with a good conscience join him in singing:

Arise, my soul, arise,
Shake off thy guilty fears;
The bleeding Sacrifice
In my behalf appears:
Before the throne my Surety stands;
My name is written on His hands.

My God is reconciled,
His pardoning voice I hear;
He owns me for His child,
I can no longer fear;
With confidence I now draw nigh,
And Father, Abba, Father! cry.[34]

But the last word belongs to John Calvin:

> Incomprehensible and immutable is the love of God. For it was not after we were reconciled to him by the blood of his Son that he began to love us, but he loved us before the foundation of the world. . . . Our being reconciled by the death of Christ must not be understood as if the Son reconciled us in order that the Father, thus hating, might begin to love us, but that we were reconciled to him, already loving, though at enmity toward us because of sin. Accordingly in a manner wondrous and divine he loved us even when he hated us. For he hated us when we were such as he had not made us, and yet because our iniquity had not destroyed his work in every respect, he knew in regard to each one of us both to hate what we had made and love what he had made.[35]

Notes to Chapter 9

1. G. E. Ladd, *A Theology of the New Testament* (Grand Rapids: Eerdmans, 1974) 450-456.
   See further F. Büchsel, *TDNT* 1 (1964) 251-259; R. Gyllenberg, *RGG* 6 (1962) 1371-1373; A. Vögtle, *LTK* 10 (1965) 734-736; R. Pesch, *EBT* 2 (1970) 735-738; H.-G. Link and H. Vorländer, *NIDNTT* 3 (1978) *s.v.*; J. Denney, *The Christian Doctrine of Reconciliation* (London: Hodder and Stoughton, 1917); V. Taylor, *Forgiveness and Reconciliation* (London: Macmillan, 1941); J. Dupont, *La Réconciliation dans la Théologie de Saint Paul* (Paris: Desclée de Brouwer, 1953); G. W. H. Lampe, *Reconciliation in Christ* (London: Longmans, 1956); L. Morris, *The Apostolic Preaching of the Cross* (London: Tyndale Press, 1955, repr. 1965); E. Käsemann, "Some Thoughts on the Theme 'The Doctrine of Reconciliation in the New Testament,' " *The Future of our Religious Past* (ed. J. M. Robinson; London: SCM, 1971) 49-64; L. Goppelt, "Versöhnung durch Christus," *Christologie und Ethik* (Göttingen: Vandenhoeck und Ruprecht, 1968) 147-164.
2. The Pauline authorship of Colossians has been contested on slender grounds, and that of Ephesians on rather more substantial grounds. Should either of them not be Pauline, they are written by close disciples of Paul, seeking to be true to his theological position. I am, however, strongly inclined to accept the authenticity of Colossians (so rightly R. P. Martin, *Colossians and Philemon* [New Century Bible; London: Oliphants, 1974], *contra* E. Lohse, *Colossians and Philemon* [Hermeneia; Philadelphia: Fortress, 1971]), and regard the balance of probability as favoring the authenticity of Ephesians (A. van Roon, *The Authenticity of Ephesians* [*NovTSup* 39; Leiden: Brill, 1974]).
3. See G. W. H. Lampe, *A Patristic Greek Lexicon* (Oxford: Clarendon, 1960-68) *s.v.*
4. For this use see also *BGU* III, 846[10]; *PGiss* I, 17[13] (J. H. Moulton and G. Milligan, *The Vocabulary of the Greek New Testament* [London: Hodder and Stoughton, 1930] *s.v.*); *Ant.* 16.4.4 § 125.
5. See further Thucydides 8.70.2; 71.3.
6. In the associated parable Matthew 5:25-26 = Luke 12:58-59 the Lukan form has the phrase ἀπηλλάχθαι ἀπό to describe the action of a man with reference to his legal adversary. The verb means "to free, release" (Heb 2:15), (middle) "to leave, depart" (Acts 19:12). Here it means "to get rid of him" or "to depart from him." The implication is that the man comes to terms with his adversary and satisfies his claims. Hence the thought is of "being reconciled" (NIV), a meaning which is associated occasionally with the verb. Cf. Matthew: "make friends with your adversary."

7. F. Büchsel, *TDNT* I, 253. The verb συναλλάσσω, which was common in Classical Greek, especially in military and legal contexts, does not occur in the LXX, and appears in the New Testament only in Acts 7:26 of the action of Moses in reconciling two quarrelling Israelites.
8. See further Herodotus 5.29; 6.108; Aristotle, *Oec.* 2.15; Thucydides 4.59.
9. See further Sophocles, *Ajax* 744; *Ant.* 5.2.8 § 137.
10. Xenophon, *Anabasis* 1.6.1.
11. See also *Ant.* 11.6.2 § 195; Philo, *Legum allegoriae* 3.134.
12. See also *OGIS* 218[105].
13. See also Aeschylus, *Septem contral Thebas* 767; Aristophanes, *Aves* 1588; Demosthenes, *Oratores Attica* 1.4.
14. See E. Lohse, *Märtyrer und Gottesknecht* (Göttingen: Vandenhoeck und Ruprecht, 1955). J. Dupont, *Réconciliation*, 13-14, while rightly recognizing the element of mercy in God's action, overlooks the fact that his wrath has been appeased by the punishment of his people.
15. It is also found in Acts 12:22 D with reference to Herod Agrippa I's reconciliation with the people of Tyre.
16. F. Büchsel (*TDNT* I, 255) argues that there is no reason to suppose that the wife left her husband in a spirit of ill-will. It is possible that she left him because he treated her harshly, but in any case she has to overcome any barriers that exist on her side to renewing the relationship with him.
17. On "peace" as the result of reconciliation see especially L. Goppelt, "Versöhnung," 160-164.
18. Paul uses the abstract term "sin" in order to avoid the dangerous implications of saying that Christ became a "sinner."
19. On the meaning of verse 19 see especially M. J. Harris, "Readers' Forum," *TSF Bulletin* 61 (1971) 27-28; J.-F. Collange, *Énigmes de la deuxieme Épître de Paul aux Corinthiens* (*SNTSMS* 18; Cambridge: Cambridge University, 1972) 270-272.
20. So rightly F. Büchsel, *TDNT* I, 256.
21. There is of course no suggestion that the whole world will necessarily accept the reconciliation, any more than this is the case in 2 Corinthians 5:18-21.
22. For details see R. P. Martin, *Colossians*, 61-66.
23. See L. Goppelt, "Versöhnung," 161, for an interpretation that tends in this direction.
24. See the summary of such views in F. Büchsel, *TDNT* I, 259.
25. R. Bultmann, *Exegetica* (Tübingen: Mohr, 1967) 228, as translated by C. K. Barrett, *The Second Epistle to the Corinthians* (*HNTC;* New York: Harper and Row, 1973) 178-179.
26. For Christ as subject see Ephesians 2:16.
27. E. Käsemann, "Some Thoughts," 53, 54. For discussion see J.-F. Collange, *Énigmes,* 266-280, esp. pp. 268-269, 275-276, who claims that Paul is incorporating traditional language known to his readers, possibly his own earlier formulation.
28. So L. Goppelt, "Versöhnung," 150-153.
29. *Contra* J. Dupont, *Réconciliation,* 14, 18.
30. The alleged echo of 2 Maccabees 3:26 in 2 Corinthians 12:7 is quite unconvincing.
31. D. Hill, *Greek Words and Hebrew Meanings* (*SNTSMS* 5; Cambridge: Cambridge University, 1967) 41-48.
32. For a similar view see L. Goppelt, "Versöhnung," 149-150, who also suggests that Paul took over the idea of "peace" from the Roman imperial ideology of the Pax Romana; here he is following E. Käsemann, "Some Thoughts," 54.
33. J. Dupont, *Réconciliation,* 14-15.
34. *The Methodist Hymn Book* (London: Methodist Conference Office, 1933), No. 368.
35. J. Calvin, *Institutes of the Christian Religion* (*LCC* 20, ed. J. T. McNeill; Philadelphia: Westminster, 1960) 506-507 (II, xvi, 4).

10: The Vocabulary of Perfection in Philo and Hebrews

CHARLES CARLSTON

Both Philo and the unknown author of the book of Hebrews are, by nearly universal consent, to be understood in terms of some kind of Platonized Hellenistic Jewish thought. In addition to this general statement, however, it is sometimes also said that the author of Hebrews is in some sense directly dependent on Philo, and it is occasionally further added that this dependence shows up with special clarity in the way the two authors understand the concept of *perfection.*

To test this correlation, if any, we shall discuss in this article the various Philonic uses of words[1] containing the syllable τελ- and compare them with the uses of the same words in Hebrews.

I

THE τελ-WORDS IN PHILO

Though many lexicons list them together, the τελ-words Philo uses break down into two distinct groups, only one of which is really significant for our purposes. One group of words seems to be related to an Indo-European root for "weight" or "lift," and includes concepts of value and worth (cf. English "ex*tol*"). The other comes from a root meaning "revolve" or "move around," and is used for notions of change, growth, maturity, and reaching an end or goal (cf. English "wheel" and Greek τέρμα, Latin *terminus*).

The former group can be passed over rather quickly. Philo uses the word τελέω in the sense of "pay what is due"[2] and ὑποτελέω in the sense of "pay tribute, make a contribution."[3] He also uses τέλος for a body of soldiers,[4] a usage which belongs here because of the relationship between a mercenary army and *payment*, as does the meaning "tax, toll, due," which occurs once.[5] In a more general sense, he speaks of οἱ ἐν τέλει, i.e., people of rank or authority, as we might speak of people "of weight,"[6] and he twice uses the noun ἰσοτέλεία, "equal rank."[7] More common are various adverbs and adjectives implying cost or profit: ἀλυσιτελής (unprofitable, worthless)[8] and its superlative, ἀλυσιτελέστατος,[9] as well as the related adverb, ἀλυσιτελῶς (in an unprofitable manner);[10] δημοτελές (at public cost)[11] and δημοτελέστατος (universal);[12] εὐτελής (easily paid for, cheap;[13] mean, worthless;[14] simple[15]) and its comparative[16] and superlative;[17] λυσιτελής (useful, profitable, advantageous, advisable),[18] also in its comparative[19] and superlative[20] forms as well as the corresponding adverb, λυσιτελῶς (profitably, with advantage or use or benefit);[21] πολυτελής (expensive, costly, sumptuous)[22] and its comparative[23] and superlative[24] forms as well as the corresponding adverb, πολυτελῶς.[25] Finally, he twice uses the verb λυσιτελέω (to pay, profit, be of advantage)[26] and frequently uses the nouns εὐτέλεια (cheapness, meanness, insignificance;[27] thrift, simplicity, economy, frugality[28]) and πολυτέλεια (great expense, extravagance, magnificence).[29] These "economic" words might be useful to a social historian—especially if they were not separated from their proper contexts, as they are here—but they contribute little to our problem.[30]

A second brief category of little direct significance for our purposes is the Pythagorean element in Philo's treatment of certain numbers as "perfect" (τέλειος). Here he is not completely consistent, though the general direction of his thought is plain. Three is a perfect number,[31] and so is four,[32] though six, which is "equal to the sum of its factors"[33] and is often designated "perfect,"[34] is called the "first perfect number."[35] He points out that 28 is also equal to the sum of its factors[36] and elsewhere designates it "perfect."[37] He also applies the term "perfect" to 10,[38] 12,[39] 50,[40] 70,[41] 90,[42] and 100,[43] so we cannot always be sure what he has in mind when he speaks of "perfect" numbers without identifying them.[44] Also Pythagorean is the use of the term παντέλεια, which "seems . . . to have been a divine name for ten in Pythagorean use,"[45] and which Philo applies once to 7,[46] but several times to 10.[47] He also speaks of 10 as a παντελὴς ἀριθμός (perfect number)[48] as well as a "most perfect" (τελειότατος) number.[49] Yet he also calls 4 the most perfect of numbers;[50] he speaks of 3 as the greatest and most perfect of numbers;[51] and he speaks of the perfecting power (τελεσφόρος) of the number 7,[52] which he specifically says is more perfect than 10[53] and of which he says that "there is nothing more perfect."[54] In a different context he speaks of 10,000 as the most perfect term in the series beginning with 1.[55] Clearly "perfect" in these cases denotes not so much the end of a process as some inherent mathematical property.

A third group of words formed on the τελ-stem have to do with the "mysteries," in which the initiate is "perfected" in the cultic rite. Such words, some of which are used of the things of God as well as of the pagans, include τελετής (= τελεστής, initiated person)[56] and τελετή (the divine rite, mystery, or initiation itself).[57] Occasionally Philo speaks of one who is ἀτέλεστος, i.e., uninitiated.[58] Much more common is the use of τελέω in the sense of "initiate," into the things of God,[59] into the priesthood,[60] into philosophy,[61] into the lesser and then the greater mysteries,[62] into pagan rites,[63] and—in what we hope Philo intends as a distinct category—into the mysteries of government.[64]

Similarly cultic, though somewhat less specific, is ἐπιτελέω in the sense of "discharge a religious duty,"[65] as well as ἐντελεχής for "whole burnt offerings" or "perpetual sacrifice."[66] Προτέλεια, originally the sacrifice offered before a ceremony, is not used in a cultic sense,[67] nor is τελεσιουργέω, which may be used for full initiation into a philosophic system.[68] In this entire category the stress seems to be on perfection as cultic performance, as fulfilling the religious obligations or rites required by God (or the gods). Since historians of religion are deeply divided over the degree to which Philo is indebted to or representative of the "mystery religions" in the technical sense, we may leave this usage at this point.

Some τελ-words emphasize the element of the "end," the "last" or "ultimate" in a series or development. (This element is almost always present, even in words which are considered below under different rubrics.) Here would be included comparatively rare words and usages like ἀκροτελεύτιον (concluding, final),[69] ἀποτελευτάω (come to an end),[70] συντέλεια (completion),[71] and συντελέω, which Philo uses in the sense of "bring to an end, complete" only in quotations.[72] Somewhat more common are τελέω to mean "fulfill, perform, bring about"[73] or "finish"[74] or even, intransitively, "be fully formed"[75] or "end up."[76] The adjective τελευταῖος is used for "last, final"[77] and adverbially for "finally, last of all"[78] in many passages; it is also used once with the neuter article (το τελευταῖον) to mean "at the extreme."[79] An especially interesting example of this emphasis is ἀτελεύτητος (endless, unbounded),[80] which Philo uses of wisdom,[81] of the bounty of God,[82] of impiety as an endless evil,[83] of endless calamities,[84] and of the unlimited rage of Gaius[85] and the enemies of the Jews.[86] Also to be included here are the verbs διατελέω, which may mean "consummate" a marriage[87] or "bring fully to an end,"[88] though its more common meaning is simply "to continue, persevere, or remain";[89] ἐπιτελέω in the sense of "complete, finish, accomplish"[90] or "execute, carry out, perform";[91] and ἀποτελέω, "bring to fullness,"[92] "bring to an end, complete, perform,"[93] "build"[94] but ordinarily simply "bring about, yield, produce, bring into being."[95] The related noun, ἀποτέλεσμα, is used for "finished product,"[96] "effect or result,"[97] and "full completion, realization, event, or act,"[98] sometimes contrasted with δύναμις (potentiality);[99] it is also used in a more technical sense for the completed elements of the universe,[100] occasionally in contrast with the στοιχεῖα or elementary elements.[101] Finally, we note τελευτάω, which Philo sometimes uses for "end (up) with,"[102] "end in or by,"[103] "issues in or extends to,"[104] and "come to an end,"[105] but which ordinarily means simply "die";[106] and τελευτή, occasionally contrasted with ἀρχή (beginning),[107] and sometimes used in the sense of "limit" or "end,"[108] but ordinarily signifying simply "death."[109]

The data are somewhat more complex in the case of the noun τέλος itself. It is very commonly contrasted with ἀρχή (beginning),[110] and it may be used in prepositional phrases as well.[111] It may suggest "limit,"[112] "sum (total),"[113] or "final form, consummation, result."[114] And it may be used in a quasi-philosophical sense for "full realization, highest point, ideal."[115] Its common meaning, however, is "end,"[116] and so Philo speaks of the end of a road,[117] a race,[118] a journey,[119] a course,[120] or an action;[121] of the "ends" (pl.) of the pious;[122] and of atheism as the "end" of polytheistic creeds.[123] He also can speak of the "end of life"[124] and note that the end of the reasonable soul is life and immortality.[125]

Closely related to these passages and in many cases hardly to be distinguished from them are the many places in which τέλος is used for "aim" or "goal."[126] Here Philo may speak of the τέλος of the godless,[127] while noting that the goal of the Logos is Truth.[128] The τέλος of happiness is to become like God,[129] of virtuous souls is to be fully conformed to God,[130] of the admonitions of the law is living according to virtue,[131] and that of Abraham, Isaac, and Jacob was virtue[132] and being well pleasing to God.[133] The goal of the thoughts, words, and choristers of the Therapeutae is piety (εὐσέβεια).[134] In sum, the best goal is knowledge of the One who truly is (ἐπιστήμη τοῦ ὄντως ὄντος).[135]

The preliminary, anticipatory character of the rare word προτέλεια is indicated in Philo's use of it for "opening" or "introduction,"[136] for the "preliminaries" of marriage,[137] and for the first elements of wisdom,[138] even though its originally cultic reference is no longer applicable.[139]

The notion of "completeness" is often suggested in Philo by words which prefix παν- (all) to the τελ- root. Here we would note παντέλεια, which is used not only of numbers,[140] but also of "full perfection" or "consummation," and is applied to priests,[141] to happiness in life,[142] to body and soul,[143] and to virtue.[144] The adverbial form, παντελῶς, meaning "completely, absolutely, utterly, perfectly," is very common,[145] as is the adverbial use of the adjective παντελής to mean "utterly, completely."[146]

Other uses of παντελής point in the direction of *totality.* It is used in the sense of "all-complete, absolute"[147] or "complete, perfect, total"[148] as well as "whole, sound,"[149] and is contrasted with what is defective (ἔνδεον) in one passage.[150] Thus the world is a perfect work,[151] the complete cosmos is the great gift of God,[152] and nothing in the realm of the sensible is more complete (παντελέστερος) than the cosmos.[153] It is hardly surprising that he once uses the expression "perfect piety."[154] The hendiadys ὁλοκλῆρος καὶ παντελής (complete and perfect), sometimes in the reverse order, is used of the bounty of the uncreated One,[155] of virtues,[156] of an action,[157] of happiness,[158] of the world before the Flood,[159] of God,[160] of the priest,[161] of both the burnt-offering[162] and the mind of which it is a symbol,[163] of parentage,[164] of justice,[165] and of the body[166] or all the parts of a healthy body.[167]

Finally, we may mention here the words ἐντελής, "complete, full, whole,"[168] used once in the superlative (with ὁλοκλῆρος, complete) of food;[169] ἐντελέχεια, "complete reality, actuality (as opposed to potentiality)";[170] and ἀτελέστερος, "less perfect, more imperfect,"[171] which is used of the lower stage of grammar[172] and of persons (contrasted with σοφός/σοφοί, wise)[173] and once (in a typical Philonian passage) of Aaron, who acquired virtue by toil and thus was less perfect than Moses, who received virtue without toil from the hands of God.[174]

The notions of perfection, completion, maturity, etc. are inherent in several words in Philo. He uses τελεσιουργέω, for example, both transitively, "bring to perfection,"[175] "finish creating,"[176] or "accomplish fully, bring to full accomplishment";[177] and intransitively, "come to perfection or maturity."[178] He also uses, mostly in an agricultural context, τελειογονέω, transitively, "to bring to full ripeness,"[179] and intransitively, "to come complete into the world,"[180] "to become ripe or complete,"[181] or "to be mature."[182] Also primarily, though by no means exclusively agricultural, is the verb τελεσφορέω, "to bring to perfection or completion,"[183] "to be fulfilled,"[184] or "to grant fulfillment,"[185] and intransitively, "to come or ripen to perfection."[186] It is hardly surprising that Philo speaks of God as bringing the world to completion[187] or of bringing Abraham's requests to pass in due season,[188] or that he suggests that the soul of the worthless man has no power to bring forth offspring.[189] Very much along the same lines is his use of the adjective τελεσφόρος for the "perfecting power" of labor pains[190] and for God's "perfecting his gifts."[191] So central is this latter notion, in fact, that Philo speaks of God as simply ὁ τελεσφόρος (θεός), the One who gives fulfillment or brings to perfection.[192]

We may conclude our study by a brief consideration of the verb τελειόω, the nouns τελείωσις and τελειότης, and the various forms of the adjective τέλειος (including its opposite, ἀτελής) as well as the adverb τελε(ί)ως. Sometimes τελειόω is used of plants, etc., either transitively, "to bring to maturity,"[193] or intransitively, "to come to maturity."[194] Somewhat similar are Philo's uses of the word for "bring to full accomplishment,"[195] or "bring about,"[196] "bring to completion,"[197] "fulfill";[198] or, intransitively, "come to fruition."[199] Once Philo seems to think of attaining perfection as an absolute, unrealizable goal, noting that it is impossible to attain perfection in any of the arts or sciences because they are always being renewed.[200] Ordinarily, however, perfection is much less absolutely conceived. Thus he notes that one is perfected after studying the Encyclica and then applying one's unfettered powers to virtue.[201] And he may contrast those who have been perfected with beginners (ἀρχόμενοι) and/or those who are making progress (προκόπτα).[202] Consequently, when he speaks of the mind's advance toward perfection,[203] or notes that a mind is not yet made perfect,[204] or urges that some are imperfect (ἀτελές) because they think their improvement is due to their own zeal, not God's help,[205] or suggests that we are not yet perfected and thus *husbandry* is necessary,[206] he is clearly combining a stress on virtue and the life of the mind with a "perfection" much less total or absolute than the corresponding English word seems to imply. Thus he may speak both of those who have advanced to perfection though still needing practice[207] and of the man of practice who comes to perfection.[208] Sometimes the stress is on teaching, especially being taught by God, as in the case of those who advance to perfection under a teacher, as contrasted with those who have been taught by God,[209] a thought that he can amplify to suggest that pupils of God are translated into "the genus of the incorruptible and most perfect" (εἰς το ἄφθαρτον καὶ τελεώτατον γένος)[210] while noting that still others (Moses, e.g.) have advanced even higher.[211] In general, however, teaching cannot be perfected without nature or practice,[212] and thus Jacob (the Practicer) is specifically said to have been perfected by practice or discipline,[213] while Abraham is said to have been perfected both by teaching[214] and by God's filling him with wisdom,[215] which is about the same thing.

The Philonic stress on both virtue and the pedagogical is also apparent in his use of τελειόω for "perfect a well-endowed soul with virtue,"[216] "perfect the naturally gifted in virtue,"[217] and for a soul "which has been perfected in contests for (the winning of) virtues (ἄθλοις ἀρετῶν).[218] His basically religious outlook is clear when he speaks of the religious means which perfect knowledge and piety,[219] and his thoroughgoing Platonic assumptions are equally clear when he notes that the soul, when perfected, will recognize itself to be a corpse-bearer.[220]

Once, but unless I am mistaken only once in the entire corpus, Philo identifies the time and mode of perfection with the time of death: "And so, when Aaron dies (τελευτά), i.e., when he is made perfect (τελειώθη). . . ."[221] The reason for the rarity of this emphasis is evident: His central concern is not with the world after death; it is with the cultivation of virtue (including, of course, the religious and intellectual life) in this one. The contrast with Hebrews could hardly be clearer, whatever other affinities in thought and language one might find.

Both nouns for perfection, τελείωσις and τελειότης, are fairly common in Philo. Τελείωσις sometimes means the execution or carrying out of something,[222] and it is used in a technical sense for the "ram of consecration (fulfillment)" (Lev 8:29).[223] These usages are not very significant, nor is the agricultural sense "ripeness, full fruition,"[224] which is also implicit in the triad "birth (γένεσις/ growth (αὔξησις)/ maturity (τελείωσις)."[225] More appropriate for our purposes are the senses "(past) fulfillment,"[226] "completion" (of the sacrifices on the eighth day),[227] and "consummation."[228] And characteristically Philonian are the uses of τελείωσις for the "perfecting" or "bringing to perfection or fullest development" of the world,[229] of the mind and reason in the eighth stage of human life,[230] of the best *types* of life[231] or of learning,[232] of the (Platonic) Ideas of mind (νοῦς) and sense-perception (αἴσθεσις),[233] or of those who have come to the edge of wisdom.[234] He notes that both word and thought may contribute to perfection,[235] and he speaks of perfecting by way of progress,[236] as well as of the perfection of both Noah's education[237] and Noah himself (in virtues).[238] He also (characteristically) thinks of Abraham as having come to perfection "by virtue gained through instruction."[239] Again, the moral, intellectual, and pedagogical elements are evident.

The other term for "perfection," τελειότης, is sometimes used absolutely[240] and very commonly contrasted with gradual progress (προκοπή, etc.) or placed at the end of it.[241] It is also used, as noted above,[242] of the numbers 6 and 100. It is ascribed to some biblical figures: Levi, as evident in his making God his refuge;[243] Israel, a name for perfection;[244] and Isaac, a symbol of perfection.[245] The moral emphasis is central in Philo's comment that repentance is second to perfection,[246] the religious in his ascription of perfection to God,[247] and the pedagogical in his exegesis of Numbers 8:24-26, in which perfection is required of him who is 25, while one who is 50 (a perfect number) is free of active labor.[248] All of these are included in his use of the phrases perfection of life,[249] of soul,[250] of one's nature,[251] and of virtue,[252] while the intellectual element predominates in such phrases as perfection of knowledge and instruction,[253] perfection of the mind (διάνοια),[254] and the supreme (ἄκραν) perfection to which Caleb's mind was changed.[255] The latter element is also central in his comment that the perfection of the whole is shared by Mind (νοῦς) when it forms a conception of the universe.[256]

We come, then, finally, to the adjectives. What does it mean to be "imperfect" (ἀτελής) or "perfect" (τέλειος)? Again, the uses are broad, but the general tendencies are extremely clear.

A common use of ἀτελής is agricultural: "unripe, immature, imperfect."[257] It may also mean "sterile,"[258] "fruitless, pointless,"[259] or "unsuccessful, inefficacious, impossible."[260] It occasionally implies failure to reach a τέλος (goal), i.e., "without end,"[261] "fragmentary,"[262] or, in a very common usage, "unfulfilled."[263] Closely related are those passages in which the word, in contrast with ὁλοκλῆρος (complete),[264] suggests either "defective, incomplete,"[265] or "imperfect."[266] Philo speaks of "incomplete" movements of the soul[267] and notes that memory without discernment is incomplete,[268] as is knowledge which has not gone from the created (world) to the Uncreated One.[269] He also speaks of those imperfectly equipped to govern,[270] and, in an especially unfortunate usage, of the female as an imperfect male.[271] Finally, he very frequently simply contrasts ἀτελής with τέλειος,[272] with which we complete our summation.

Some of the uses of τέλειος are comparatively rare. Thus, e.g., he once speaks of ἡ τέλεια as the full point (consummation) of the moon[273] and once uses the same expression for "(falling short of) perfection."[274] And in what may be of some significance, the adverb τελείως/τελέως (finally, absolutely, completely, utterly, perfectly)[275] is very substantially less frequent than the adjective, which is itself occasionally used adverbially.[276] The adjective also occurs with the neuter article το τέλειος (the perfect),[277] and once without the article in the same sense.[278]

Occasionally τέλειος looks to the *end* of an action or process and means "completed, finished"[279] or "total";[280] it may be used as a grammatical term[281] or of a fully trained fighter (still unpracticed in virtue).[282] And it occurs numerous times in the sense of "fully developed"[283] or "full-grown, mature."[284] Various contrasts make this emphasis clear: It is contrasted with babes (βρέφοι, etc.),[285] with the "earliest years" (ἐκ πρώτης ἡλικίας),[286] with childhood or the things of childhood (νήπιοι, etc.),[287] with youth (νεότης, etc.),[288] or with several of these stages (νήπιοι, βρέφοι, and παιδικοί).[289] It may also be contrasted with a halfway stage (μέσος)[290] or, in the feminine, with virgins (παρθένοις).[291] Closely related is the contrast between marriage and harlotry.[292] And the absolute, το τέλειος (the fully mature) is once contrasted with το ἀρχόμενον (that which is just beginning).[293] A similar sense lies behind the concept of sins brought to perfection, i.e., to *perpetration.*[294]

Other passages in Philo speak of God as perfect,[295] of God's perfect goodness,[296] of God the perfect Teacher,[297] or of God's gifts as perfect.[298] And God is Lord and God of the perfect (pl.)[299] as well as of the perfect nature (φύσις).[300]

Now the interest has shifted to *human*[301] perfection, a major emphasis in Philo's thought. Often the perfect man is not really defined,[302] or he is simply contrasted with one who is progressing,[303] with the imperfect (ἀτελεῖς),[304] or with the practicer (ἀσκητής).[305] Often, however, specifics are given. The perfect man, formed after the divine image,[306] and complete from the first,[307] honors God[308] and seeks quietude (ἠρεμία),[309] though as a created being he does not escape sinning,[310] a thought that is not really inconsistent with Philo's paralleling of a perfect man and one of "truly harmonious character" (πρὸς ἀλήθειαν εὐάρμοστος).[311] A very common note is the description of the perfect wise man (τέλειος σοφός)[312] whose perfection (or Wisdom, the perfect Way[313]) is defined in highly Platonic terms: God, by the same Logos by which he made the universe, draws the wise/perfect man from earthly things toward himself.[314] Or the perfect man (here expressed as pure Mind) has left (the realm of) the passions, i.e., "has passed elsewhere and resolved no longer to dwell in the same city as they."[315] Or the perfect (pl.) are those whose perfecting begins with the body and the senses but ends in the wisdom of God.[316] Equally Platonic but more ethically conceived is the definition of a perfect man as one who expresses conceptions of the Good in action, i.e., "to whom it is given to set their image in the eye of the soul, not at rest but in motion and engaged in their natural activities."[317]

This ethical stress, "perfect virtue(s),"[318] or "perfect in virtue,"[319] or "not perfect in virtue,"[320] is extremely common, and we find variations of it like "perfect ordinances of virtue,"[321] "perfect offspring of virtues,"[322] and "good and perfect character,"[323] as well as the note that justice in the soul is "perfect."[324] Essentially similar are the notes that some are not perfect but are making progress[325] and the description of noble deeds as perhaps constituting the perfect reward.[326] Philo once even speaks of the perfect form (εἶδος!) of virtue.[327] And he often uses, with a variety of referents, the phrase "perfect good(s)."[328]

It is, naturally, an important aspect of Philo's religious philosophy, as it was of Plato's, that the world is perfect,[329] complete.[330] Hence Philo speaks of "perfect parts" (of the universe)[331] and insists that the world and its parts are perfect,[332] that the world is perfect and complete (τέλειος . . . ὁλοκλῆρος) in all its parts,[333] that the things of nature are perfect,[334] that the world is made of a perfect substance (ἐκ τελείας οὐσίας),[335] that the world was created with a complement of perfect parts,[336] that the elements of the world are perfect branches of the whole,[337] that the world, in short, is a perfect work of perfect parts,[338] or, to put it somewhat differently, perfect parts (elements) were used to make the most perfect (τελειότατος) universe.[339] It is not inconsistent with any of this to suggest that while nothing in creation is perfect (complete) *in itself*,[340] the plants and shrubs were perfect at creation[341] and that a living animal is made of parts perfect (complete) in themselves in a harmonious whole.[342]

Many human faculties, habits, experiences, etc. may also share in this perfection. Thus Philo speaks of perfect thoughts,[343] perfect sense or wisdom (φρόνεσις),[344] perfect reason,[345] perfect mind,[346] a perfect soul[347] and of perfections in relationship to the soul,[348] a perfect life,[349] perfect enjoyment,[350] perfect happiness (εὐδαιμονία)[351] perfect gladness (εὐφροσύνη),[352] and perfect freedom from passion (τελεία ἀπάθεια).[353] He notes that the ideas, thoughts, etc. of the mind which come from God are perfect,[354] and similarly, in a different context, that what sense sees and hears under the direction of the mind (νοῦς) is perfect.[355]

In addition to this anthropological emphasis, Philo often stresses the perfection of many matters relating to worship. Thus he speaks of perfect mysteries (of God),[356] perfect prayers,[357] perfect knowledge of God,[358] perfect blessings for all people,[359] perfect priestly rites,[360] a (purified and) perfect (= fully consecrated) priest,[361] a high priest who is not perfect,[362] as well as perfect cleansing or purification.[363] He mentions perfect sacrifices[364] and perfect sheep for sacrifice;[365] notes that gifts brought to God are to be perfect[366] and that Cain's sacrifices were not;[367] and he insists that a sacrifice is perfect in giving thanks,[368] while the confession of thankfulness (ἡ ἐξομολόγησις) is the perfect fruit.[369]

Some biblical characters are also discussed in τέλειος-terms. The word "perfect" is used of Noah in several instances.[370] Abraham is called perfect[371] and said to have lived a laudable and perfect life;[372] when (as Abram) he was still only inquiring into supramundane things, Philo says, he had not yet become perfect,[373] but when he had been filled with wisdom, he had.[374] Isaac was perfect in virtue,[375] but Joseph never acquired perfect seniority of the soul.[376] Levi's life, on the other hand, was one of perfect virtue.[377] Aaron is a man of progress and thus not among those who live in perfect happiness;[378] he is specifically contrasted, as a perfect interpreter, with the most perfect (τελειότατος) Moses.[379] Moses indeed is described as perfect,[380] as a perfect athlete,[381] and as a perfect worshipper of God.[382] The ethical, religious, and intellectual elements in the term "perfect" are evident in these brief biographical notes.

In a few instances a direct pedagogical note is also sounded. Though he observes that no one but God is really perfect in any pursuit,[383] Philo speaks of being perfect in any subject of study,[384] of perfect art[385] and a perfect portrait (γραφή),[386] and of a perfect master of music or letters.[387] He also insists that the only perfect king is one skilled in shepherding.[388]

The remaining uses are not easy to categorize. Philo speaks of perfect harmonies,[389] perfect music[390] and the perfect music of the spheres,[391] perfect signs,[392] perfect light,[393] the perfect powers of leaders,[394] and perfect exercises in evil.[395] He notes that the month, the complete cycle of the moon, is perfect.[396] Finally, that race (γένος) is perfect which is subject to neither war[397] nor slavery.[398]

The comparative (τελειότερος/τελεώτερος) and superlative (τελειότατος/τελεώτατος) forms of the word confirm, without adding very much except further examples, the general tendencies described above.

Many of the τελειότερος-phrases contain nothing very significant, once the notion of "more perfect" becomes familiar to our English-speaking ears. Sometimes the term means merely "more advanced, surpassing,"[399] and it may be applied to a more advanced stage of grammar.[400] He also speaks, however, of "more perfect joy,"[401] a "more perfect victory,"[402] a "more perfect" God-inspired soul,[403] a "fuller" vision,[404] a more complete eclipse,[405] as well as of any perfection greater than blessedness, happiness, etc.,[406] of a true feast which is "more perfect" than human nature could comprehend,[407] of a tribe as a kind of "more complete" (all-embracing) kinship,[408] of the "more perfect" parts of the body,[409] of Isaac as a more perfect son than Abraham and Sarah had hoped for,[410] of a plant of sound sense as a "more perfect thing,"[411] and, in a violation of that very standard, of the male as "more complete" than the female.[412] He also notes that there is something "more perfect" than gifts,[413] while he urges his readers to preserve God's gifts as "(more) perfect."[414]

The anthropological element is clear in his speaking of men of "more perfect" thoughts and feelings (φρονημάτων)[415] and of "more perfect" natures,[416] while noting that Abraham's nature was "of a more than human perfection."[417] And the ethical definition of this element shows in his use of the word for "more mature," as in his speaking of "virtues perfect beyond one's years,"[418] or of virtues as "grown-up" food (τελειότερας) contrasted with the simple and milky foods of infancy (τῇ βρεφώδει).[419] A related pedagogical interest is evident in the statement that men of practice enjoy "more perfect" things only after having participated in earlier stages of culture.[420]

The intellectual element, with its "Platonic" assumptions, is also evident. The contemplative life, he asserts roundly, is a "more advanced" contest than the practical life,[421] since what is perceived by the mind is "more perfect" than the cosmos,[422] while Moses is, among other things, "a more perfect Mind."[423] There is, in short, no more perfect good than philosophy.[424]

Philo's "philosophy" is, of course, profoundly religious. Nothing in the realm of the intelligible is more perfect than God,[425] and the soul of the most perfect (τελειοτέρων) is fed by the whole Word.[426] When Philo comes to the rhetorical question, "What could be more perfect?",[427] therefore, he specifies by two more rhetorical questions: What more perfect good can we find than God?[428] and, What can be more perfect than the sight of God?[429]

We conclude our study with the superlative (τελειότατος/τελεώτατος), which follows very much the lines already set out. The use of the word in connection with 3, 4, 10, and 10,000 has already been mentioned;[430] allied to it is the phrase "more perfect concord (σύστημα) of numbers"[431] as well as the mathematical note that the circle is the most perfect of figures.[432] He also occasionally uses the word in an agricultural sense, "fully mature, full grown."[433] A musical context or metaphor is occasionally evident: he speaks of "most perfect melodies"[434] and notes that the voice is the "most perfect of (musical) instruments"[435] and the soul of the Sage a "most perfect instrument."[436] Sometimes the term occurs in a cultic context: "a most perfect thank-offering"[437] is really a metaphor of the intellectual life, but Philo includes the literal as well in speaking of the "most perfect purification,"[438] or of "most perfect sacrifices,"[439] as in pointing out that the high priest is to be completely perfect, that is, without defect,[440] and in suggesting that the most perfect way of releasing dedicated property is for the priest to refuse it.[441] It is not, of course, directly cultic to insist that each portico of the temple was a most perfect work[442] or that the ephod was wrought with perfect knowledge.[443] And it is only typically Philonian to say that noble living is the best and most perfect sacrifice[444] and that fasting and perseverance are the most perfect of offerings.[445]

Many of the uses are not particularly trenchant or significant for our purposes. The "perfection" of wickedness,[446] the "greatest and most perfect wealth,"[447] a "truly perfect ruler,"[448] a "most perfect mark (τύπος),"[449] the "most perfect types of being (φύσεις)"[450] and the "most perfect judgment (γνώμη)" of nature,[451] and a sense of hearing at its fullest[452] are simple superlatives (a common Greek construction), while the note that slavery is the most perfect good for the fool[453] is perhaps best left unnoticed.

Other passages, however, directly confirm the stresses already noted. The intellectual element is evident in his insistence that philosophy is the most perfect of studies,[454] that reason (λογισμός) is a most perfect thing,[455] that memory and the capacity to distinguish are, in partnership, most perfect,[456] and, in highly Platonic terms, that the heavenly model of the world is the most perfect object of intelligence (ὅσα . . . νοετά).[457] A combination of the intellectual and the ethical is evident in Philo's remark that for the worthless person (φαῦλος) pleasure is a "most perfect good."[458]

The ethical note is all-pervasive. Thus he speaks of "most perfect virtue,"[459] of the perfection of virtue (ἀρετήν . . . τελειοτάτην) in the good,[460] of God as willing to be God and Lord of the best and most perfect,[461] of faith as the most perfect of virtues.[462] He says that virtues have women's titles but the powers and activities of most perfect (consummate) men,[463] and he notes that the offspring of virtue are the most perfect of all.[464] The ethical is a part—though only a part—of the qualities of Moses, the "most perfect of men,"[465] the "most perfect of prophets,"[466] the "most perfect" one in contrast to Aaron, who is merely "perfect."[467] Once he speaks of continence as the most perfect of blessings (συμφέρον),[468] but it is somewhat more characteristic of him to call abstinence from idolatry and perjury the "most perfect reward."[469] For when all is said, to be well pleasing to God is the most perfect of virtues.[470] The most perfect praise of created things is to be found in God;[471] indeed, the most perfect of all accomplishments is the praise of God.[472]

For, finally, God and God's world are what constitute the truly perfect. God is fully perfect,[473] as is His nature.[474] He is the most perfect Good,[475] the most perfect Mind,[476] the most perfect Source (αἴτιος) of good things to the blessed[477] and the creator of most perfect knowledge (ἐπιστήμη).[478] Hence Philo can speak of God's "most perfect joys"[479] and note that to possess God is the most perfect happiness.[480] Those who have dispensed with human instruction and are taught by God belong to the genus of the imperishable and fully perfect.[481] God is, in sum, the most perfect Planter and his plants the most perfect in the universe.[482]

For the world, like God, is most perfect,[483] the most perfect of God's work,[484] the most perfect work known to our sense[485]—for the works of God are made with most perfect skill and knowledge.[486] The universe (ὁ κόσμος ἅπας) is the most perfect flock of God,[487] the most perfect Man.[488] The Great City, inhabited by spiritual and divine natures, is the dwelling of those who have "been enrolled in the greatest and most perfect Commonwealth,"[489] for heaven is the most perfect of indestructible things, just as man is the most perfect of mortal things.[490] That ethics, philosophy, and religion are all ultimately centered in God in Philo's thought is obvious.

The above statistics, whatever their shortcomings as dramatic narrative, have at least one virtue: they include (except for errors and accidental omissions) every occurrence of every *tel*-word in the Philonic corpus.[491] They thus provide a statistical base for some generalizations about Philo's understanding of perfection, a base so broad that though they could be confirmed also by a study of the larger concepts (not simply the individual words) used, such a confirmation, impossible in a brief article anyway, is hardly necessary. Such generalizations would include the following:

1. Absolutely fundamental to the Philonic system is the Platonic cosmology.[492]

2. Since the heavenly realm is perfect, one may attain perfection by entering it. Once Philo speaks of this as accomplished by death,[493] and there are many passages in his writings which suggest that he accepts traditional views of life after death in the heavenly world.

3. His main emphasis, however, lies elsewhere, in the soul's ascent,[494] in the "mystic vision of God,"[495] in escape from the world of sense-perception,[496] in contemplation of the heavenly Ideas, etc. Saint and Sage are indistinguishable in Philo.

4. Hence his religious pedagogy, for all its emphasis on God as drawing the Sage upward, is intrinsically ethical. Virtue leads some to the heavenly region; vice pulls others down.[497] It is unthinkable to Philo that access to the heavenly realm should be available to any but the worthy.

5. Perfection in Philo, then, includes elements of the religious, the philosophical, the pedagogical, and above all the ethical.

II

THE τελ-WORDS IN HEBREWS

Here of course the statistical base is much more limited. Τελ-words which occur in Philo but never in Hebrews are 33 in number,[498] while only one word, τελειωτής, occurs in Hebrews but not in Philo. There are, however, twenty-five occurrences in Hebrews of Philonic τελ-words.

Some are not very significant. 'Αλυσιτελές, e.g., occurs once[499] and means, as in Philo, "unprofitable." Συντέλεια also occurs once,[500] where it suggests the end of the world, and συντελέω once,[501] of the completing of a covenant. Both uses are non-Philonic. Τελευτάω means, as commonly in Philo, simply "die."[502] And παντελής occurs only in the phrase εἰς το παντελής,[503] where it means "completely, utterly," as παντελής does in Philo.

The seven other terms—ἐπιτελέω, τέλος, τελειόω, τελείωσις, τελειωτής, τελειότης, and τέλειος—are significant not only for understanding the relationships between Philo and the unknown author of Hebrews but for understanding the theology of Hebrews itself.

First, ἐπιτελέω. In 8:5, in which Exodus 25:40 is quoted,[504] the word means "finish, complete, make."[505] In 9:6 it means "perform a religious duty."[506] Both usages are Philonic, as is the fascination with Exodus 25:40, which must have seemed to every kind of Platonist to ground Platonism solidly in scripture.

Τέλος is more common.[507] but the range of use is quite narrow. It always means "end," with the nuance of "destiny" in 6:8 and the contrast "beginning of days/end of life" in 7:3.[508] The threefold "until the end" (μέχρι/ἄχρι τέλους) is particularly striking. The end of all things is not, as in Philo, a theoretical hope; it is, as in most strata of the New Testament, a concrete and imminent possibility. The traditional "horizontal" eschatology has in these instances been taken over for parenetic purposes; it has not been transformed into the Platonic "vertical" scheme which is central to so much of the book.

Τελειόω is by far the most common of the τελ-words in Hebrews.[509] The basic meaning, "to make 'perfect'," is common to them all, but the meaning is not immediately clear. If we assume, however, that the one clear passage (12:23) provides the key to the others, all may be fitted easily into the same framework, one which is totally consistent with the author's Platonism and his Christology as well. This passage, "But you have come to . . . the heavenly Jerusalem . . . , to the general assembly and church of the firstborn, . . . and to the spirits of just men made perfect," shows that while virtue is of course required ("*just* men"), it is not perfection; to be made perfect is rather to have been translated into the heavenly realm. (There is no stress on leaving the world of sense-perception, as in Philo, and a central emphasis is on being with Jesus in the heavenly realm.) If this pattern is maintained, most of the other passages fit into it. "It became him, in bringing many sons into glory, to make the captain of their salvation perfect through sufferings" (2:10), might, taken alone, sound pedagogical; but in the context the suffering is identified with death, which for Jesus was the route to "being made perfect." 5:9 is similar: Jesus "learned obedience" by the things which he suffered—and being made perfect, he became the author of eternal salvation. Clearly he was made perfect by dying. In 7:28, no other meaning is even possible: the Son has been made perfect forever. The stress in both wording and context is on the high priest "exalted above the heavens" (v. 26), who offered up himself and thus has been made perfect forever. So also 10:14, "by one offering [his sacrificial death], Jesus has made perfect forever them that are sanctified." Whether already sharing in the heavenly realm or living in it only by anticipation, the "sanctified" have been "perfected" by Jesus' death. That there is no intellectual, pedagogical, or ethical element here is evident. And it is probable, though not quite so clear, that 11:40 should be interpreted the same way: the heroes of the old dispensation did not receive the Promise, but God provided a better thing "for us, that they without us should not be made perfect." Again, the perfection has no pedagogical or ethical content; it is rather a way of speaking of the fulness of the Promise in the heavenly realm (which is in some way also the world to come.) The "vertical" eschatology of the author's Platonism is here put to very good use.

The three remaining passages (7:19; 9:9; 10:1)[510] are somewhat different, though they too make no distinction in virtue or spiritual progress between those that are imperfect and those that are not—as Philo often does. The suggestion is rather of incompleteness, imperfection in the sense of "not so total" as the corresponding Christian ordinances—the "better hope" (7:19), the once-for-all sacrifice of Christ in his death (9:12, 14, 15), the one offering for sin forever (10:12). To be made perfect, consequently, is either to be translated (by death) into the heavenly realm or to anticipate in this life the benefits purchased in that realm by Christ's death. The "Platonism" is as clear as the Christianizing of it.

"Perfection" (τελείωσις) in 7:11[511] is to be understood in this latter sense. The old priesthood is incomplete; the new priesthood does what it cannot do, bring "perfection" to the worshipper.

The "perfecter" (τελειωτής)[512] of our faith (12:2) is Jesus. Two nuances belong to the word here. One is the contrast, "author, beginner/finisher, perfecter." The other is Jesus' death and session at God's right hand.

In 6:1, perfection (τελειότης) is contrasted with the "first principles" of Christian doctrine, which are then defined (6:1-2) in phrases which by common consent represent something like a fixed formula of Hellenistic missionary preaching. But the nature of that perfection is not particularly clear. What it is not—and the possibility is a merely theoretical one—is *apostasy*, falling away from God (6:6) instead of holding fast to the end (6:11). It is an admonition, but a general one, not to virtue but to perseverance, not to growth but to holding fast on the road whose end is "perfection."

Τέλειος, perfect, occurs only twice in Hebrews, in quite different senses (both used by Philo). In 5:14 it means "mature, full-grown" and is contrasted with a child (νήπιος, 5:13). The context is parenetic and, like 6:1, it contrasts the perfect with "first principles." The emphasis, not entirely clear, seems to be on advanced *doctrine*. In 9:11, on the other hand, a "greater and more perfect tabernacle" (τελειοτέρας σκηνῆς) is contrasted with the former, earthly one. Again, since Christ is the high priest in this heavenly sanctuary, the combination of "Platonism" with a particular Christology is clear.

This concludes our rapid survey of the vocabulary of perfection in Hebrews. To generalize:

1. The "Platonic" cosmology is central to the author's thought. It enables him to conceive of a contrast between the heavenly and earthly realms and, by placing Jewish ordinances in the earthly realm, to make them at once good and yet imperfect. No Platonist would find it difficult to understand this scheme.

2. Nevertheless, the Christian kerygma has modified this scheme in many ways. The "horizontal" eschatology of primitive Christian preaching is crucial in the warnings about holding fast to the end and in the promise of Christ's coming (9:28). The heavenly sacrifice, the heavenly tabernacle, the heavenly high priesthood are all understood in Christianized Platonic terms as Christ, in his death, is seen as having offered a once-for-all sacrifice in the heavenly temple. It would be hard to imagine anything more foreign to Philo's mode of thought.

3. Finally, crucial Philonic emphases are missing: the interest in philosophy, the notion of progress in virtue, the strong stress on the ethical, and a sense of "training" or pedagogy.

In short, the unknown author of Hebrews lived in the same generally "Platonic" world as Philo. But, as the analysis of perfection makes clear, they were citizens of quite different countries.

Notes to Chapter 10

1. Where I have not made my own translation I have used that of F. H. Colson and G. H. Whitaker in The Loeb Classical Library series, © Harvard University Press. I am grateful to Harvard University Press for permission to cite this edition.
2. *9* 58; *20* 243; *24a* 78. See also nn. 69, 70 below. (For number references, see the list of works following these notes.)
3. *20* 240; *28* 59. This is always the meaning of συντελέω (*19a* 59, 116; *20* 240; *24* 67) in Philo except in quotations; see below, n. 72.
4. *11* 115.
5. *24* 143 (pl.).
6. *20* 93, 260; *21* 98, 250; *22* 46, 91, 122, 168, 221; *24b* 13; *27* 127; *30* 4, 141, 183; *33* 26, 108, 110, 144, 222, 252, 300, 303.
7. *3* 120; *24* 53.
8. *2b* 61; *9* 39, 47; *11* 16, 20; *19a* 275; *20* 18; *24c* 151; *28* 20; *30* 137; *32a* 37, 37; Gr. Frag. Ex. #17 (p. 261).
9. *2b* 222; *24* 100; *26* 20; *30* 19; *33* 218; Gr. Frag. Gen. #10 (p. 236).
10. *24c* 151.
11. *1* 116; *19a* 144; *24b* 183; *26* 171; *33* 280.
12. *24* 183.
13. *19* 93, 124; *19a* 56; *26* 99; *28* 37, 69; *31* 380.
14. *22* 111; *24a* 34; *25* 49; *30* 78. Of seed, *1* 68.
15. *28* 24.
16. *14* 106; *15* 158; *21* 204; *22* 112.
17. *5* 14; *15* 158; *16* 51; *19* 6; *19a* 48; *24* 271; *28* 38.
18. *1* 10; *2b* 19; *6* 181; *8* 19; *9* 41, 77, 88; *11* 22; *13* 6, 12, 164, 195; *14* 86; *15* 244; *16* 158;
19. *9* 85; *24a* 184, 239; *24c* 221; *26* 7; *33* 242.
99, 369; *35a* #13 on Exodus xxiii.20-21, #17 on Exodus xxiii.24c.
20. *9* 122; *12* 3; *16* 176; *18* 118; *19* 132; *24* 120; *24a* 18, 256; *30* 4; *33* 109.
21. *19* 233.

22. *1* 158; *2b* 156; *3* 104; *4* 21, 21, 23; *5* 20; *6* 142; *8* 146; *11* 211; *15* 158, 158; *16* 19; *17* 31; *19* 123, 124, 125, 224; *19a* 33, 54, 57; *21* 196, 205; *22* 275; *22a* 23, 72, 112; *23* 133; *24* 87, 176; *24a* 193; *25* 39; *27* 66; *28* 37, 69, 74; *30* 69; *32* (336).
23. *21* 234; *22a* 42; *24a* 193; *33* 358.
24. *10* 65; *22* 317; *24* 271; *32a* 29; *33* 151, 319.
25. *21* 23; *22a* 95; *33* 185.
26. *5* 68; *33* 36.
27. *8* 161; *25* 18.
28. *1* 164; *22* 153; *22a* 185; *24* 173; *24a* 19, 160, *33* 274.
29. *1* 164; *22* 152, 153, 256; *23* 71; *24* 71, 73, 95, 176; *24a* 19, 20; *24c* 101; *25* 8; *26* 99; *28* 48, 53; *30* 91; *31* 380; *33* 14, 157, 344.
30. We omit as irrelevant in this connection the word τελματώδης (swampy, *15* 32), which is probably related to the root for "heavy."
31. *15* 126.
32. *1* 47; *25* 158.
33. *23* 28; *24a* 177 (where six is also seen as the starting-point of perfection). Technically the word "perfect" should be applied only to such numbers, i.e., 6, 28, 496, 8128, etc.
34. *1* 13, 14, 89; *2* 3, 15.
35. *34a* #42 on Genesis viii.11; *34b* #38 on Genesis xvi.16. (Not confirmed by Greek fragments.)
36. *22a* 84.
37. *1* 101; *24a* 40; cf. *35a* #87 on Exodus xxvi.2.
38. *6* 48, 96, 173; *16* 88, 116; *22* 96; *24* (177); *24a* 41, 201.
39. *17* 184; *26* 65.
40. *5* 64. Since 50 is a perfect number, one who is 25 must strive for perfection, but one who is 50 is free of active labor (Num 8:24-26).
41. *14* 169.
42. *18* 192, 192.
43. *18* 189. In *18* 2, the number 100 is seen as a symbol of perfection.
44. *16* 113; *18* 88, 188.
45. F. H. Colson in the Loeb edition of Philo's works, VI, 598.
46. *24a* 58.
47. *1* 47; *20* 244; *22a* 79, 84; *23* 20; *24a* 220, 220; see also below, nn. 140-144.
48. *24* 178; το παντέλειον ἀριθμόν, Gr. Frag. #17 (p. 237).
49. *16* 90; *24c* 105.
50. *34b* #12 on Genesis xv.16; note that he describes 4 as "the root and base of the most perfect decad" (Armenian only).
51. *34b* #61 on Genesis xvii.24-25.
52. *1* 102, 103, 106, 107. Τελεσφορέω is used in the same connection in *1* 102.
53. *6* 173.
54. *35a* #87 on Exodus xxvi. 2 (Armenian only).
55. *10* 76.
56. In Philo used only of initiation into the things of God: *3* 42, 48.
57. Used of the things of God in *3* 42, 43, 48; *4* 60, 62; *7* 54; *11* 129; *19* 82; *20* 122; *22a* 149, 153; *23* 41; *26* 141; *34c* #8 on Genesis xviii. 6-7; Gr. Frag. Ex. #20 (p. 262). Used of pagan rites in *3* 94; *18* 107 (Baal Peor); *24* 56, 319 (τελετὰς καὶ μυστήρια), 319; *24b* 40 (μυστήρια καὶ τελετάς); *27* 14.
58. In general: *19* 191; in the things of God, *19* 164; Gr. Frag. Ex. #20 (p. 262). The contrast with σοφός/σοφοί (wise) in *15* 19 probably also belongs here. See below, n. 173.
59. *3* 48; *7* 54; *20* 122; *23* 41; *28* 25.
60. *22a* 150.
61. *18* 36.
62. *22* 62.
63. *18* 107 (Baal Peor); *22* 303 and *24* 56 (these two references to Phinehas and Num 25), 319, 319, 323.
64. *33* 56.
65. *10* 165 (offer sacrifice); *11* 129 (Aaron/reason offering "unseen rites," τελετάς); *15* 82 (high priest); *17* 37 (Levites); *19* 214, 215; *22* 87, 253 (vows), 287, 298 (sacrifices); *22a* 94,

147, 154, 221; *24* 3, 56, 97, 98, 113, 221, 297; *24a* 145; *24b* 56, 125, 171; *26* 79 (divine commandments); *27* 140; *33* 157, 157, 317. See also nn. 90, 91 below.
66. *33* 157, 280, 291, 317 (= ἐντελής).
67. See below, n. 139.
68. See below, nn. 175-178.
69. *15* 8; *28* 80.
70. *29* 135.
71. *15* 17, 17 (a completed action); *24a* 58. In *10* 90 the Loeb editors conjecture ἐπιτέλεια (accomplishment, completion).
72. *2* 1, 2, 3; *11* 53; *15* 122; *18* 270; *19a* 23, 29; *34c* #96 on Genesis xxiv.15. See n. 3 above.
73. *24b* 131, 190; *25* 76.
74. *1* 104, 104 (quote). See also n. 2 above.
75. *8* 39 (fruit).
76. *19a* 144 (conj.).
77. *1* 108, 109, 110, 110; *11* 15; *16* 109; *17* 166; *19* 14; *20* 95, 195, 219; *21* 23, 175, 187, 217, 249; *22* 195; *22a* 2, 153, 233; *23* 106; *24* 222; *24a* 157, 186, 204, 211, 243; *24c* 28, 78, 207; *25* 72; *26* 110; *28* 54; *30* 61, 72, 115, 156, 175, 187; *33* 15, 135, 239, 267, 274, 290, 302.
78. *1* 83, 95; *2b* 41; *4* 63; *10* 85; *19* 218; *19a* 281; *20* 50; *22* 134, 311; *22a* 146, 187; *23* 142; *24b* 39; *32a* 40; *33* 308.
79. *24c* 23.
80. *11* 52; *19* 24; *19a* 44, 133; *24c* 122; *25* 37; *26* 70; *29* 53, 75, 116; *30* 167; *35a* on Exodus xii.2.
81. *19* 12.
82. *1* 23.
83. *17* 61.
84. *33* 100.
85. *30* 180.
86. *30* 71.
87. *9* 152.
88. *2b* 34; *19a* 106.
89. *2a* 32, 54; *2b* 94, 101; *9* 45, 123; *10* 23, 148, 162; *11* 148; *13* 12, 167; *14* 119; *17* 166, 199; *18* 17, 80; *19a* 144; *20* 34, 85, 155, 209; *21* 103, 223; *22* 40; *23* 49, 117; *24* 113, 115, 304; *24a* 168, 207; *25* 113, 115, 304; *24a* 168, 207; *25* 136, 217; *28* 10, 47, 63; *29* 19, 61, 93; *30* 122; *32a* 21; *33* 123; *34* 4.
90. *17* 161; *22* 304; *24b* 72.
91. *1* 61; *3* 14; *14* 97; *19* 90; *19a* 153; *21* 208; *23* 162, 164; *24* 217; *24c* 67; *25* 98, 100; *26* 126, 131; *27* 36; *28* 71; *30* 97; *33* 218; *34a* #16 on Genesis vii.5; *35a* #16 on Exodus xxiii.22. See also n. 65 above.
92. *4* 108, 109 (right living is brought to fulness by true nourishment).
93. *2a* 13; *8* 46; *15* 149; *16* 142; *17* 26; *22* 207, 210; *22a* 34; *30* 117.
94. *1* 17; *2b* 98.
95. *1* 19, 92, 92, 95, 96, 97, 102, 116, 126, 126, 136; *2* 2, 7, 8, 23; *2a* 37, 37, 37, 74; *4* 69, 74; *5* 54, 87, 120; *6* 169; *8* 84, 88; *11* 116; *13* 186, 186, 187; *14* 6, 136, 180; *15* 141, 149, 150, 197, 214, 233, 266; *19* 35; *19a* 165; *21* 84; *22* 71, 96, 97; *22a* 74, 124, 126, 127, 256, 282; *23* 26, 31; *24* 87; *26* 102; *24a* 40; *24c* 87, 91, 161; *26* 97; *28* 88; *29* 41, 79, 88, 94, 98, 99, 135.
96. *1* 28, 129; *2a* 40; *17* 133; *22a* 76; *24b* 191.
97. *2b* 250; *12* 48; *29* 101.
98. *2a* 62, 63; *2b* 34, 204; *14* 43; *24a* 189.
99. *2* 100; *10* 125.
100. *15* 226; *28* 5.
101. *15* 209, 226, 227. See also *22* 96-97.
102. *18* 228; *24a* 41; *35a* #26 on Exodus xxiii.33b.
103. *30* 50.
104. (Of numbers) *6* 173.
105. *24a* 142.

106. *2a* 46 (quote); *2b* 45, 212, 212 (quote); *4* 8, 253; *5* 75, 94, 94 (quote), 95, 151; *6* 5, 181; *9* 95, 155; *14* 177; *15* 202, 292; *17* 55, 59 (quote), 83, 83, 107, 113 (quote); *18* 62; *19* 10, 26, 31; *20* 245; *21* 216, 261, 264, 268; *22* 100, 136, 145; *22a* 225, 231, 235, 235, 291, 291; *24* 105, 108, 129, 161, 250; *24a* 2, 124, 127, 127, 131, 139; *24b* 14, 20, 30, 106, 107, 133, 148, 148, 206; *24c* 36, 169, 202, 202; *27* 112; *28* 13; *29* 23, 86, 97, 97, 129, 143; *30* 9, 12, 66, 71, 75, 84; *33* 26, 58, 168, 268, 325; *34* #70 on Genesis iv. 10; *34* 376 on Genesis xv.15; Gr. Frag. Ex. #14 (p. 261).
107. *15* 126, 209; *17* 17; *32a* 25.
108. *9* 156; *13* 42 (of life); *15* 31; *19* 11; *22a* 281, 292; *23* 99, 117 (all four: of life); *24a 95* (= θάνατος, death); *29* 111; *33* 141 (of life).
109. *2a* 6; *5* 178; *8* 75; *9* 25; *11* 143 (quote); *14* 16; *19* 47; *20* 230, 255; *21* 128 156, 179, 226, 262; *22a* 34, 226, 234; *24* 102, 112, 159; *24a* 16, 16, 42; *24b* 123, 131, 161, 205; *24c* 119; *25* 52, 67; *27* 110, 113, 133, 135; *29* 20, 60, 74; *30* 2, 74; *32a* 50; *33* 8, 72, 160, 192; *34c* #145 on Genesis xxiv.67.
110. *1* 44, 44, 44, 44, 82, 82, 82, 82; *2* 6, 6; *2b* 205, 253; *4* 253; *5* 88; *7* 14; *9* 169, 180, 181; *10* 76, 93; *14* 56; *15* 120, 120, 121, 121, 122, 315; *17* 171, 172; *18* 102; *19* 151; *20* 46, 46; *21 246* (pl.); *22* 251, 327; *22a* 181, 181, 181, 181; *23* 25, 51; *24* 188, 188, 266; *24a* 38, 142 (pl.), 157, 157, 157; *24b* 29; *24c* 12; *26* 23; *35* #1 on Exodus xii.2 (twice); *34* #96 on Genesis vi.8.
111. Εἰς τέλος, "at last," *6* 29 (quote); ἐπὶ τοῦ τέλους, "at last," *2* 89; adv., "finally," *29* 36.
112. *3* 86; *18* 216; *24b* 54.
113. *14* 139, 139; *19* 66; *24* 345 (the knowledge of God is the sum total of happiness).
114. *8* 25; *10* 49, 168; *11* 218; *15* 172, 172; *22* 329; *24* 336; *24a* 236; *24b* 86, 125; *25* 75.
115. *2a* 73; *2b* 249; *21* 1.
116. *4* 113; *6* 152; *9* 76, 125, 126; *11* 202, 204; *12* 60; *13* 155; *14* 103, 143; *19a* 29; *22a* 290; *23* 121; *24b* 98; *26* 142; *31* 256; *33* 25.
117. *20* 172.
118. *10* 76; *14* 133; *19* 171.
119. *22* 194; *35a* #26 on Exodus xxiii.33b.
120. *10* 99.
121. *20* 177; *22a* 187; *25* 182 (pl.).
122. *21* 122.
123. *26* 162.
124. *1* 103; *4* 42, 125; *14* 153 (pl.); *19a* 11 (pl.), 107, 141, 142; *20* 230; *27* 160; Gr. Frag. Gen. #12 (p. 236).
125. *10* 37.
126. *1* 158, 162; *2* 84; *2b* 37, 47; *3* 91; *4* 115; *6* 21, 53, 80, 157, 174; *7* 53; *8* 61, 67, 98, 100; *9* 5, 91, 173; *10* 80, 90 (conj., ἐπιτέλεια), 161; *11* 202; *14* 128, 131, 134, 134, 225; *15* 246; *16* 12, 141; *19* 8, 230; *19a* (250); *20* 49, 130, 235; *21* 43; *22* 151; *22a* 151; *23* 50, 123; *24* 317, 333, 344; *24b* 86; *26* 28, 28; *34c* #86 on Genesis xxiv.2; *34c* #200 on Genesis xxvii.8-10.
127. *5* 114.
128. *2b* 45.
129. *23* 73.
130. *1* 144.
131. *25* 15; cf. also *35* #7 on Exodus xii.5a.
132. *19* 167-168.
133. *26* 24.
134. *28* 88.
135. *23* 81. Cf. (and contrast) "Man's chief end is to glorify God and enjoy him forever."
136. *20* 89.
137. *16* 5.
138. *8* 148.
139. See above, n. 67.
140. See above, nn. 42-44.
141. *22a* 149.
142. *24c* 95.

143. *24* 82.
144. *1* 156.
145. *5* 32, 38; *6* 72; *8* 43, 182; *9* 101; *11* 154, 223; *16* 150; *17* 80, 153; *18* 49, 50, 229; *19* 8; *19a* 18, 163; *20* 223; *22a* 264; *23* 68; *24* 111, 259; *24c* 14, 145, 181; *25* 38; *26* 95; *28* 27; *31* 356; *34* #77 on Genesis iv.23.
146. *2b* 15, 112; *3* 3; *5* 38, 46, 51; *6* 156, 167; *9* 160; *15* 278; *17* 39; *18* 36, 84; *19* 31, 148; *20* 247; *24* 344; *24a* 47, 55, 67, 123; *24b* 98.
147. *17* 81, 187 (virtue); *18* 228; *33* 28 (power).
148. *2a* 33; *2b* 99, 215; *3* 92, 96; *4* 122 (freedom), 57; *5* 46, 51, 54 (knowledge), 63 (release and freedom), 65, 143, 168, 178; *6* 42, 82, 95, 164, 185; *8* 16, 173; *9* 94, 96, 125 (knowledge), 130, 157; *11* 4, 5, 21, 23, 29, 72, 84, 111, 116 (courage), 162, 166 (insensibility); *13* 67, 195; *14* 2, 124; *15* 271 (freedom), 284, 299; *16* 108, 119; *18* 84, 228 (release to freedom); *19* 86; *19a* 163, 292 (pardon); *20* 140, 202; *22* 81; *22a* 107; *23* 92; *24* 164, 215 (remission of sins), 237 (health), 242 (amnesty), 344; *24c* 211, 213; *26* 127; *27* 26; *29* 5, 6, 23, 37, 62, 71, 81, 100, 145; *30* 10, 16, 84; *31* 356; *32* (336); *33* 18, 104, 134, 144, 257 (destitution), 293, 330; cf. *34a* #64 on Genesis ix. 13-17.
149. *9* 130; *11* 135; *19a* 144.
150. *6* 95.
151. *3* 112.
152. *11* 118.
153. *29* 1.
154. *24a* 197.
155. *4* 57.
156. *18* 258; *20* 146; *22a* 8.
157. *20* 177.
158. *15* 86.
159. *20* 44.
160. *18* 258.
161. *11* 135; *24* 80.
162. *24* 196, 196.
163. *24* 253, 283.
164. *24b* 21.
165. *24c* 143.
166. *9* 130.
167. *26* 119.
168. *18* 50; *24c* 144; *33* 317 (=ἐντελεχές).
169. *24a* 184.
170. *1* 47; *2* 100; *2a* 73. Cf. *34a* #79 on Genesis x.1.
171. *5* 46; *12* 12; *29* 43.
172. *16* 148.
173. *15* 19. See above, n. 58.
174. *2b* 135.
175. *3* 102 (reason, διάνοια); *4* 83 (reason, λόγος); *25* 94. Note Philo's comment that "nature *brings forth* no *finished product* in the world of sense without using an incorporeal pattern" (*1* 130).
176. *2a* 24; *13* 156, 158, 175; *19* 207; *24b* 33.
177. *2b* 227; *20* 147.
178. *6* 171 (seeds). See also n. 68 above.
179. *1* 124; *22a* 66 (fruits of virtue), 104 (seeds); *25* 49 (grain), 145 (grain), 154 (trees); *26* 130 (fruit); *29* 60 (men), 98 (seed).
180. *1* 36.
181. *1* 116; *22a* 222; *24* 172; *24b* 111 (fetus).
182. *25* 156, 158.
183. *1* 59, 102; *4* 124; *6* 97 (hopes); *8 39* (fruit); *10* 151 (fruit); *16* 138 (fetus), 162; *17* 170; *24* 16, 179; *24a* 59 (fruit), 260 (all things at creation).
184. *11* 126 (prayers); *24b* 188; *25* 77 (benedictions); *26* 126 (blessings).
185. *22a* 5 (prayers).

186. *1* 113; *8* 40; *24a* 143; *22* 226; *24* 172.
187. *10* 127.
188. *5* 60.
189. *2* 76.
190. *8* 5 (Hannah); *11* 30.
191. *9* 173.
192. *14* 31, 139; *19* 115; *19a* 76, 142, 272; *24a* 204. On the "perfecting power" of the number 7, see above, n. 52.
193. *25* 157 (fruit); *32a* 43.
194. *24a* 158; *24c* 209; *26* 127, 128, 131; *35* #1 on Exodus vii.2.
195. *2a* 61; *20* 62; *5* 39 (rhetorical qualities).
196. *22a* 261; *26* 9; Gr. Frag. Gen. #14 (p. 237).
197. *1* 89; *2* 6; *9* 158; *13* 89 (a building), 155, 155 (Babel), 158; *17* 172 (learning); *19a* 45 (the whole universe); *22* 283; *25* 69; *29* 71 (the world). In *2* 10 Philo argues that during the second seven-year period of human life one is brought to complete perfection or consummation, because (s)he is capable of reproducing his/her likeness. (See n. 225 below.)
198. *22a* 275 (prediction).
199. *3* 35 (good or evil).
200. *10* 81.
201. *2b* 245. Similarly, of Jacob, in *16* 35.
202. *9* 159, 165.
203. *14* 139.
204. *2a* 91.
205. *9* 169.
206. *10* 94.
207. *9* 159, 160.
208. *25* 36.
209. *4* 7.
210. Ibid.
211. *4* 8.
212. *20* 53.
213. *9* 42; *13* 181; *14* 214 (by quitting the dwelling-place of the senses, i.e., by contemplation); *18* 85. On the symbolic triad of perfection (Abraham, Isaac, and Jacob), see below, n. 245.
214. *18* 270. See below, n. 245.
215. *26* 49. Thus in *14* 174-175 Philo can use τελειόω with οὐ (to fall short of perfection) to contrast it with arriving at full knowledge (ἐπιστήμη).
216. *19* 200.
217. *24a* 39.
218. *19* 13.
219. *28* 25.
220. *2b* 74.
221. *2b* 45. (See below, n. 493.)
222. Of a work begun, *22a* 141; of a vow, *24a* 9, 38.
223. *2b* 129 (quote), 130; *14* 67; *22a* 149 (quote), 152 (quote).
224. Of crops: *23* 161; *25* 154; of fruits: *24a* 204; of anything imperfect (ἄτελες) at first, but growing to perfection: *29* 71, 100.
225. *24b* 58. Cf. also *2* 10, the "perfection" of the child at puberty; see n. 197 above.
226. *22a* 288.
227. *15* 251.
228. Of the ψυχή (soul): *2b* 213; of the world in fire (according to the Stoics) *29* 99.
229. In 6 days, *23* 99; in 7 days, *24a* 58.
230. *1* 103.
231. *26* 11.
232. *15* 311.
233. *2* 1.
234. *9* 161.

235. *16* 33.
236. *6* 97.
237. *6* 174.
238. *8* 122.
239. *26* 27.
240. *9* 133, 158; *10* 135; *11* 85; *14* 73; *15* 156; *17* 115.
241. *6* 132; *9* 157, 165, 168; *11* 82, 82; *13* 72; *17* 172; *18* 24.
242. See nn. 33-35, 43 above.
243. *4* 120.
244. *11* 82.
245. *18* 12. (See nn. 208, 209 above.) On Isaac, see *5* 124-125. On the educational triad of perfection, Abraham (teaching), Isaac (nature), and Jacob (practice), see *4* 57 (and the notes in the Loeb Edition, II, 488); *19* 167-172; *20* 52-54; *21* 1; *26* 24-51; Colson's notes in Loeb, VI, x and VIII, 453-454 as well as Earp's list of passages in X, 325 n.[a] and 346 n.[a]. Note that the perfection these figures symbolize represents the acquisition of *wisdom* or *virtue* by three differing means.
246. *20* 26.
247. *6* 143; *8* 26; *15* 121.
248. *5* 64.
249. *20* 54; *24c* 69.
250. *9* 146; *24* 80.
251. *22a* 58.
252. *15* 310.
253. *7* 26.
254. *24a* 64.
255. *18* 123.
256. *5* 90.
257. *1* 42 (plants); *12* 24 (the lover of pleasure); *24a* 158, 158, 158; *25* 156, 156; *26* 127; *29* 71.
258. *20* 135.
259. *2* 80; *4* 113, 114; *8* 93; *17* 141; *24b* 32; *26* 166.
260. *2b* 47; *4* 29; *19a* 213; *24* 11; *24b* 85.
261. *17* 162.
262. *2* 23.
263. *3* 94 (vows); *13* 137 (ambitions); *15* 269; *24b* 11 and 34 (hope of offspring); *24c* 32 (oaths), 158 (hopes); *25* 29 (hopes), 209 (prayers); *26* 110 (of an early death), 142 and 149 (hopes).
264. *14* 242.
265. *1* 63; *9* 54, 141; *14* 55; *15* 116; *29* 48, 49.
266. *2b* 213; *4* 57, 129 (murderer!); *6* 85; *9* 169; *17* 207; *29* 99.
267. *2a* 97.
268. *9* 145.
269. *16* 48.
270. *26* 56.
271. *24* 200; *35* #7 on Exodus xii.5a.
272. *2b* 135, 207, 249; *4* 43, 65; *6* 96, 171; *7* 45; *9* 140, 160; *14* 73; *15* 275; *16* 137; *17* 13; *18* 122, 122, 230; *19* 213, 213; *25* 156, 156, 184; *31* (379); *34c* #104 on Genesis xxiv.18; Gr. Frag. Gen. #8 (p. 235).
273. *24c* 234.
274. *26* 161.
275. *2a* 27, 102; *2b* 35, 241; *5* 144, 175; *8* 183; *10* 64; *12* 62; *15* 156; *16* 13; *17* 41, 128; *18* 205; *21* 110; *22a* 50; 24a 11; *28* 7, 41, 55.
276. *9* 50; *18* 50, 227, 227.
277. *2b* 135; *10* 93. See below, n. 293.
278. *4* 115.
279. *5* 96; *15* 306; *16* 137.
280. *14* 199; *15* 293; *24* 178.

281. *9* 140. See note in Loeb, III, 493.
282. *9* 160.
283. *15* 125 (speech); *24b* 134 (character).
284. *1* 41 (plants); *2b* 89, 89; *14* 55, 55; *25* 156 (animals); *29* 57, 59, 60; *30* 15; *34c* #88 on Genesis xxiv.3; *35a* 21 on Exodus xxiii.27a.
285. *24b* 119; Gr. Frag. #52 on Genesis xvii.14 (p. 212).
286. *24a* 233.
287. *9* 9, 9; *12* 9; *14* 46; *16* 154, 154; *24a* 32; *31* 361.
288. *2b* 179; *3* 114; *12* 15; *17* 40; *24b* 134.
289. *19a* 10.
290. *5* 65.
291. *24b* 169.
292. *25* 112.
293. *6* 172.
294. *15* 306; *22* 96.
295. *7* 45.
296. *8* 73.
297. *4* 65.
298. *14* 73; *16* 38.
299. *18* 23.
300. *2b* 219.
301. I hope that my use of the masculine for the human in this section and elsewhere will not be taken amiss by contemporary readers. My attitude toward Philo's biases is perhaps adequately suggested elsewhere in the article.
302. *5* 64; *2b* 196 (pl.), 207 (pl.); *14* 223; *18* 24, 230; *19* 213; *19a* 33, 234.
303. *2b* 140, 140, 159; *19a* 236; *34c* #30 on Genesis xix.1 (twice).
304. *4* 43.
305. *2b* 144; *19* 213.
306. *2* 94, 94.
307. *20* 47.
308. *16* 105.
309. *8* 23.
310. *24* 252.
311. *6* 88.
312. *2b* 147. Cf. *14* 27: those who are to become wise are essentially defined as τέλειοι.
313. *8* 142.
314. *4* 8.
315. *11* 103.
316. *15* 315.
317. *24c* 140.
318. *2* 61; *2b* 244, 244, 244, 249; *4* 43 (pl.), 78, 111 (pl.), 111 (pl.), 120; *5* 60; *6* 130; *8* 154 (pl.); 9 157; *11* 148; *17* 43; *19* 177, 200 (pl.); *20* 100 (pl.); *22a* 180; *24* (201), 287 (pl.); *24a* 23; *25* 60; *27* 92 (pl.).
319. *20* 26.
320. *2* 34. Cf. *16* 138 (twice): not perfect in virtue but in some other act.
321. *2a* 55.
322. *3* 43. Cf. *18* 68: perfect offspring of the soul.
323. *19* 162.
324. *16* 90.
325. *9* 165.
326. *19a* 34.
327. *22* 159.
328. *2a* 17; *2b* 135 (pl.), 196 (pl.); *4* 10, 36 (pl.), 37 (pl.); *5* 7 (pl.), 157 (pl.); *6* 26, 95 (the beautiful); *9* 53 (pl.), 100; *14* 36, 44 (faith); *16* 45, 130, 160; *17* 43, 213 (pl.); *18* 188; *19a* 270; *21* 57 (pl.); *24a* 53 (pl.), 203 (pl.); *24c* 95, 182; *28* 21; *33* 318 (pl.).
329. *29* 50, 73.
330. *10* 128.

331. *29* 103.
332. *29* 26, 26, 26 (a quotation from Plato).
333. *32* (336).
334. *35a* #1 on Exodus xx.25b.
335. Ibid.
336. *10* 6. Cf. *17* 12: the perfect form (εἶδος) of created things.
337. *10* 4.
338. *24a* 59.
339. *5* 154.
340. *3* 109.
341. *1* 42.
342. *4* 85.
343. *19* 199.
344. *14* 166; *25* 129.
345. *2* 19; *7* 5; *11* 33. Cf. *17* 12: the perfect Logos, and *19* 198: two perfect ways of thinking (λόγοι).
346. *9* 80.
347. *3* 59 (which needs both the mind and the powers of sense-perception); *4* 10; *5* 65 (pl.), 132; *14* 96; *26* 65.
348. Perfect, full-grown in soul, *14* 208; perfect (ripe) fruits of the soul, *14* 202; perfect growth within the soul, *11* 164.
349. *5* 60; *27* 91.
350. *6* 148.
351. *8* 92; *10* 37; *19a* 235; *28* 11.
352. *8* 96.
353. *2b* 131.
354. *14* 33.
355. *4* 105.
356. *4* 60.
357. *2b* 192. Cf. *24* 63, perfect duties toward God (not divination, etc.).
358. *22a* 5.
359. *18* 230.
360. *22a* 5.
361. *8* 132; *22a* 150. Cf. *4* 132: the perfect priesthood, which legislates for reward, not punishment.
362. *15* 82.
363. *22a* 196; *24a* 262 (from impurity); *25* 189 and *26* 120 (pl., of the mind); *34c* #8(b) on Genesis xviii.6-7.
364. *10* 161; *17* 18; *23* 158.
365. *35* #7 on Exodus vii.5a (quote).
366. *4* 111.
367. *9* 127.
368. *24* 286.
369. *19* 37.
370. *8* 117 (quote), 118; *20* 31 (quote), 34, 36 (quote). In the last passage "perfect in his generation" (Gen 6:9) is explained to mean "he was not good absolutely but in comparison with the men of that time."
371. *2b* 203, (244); *8* 4; (*15* 275).
372. *20* 271.
373. *2b* 244.
374. *18* 270.
375. *12* 8. The adjective τέλειος is not applied to Jacob. But see 9 42 and nn. 213, 245 above.
376. *12* 13.
377. *4* 120.
378. *19a* 235.
379. *5* 132.
380. *2a* 91; *2b* 131, 134, 140.

381. *14* 27.
382. *5* 160.
383. *15* 121.
384. *6* 152.
385. *11* 90.
386. *9* 168.
387. *2* 94.
388. *22* 62.
389. *23* 33.
390. *18* 184; *19* 36.
391. *1* 54, 70.
392. *19* 213.
393. *2* 18.
394. *11* 115.
395. *13* 75.
396. *24* 177.
397. *18* 248.
398. *15* 275.
399. *21* 210; *22* 19.
400. *16* 148 (see note in Loeb, IV, 580); *19* 205. 7 is "more perfect" than 10; see above, n. 53.
401. *8* 81.
402. *9* 83.
403. *18* 128.
404. *26* 58.
405. *22* 123.
406. *33* 5.
407. *24a* 51.
408. *24a* 128.
409. *10* 31.
410. *20* 254.
411. *9* 18.
412. *24* 200.
413. *15* 26.
414. *15* 114.
415. *19* 39.
416. *19* 59.
417. *25* 217.
418. *20* 168.
419. *16* 19. Cf. *24b* 200: "more adult" (food).
420. *11* 48.
421. *17* 36.
422. *20* 84.
423. *2b* 100.
424. *1* 54.
425. *29* 1.
426. *2b* 176.
427. *14* 106. The answer implied in this passage is ethical: "to be by nature good . . . and worthy of blessing."
428. *24a* 171.
429. *11* 83.
430. See above, nn. 49-51, 55.
431. *1* 48.
432. *24* 205.
433. *1* 141; *17* 46 (contrasted with παιδικός). See also *22* 77: Moses' rod becomes a full-grown serpent.
434. *19a* 27. Cf. *24a* 200: the most perfect sum (πλήρωμα) of musical truths.
435. *6* 103.

436. *8* 25.
437. *3* 106.
438. *18* 240.
439. I.e., those where "perfection" is most necessary; *25* 146.
440. *11* 135.
441. *31* 358.
442. *24* 71.
443. *22a* 111.
444. *24* 272.
445. *14* 98.
446. *22a* 218.
447. *22* 155.
448. *22a* 187.
449. *19* 216.
450. *3* 9.
451. *24a* 231.
452. *20* 160.
453. *27* 57.
454. *11* 51.
455. *18* 223.
456. *10* 135.
457. *29* 15.
458. *2a* 17.
459. *19a* 22; *20* 116; *24a* 68.
460. *29* 75.
461. *18* 19.
462. *15* 91.
463. *17* 51.
464. *2a* 48.
465. *11* 94; *22* 1.
466. *23* 175.
467. *5* 132.
468. *24* 149. Cf. *17* 3: the "most profitable of virtues" (ὠφελιμωτάτην τῶν ἀρετῶν).
469. *24a* 258.
470. *8* 118.
471. *10* 128.
472. *10* 135.
473. *10* 49; *24* 35, 277.
474. *3* 86.
475. *13* 180; *23* 81.
476. *24* 18.
477. *10* 91.
478. *28* 5.
479. *15* 76.
480. *10* 66.
481. *4* 7.
482. *10* 2.
483. *1* 9, 13; *5* 154; *10* 6, 6, 131; *15* 199; *20* 2; *22a* 134 (= God's "son"); *24* 210; *29* 73.
484. *8* 106. Cf. *5* 125: nature's most perfect works.
485. *13* 97; *29* 15-16. *1* 82: heaven is the most perfect of the objects of sense.
486. *29* 41.
487. *9* 52.
488. *14* 220. The argument is that in thought the Mind should travel through man and also through the universe, the "most perfect Man."
489. *1* 143.
490. *26* 1.
491. I have included in the listing all Greek occurrences in the first ten volumes of the Loeb

series. (I have included from Vols. XI and XII only those passages where Greek fragments roughly confirm the Greek original, even though Prof. Marcus' retranslation from the Armenian is almost certainly correct in a very high percentage of cases.) Although I originally compiled my own list, I have profited greatly from comparing my notes with the very accurate work of Günter Mayer, *Index Philoneus* (Berlin/New York: Walter de Gruyter, 1974).

492. Especially the world of Ideas and the dialectic between heavenly pattern and earthly copy. For this, see Vols. XI and XII of the Loeb edition, *passim*, and such passages as *1* 16, 24-25, 29, 36, 54-55; *2* 1; *2b* 96; *3* 86; *5* 86-90; *8* 311; *11* 132, 133; *13* 73, 172; *14* 12; *18* 135, 183; *19* 188; *19a* 45; *20* 3, 84; *22a* 74-76, 127; *25* 12; *27* 3; *29* 15 (a summary of *Plato's* views). In *2b* 102, Philo interprets the tabernacle and its furniture (quoting Exod 25:40) in terms of heavenly pattern and earthly copy.

493. See above, n. 221.

494. *2b* 71; *5* 114; *15* 69-70, 85; *17* 62; *19* 225-226; *24* 37-38; *34* 86-87.

495. *1* 55; *2b* 100; *14* 34-35; *19* 148-151; *20* 122; *24a* 165; *28* 11-12; *33* 5-6; *34c* 20; *35a* 29, 40.

496. *2a* 42, 44; *5* 158-160; 7 61; *14* 2, 184-195, 214-221; *15* 69-71, 275-280; *24* 17.

497. *15* 241.

498. ἀτελής, ἀκροτελεύτιον, ἀποτελέω, ἀποτέλεσμα, ἀποτελευτάω, ἀτελεύτητος, ἀτέλεστος, διατελέω, δημοτελής, εὐτέλεια, εὐτελής, ἐντελέχεια, ἐντελεχής, ἰσοτέλεια, λυσιτελέω, λυσιτελής, λυσιτελῶς, παντέλεια, πολυτέλεια, πολυτελής, πολυτελῶς, προτέλεια, τελειογονέω, τελέω, ἐν τέλει, τελεσιουργέω, τελεσφορέω, τελεσφόρος, τελετή, τελετής, τελευταῖος, τελευτή, ὑποτελέω.

499. 13:17. Bad citizenship if "unprofitable for you."

500. 9:26. Christ has appeared at the consummation (end) of the world to put away sin.

501. 8:8 (quotation). ". . . I will establish a new covenant with the house of Israel."

502. 11:22, "Joseph, when he died. . . ."

503. 7:25. Christ is able to save completely.

504. See above, n. 492.

505. Moses, when he was about to make the tabernacle, was warned to make it according to the pattern shown him in the mountain.

506. The priests went into the first tabernacle, performing the (divine) service.

507. 3:6, 14; 6:8, 11; 7:3.

508. 3:6, ". . . if we hold fast the confidence *until the end* "; 3:14, ". . . if we hold fast the beginning of our confidence *until the end*"; 6:11, ". . . show . . . diligence in . . . the assurance of hope *until the end*"; but 6:8, ". . . whose end is to be burned," and 7:3, ". . . without beginning of days or end of life."

509. 2:10; 5:9; 7:19, 28; 9:9; 10:1, 14; 11:40; 12:23.

510. 7:19, "The law made nothing perfect"; 9:9, ". . . gifts and sacrifices that could not make perfect in conscience the one who did the service"; 10:1, ". . . the sacrifices of the law, offered continually can never make perfect those who come to them."

511. "If therefore perfection were by the Levitical priesthood. . . ."

512. A word Philo does not use.

List of Philo's Writings

Loeb vol.	Code number	Latin title	English title
I	1	*De opificio mundi*	On the Creation of the World
	2	*Legum allegoriae(rum)*, Bk. 1	Allegorical Interpretation of the Laws
	2a	Bk. 2	
	2b	Bk. 3	

II	3	*De cherubim*	On the Cherubim
	4	*De sacrificiis Abelis et Caini*	On the Sacrifices of Abel and Cain
	5	*Quod deterius potiori insidiari soleat*	The Worse Attacks the Better
	6	*De posteritate Caini*	On the Posterity and Exile of Cain
	7	*De gigantibus*	On the Giants
III	8	*Quod Deus immutabilis sit*	On the Unchangeableness of God
	9	*De agricultura*	On Husbandry
	10	*De plantatione*	On Noah's Work as a Planter
	11	*De ebrietate*	On Drunkenness
	12	*De sobrietate*	On Sobriety
IV	13	*De confusione linguarum*	On the Confusion of Tongues
	14	*De migratione Abrahami*	On the Migration of Abraham
	15	*Quis rerum divinarum heres*	Who is the Heir
	16	*De congressu quaerendae eruditionis gratia*	On the Preliminary Studies
V	17	*De fuga et inventione*	On Flight and Finding
	18	*De mutatione nominum*	On the Change of Names
	19	*De somnis,* Bk. 1	On Dreams
	19a	Bk. 2	
VI	20	*De Abrahamo*	On Abraham
	21	*De Iosepho*	On Joseph
	22	*De vita Mosis,* Bk. 1	On the Life of Moses
	22a	Bk. 2	
VII	23	*De Decalogo*	On the Decalogue
	24	*De specialibus legibus,* Bk. 1	On the Special Laws
	24a	Bk. 2	
	24b	Bk. 3	
VIII	24c	Bk. 4	
	25	*De virtutibus*	On the Virtues
	26	*De praemiis et poenis*	On Rewards and Punishments
IX	27	*Quod omnis probus liber sit*	Every Good Man is Free
	28	*De vita contemplativa*	On the Contemplative Life
	29	*De aeternitate mundi*	On the Eternity of the World
	30	*In Flaccum*	Flaccus
	31	*Apologia pro Iudaeis*	Hypothetica
	32	*De providentia,* Bk. 1	On Providence
	32a	Bk. 2	
X	33	*De legatione ad Gaium*	On the Embassy to Gaius
XI (= Supp. I)	34	*Questiones et solutiones in Genesis,* Bk. 1	Questions and Answers on Genesis
	34a	Bk. 2	
	34b	Bk. 3	
	34c	Bk. 4	
XII (= Supp. II)	35	*Questiones et solutiones in Exodum,* Bk. 1	Questions and Answers on Exodus
	35a	Bk. 2	

(Greek Fragments, listed by number and page in Vol. XII of Loeb)

11: The Melchizedek Argument of Hebrews: A Study in the Development and Circumstantial Expression of New Testament Thought

RICHARD LONGENECKER

There is probably no more enigmatic a figure in all of scripture than Melchizedek, and no more difficult a problem in biblical studies than tracing the Melchizedek tradition through its various developments in Jewish and Christian literatures. He appears in the Old Testament only in Genesis 14:18-20 and Psalm 110:4, and in the New Testament only in Hebrews 5:6, 10 and 6:20-7:28 (principally, of course, in 7:1-10). He also appears in a number of writings that can be assigned to the period of Late Judaism, with Jubilees, 1 Maccabees, The Assumption of Moses, various Targumim, Philo, and Josephus suggesting either explicitly or inferentially that he was the subject of rather fervent debate within various Jewish circles just prior to and during the first Christian century. The Talmudic writings also lend support to the existence of such a discussion and add their evidence as to an earlier Pharisaic attitude toward his person and significance. But the references and allusions to Melchizedek in the materials of Late Judaism and of later Rabbinic Judaism are at best somewhat indeterminate, allowing a wide range of opinion among scholars as to the nature of pre-Christian Jewish views on the subject. With the discovery and publication of the Melchizedek Scroll from Qumran, however, interest in the subject has been renewed and a measure of clarification has come about—both as to the attitudes toward Melchizedek within Late Judaism and (I propose) as to the employment of Melchizedek by the writer of the Letter to the Hebrews.

It is not my purpose here to take up the thorny question of the precise identification of Melchizedek in the narrative of Genesis 14, or to attempt any treatment of his significance in Psalm 110; nor, on the other hand, to comment on the employment of the Melchizedek figure in later Christian theology, whether "orthodox" or "heretical."[1] I assume that Melchizedek was originally an early Canaanite king-priest who ruled over the Palestinian city-state of Salem and who was used by God for his own purposes in dealing with Abram,[2] and that Psalm 110 was composed as something of a "royal" psalm in the time of the United Monarchy, probably during the early reign of David.[3] Beyond that, I am willing to leave the further Old Testament issues and the additional Christian materials from the patristic period on to others more qualified. What I am interested in here, and what I want to explicate in what follows, are three matters: (1) the varied attitudes taken toward Melchizedek in Late Judaism; (2) the argument of the Letter to the Hebrews in relation to these various strands of thought then current; and (3) the significance of Hebrews' Melchizedek argument for an appreciation of theological development and circumstantial expression in New Testament thought.

I

ATTITUDES TOWARD MELCHIZEDEK IN LATE JUDAISM

The expression "Late Judaism" is roughly synonymous with the somewhat misleading Christian cognomen "Intertestamental" that is widely employed to identify the period from about 200 B.C. to about A.D. 100—though, of course, "Late Judaism" has reference to events and developments within Judaism itself, apart from Christianity, that occurred from roughly the Maccabean rebellion through the first destruction of Jerusalem by the Romans. It coincides with the period of Jewish national independence (such as it was) under the Hasmoneans and the Herodians, and it bridges the span religiously between "Early Judaism" and later "Rabbinic Judaism." It is probably best known to Christians as the period that saw the rise of such groups as the Sadducees, the Pharisees, and the Essenes. And it is within such groups that various attitudes toward the person and significance of Melchizedek can be discerned.

1. *Hasmonean-Sadducean Views.* There are a number of indications in various Jewish writings that the Hasmoneans began to think of their reign in messianic terms and to justify their priestly-royal prerogatives by reference to Melchizedek, and that their successors the Sadducees continued to view matters in the same light. The writer of Jubilees, who wrote sometime during the reigns of Jonathan, Simeon, and John Hyrcanus (i.e., 152-104 B.C.), appears to have viewed the messianic kingdom as already inaugurated with the Hasmonean supremacy. This is suggested by his portrayal of the Messianic Age as a process that will come to final realization only gradually in history (23:23-30), by his depiction of the ascendancy of Levi over Judah in the messianic blessings of the patriarch Isaac (31:9-20), and by his employment of the Melchizedekian title for Jacob and his two sons, Levi and Judah: "they ordained and made him the priest of the Most High God, him and his sons for ever" (32:1)—with particular emphasis in the context upon Levi. If only we knew what had been written originally in what is now the lacuna of 13:25*a*, our understanding of Jubilees' attitude toward the Hasmonean claim would undoubtedly be clarified. Of that lacuna, however, we must speak later. Suffice it here to say, Jubilees suggests that sometime during the reign of Jonathan (152-142 B.C.), Simeon (142-134 B.C.), or

John Hyrcanus (134-104 B.C.), an identification of the Messianic Age with the Hasmonean dynasty began to be made. Such a consciousness also comes to the fore in the hymn of praise to Simeon in 1 Maccabees 14:4-15, particularly in the attribution of the words of Zechariah 8:4 and Micah 4:4 to his reign, and it may be involved as well in the designation of Simeon in 1 Maccabees 14:41 as "ethnarch and high priest for ever" (εἰς τὸν αἰῶνα).[4]

That the Hasmoneans claimed Melchizedekian support for their prerogatives is indicated rather directly in materials that have no Sadducean connections. The Assumption of Moses 6:1, for example, after detailing the sacrilege of the Seleucids and before describing Herod the Great, summarizes the Hasmonean period in the terse words: "Then there shall be raised up unto them kings bearing rule, and they shall call themselves priests of the Most High God (ἱερεὺς τοῦ θεοῦ ὑψίστου)"—the exact title of Melchizedek in Genesis 14:18. Josephus in *Antiquities* 16.163, speaking of Caesar Augustus, writes that Augustus decreed that "the Jews may follow their own customs in accordance with the law of their fathers, just as they followed them in the time of Hyrcanus, high priest of the Most High God (ἀρχιερέως θεοῦ ὑψίστου)"; and b. Rosh Hashanah 18*b* relates: "The Grecian [Seleucid] government had forbidden the mention of God's name by the Israelites, but when the government of the Hasmoneans became strong and defeated them, they ordained that they should mention the name of God even on bonds; and they used to write thus: 'In the year so-and-so of Johanan, High Priest of the Most High God'." Likewise, there are suggestions of this joining of the Melchizedekian appellative and the Hasmonean dynasty in Tos. Sotah 13:5, b. Sotah 33*a*, and Testament of Levi 18:14 (if, indeed, the Greek Testament of Levi reflects a pre-Christian stance at this point).

Psalm 110, of course, has been commonly associated with the Hasmonean rise to supremacy, usually on the basis of its acrosticon "Simeon" (*šm'n*) formed by the first letters of each of the four verses in the oracle, beginning with the word *šb,* and therefore understood as a piece of Maccabean propaganda written in support of Simeon's claim to priestly and kingly powers in 141-140 B.C.[5] The acrostic argument for Maccabean provenance, however, has been widely judged somewhat weak, and the psalm in its ascription of priesthood to a royal figure does not quite fit the Hasmoneans, who were priests by birth and required legitimacy for their royal assertions.[6] Nevertheless, as David M. Hay points out, "while the Hasmoneans probably did not compose the psalm, they probably did use it to defend their claims to priestly and royal prerogatives."[7] Mattathias' initial rebellion against the Seleucids is supported in 1 Maccabees 2:26 and 54 by appeal to the action of the righteous and zealous priest Phinehas, who received for himself and his posterity the promise of a perpetual priesthood because of his valiant activity in rooting out apostasy and protecting his people (cf.

Num 25:12-13). But Phinehas was not a king! Thus when Jonathan, Simeon, John Hyrcanus, and their successors assumed kingly powers, it became necessary to find a more substantial biblical prototype.

It was just such a prototype that the Hasmoneans and their Sadducean descendants seem to have found in the Canaanite king-priest of Genesis 14:18-20. Melchizedek had already been disinfected of his earlier Canaanite associations and rebaptized into the religion of Israel by his employment in Psalm 110, and they could therefore probably easily reemploy him in support of their priestly-kingly position. It therefore seems that we should understand that both Psalm 110 and its Melchizedekian ascription "entered the NT age trailing associations of the dusty glory of the Hasmoneans."[8]

2. *Quietistic Reactions.* Not everyone within Late Judaism, however, seems to have been prepared to concede the legitimacy of the Hasmonean-Sadducean claim or to accept their appeal to Melchizedek in support of that claim. The copyist of the Book of Jubilees evidently could not, as is indicated by the lacuna of an entire line at what should be Jubilees 13:25*a* —the line that in context undoubtedly spoke originally of the meeting of Abraham with Melchizedek. Just when this lacuna first appeared in the text of Jubilees, of course, is somewhat difficult to determine exactly. The Latin version of Jubilees offers no help here, for only about one fourth of the text of Jubilees is extant in that version and chapter 13 is not one of those portions preserved. Nor does the existing Greek fragment of Jubilees (i.e., 2:2-21), or the Greek quotations of the book in the patristic writings, or the recently discovered Aramaic portions, since none of these materials contains either this particular verse or its context. Nevertheless, the fact that in all four of the extant Ethiopic manuscripts of Jubilees there is a lacuna at what should be 13:25*a*—with no such lacuna appearing anywhere else in the entire text—suggests that the lacuna was present in the Greek manuscript of the book from which the Ethiopic version was translated, and that probably it appeared as well in an Aramaic transcription.

The question, of course, is: How should we understand the lacuna of Jubilees 13:25*a*? Certainly the original author of Jubilees, as R. H. Charles commented, "would naturally be interested in the first man who bore the title assumed by his heroes, the Maccabees."[9] But what about the copyist? Why did he leave the line at 13:25*a* blank? It seems too much to believe that it occurred only through "technical inadvertence," as some have rather lightly proposed. Evidently the copyist was so opposed to something in the original text itself or to some contemporary usage of the text that he could not bring himself even to copy out the line that spoke of Abraham's meeting with Melchizedek. And in view of the Hasmonean-Sadducean employment of the Melchizedekian figure in support of their cultic-royal prerogatives, it does not seem too much to postulate that at least one quietistic Jew with a priestly background (perhaps Essene and/or Qumranite), while generally applauding the message of Jubilees, found the explicit reference to Melchizedek in Jubilees 13:25*a* just too much to take—either because of what it said directly or of how it was then being used.

The Assumption of Moses, written sometime between A.D. 6-30, probably characterizes such a quietistic attitude as well, though in this case from a more Pharisaic perspective than the priestly stance of either the author or the copyist of Jubilees. The Assumption of Moses expresses its attitude toward the Hasmonean claims not only in its very brief reference to Hasmonean supremacy, saying only in 6:1*a* (as noted above), "Then there shall be raised up unto them kings bearing rule, and they shall call themselves priests of the Most High God," but also more directly in its rather caustic comment by way of evaluation in 6:1*b* , "And they shall assuredly work iniquity in the holy of holies."

3. *Pharisaic Stances.* The Pharisaic materials treat Melchizedek in three ways. In b. Nedarim 32*b* he is identified as Shem, the son of Noah, by Rabbi Zechariah in the name of the early second-century teacher Rabbi Ishmael; and this is supported by Targum Neofiti on Genesis 14:18, "And Melchizedek, king of Jerusalem—that is the great Shem—brought bread and wine, for he was a priest and exercised the sovereign priesthood before the Most High God,"[10] and by Targum Pseudo-Jonathan on the same passage, "And Melchizedek, who is Shem, the son of Noah, went out to meet Abraham."[11] In Song of Songs Rabbah 2.13.4 and b. Sukkah 52*b* Melchizedek is included among the four eschatological craftsmen (i.e., the *ḥršym)* by whom the Age to Come is to be built: "It is written in Zechariah [2:3]: 'The Eternal showed me four workmen'. R Hanna ben Gizna says in the name of R. Simeon the Hasid: 'these four workmen are the Messiah the son of David, the Messiah the son of Joseph, Elijah and Melchizedek' " —though later in b. Sukkah 52*b* Rabbi Shesheth is recorded as strenuously objecting to the inclusion of Melchizedek. And, finally, in Leviticus Rabbah 25.6 and b. Nedarim 32*b*, Melchizedek is portrayed as an irreverent priest who relinquished the rights of his office to Abraham because of his inappropriate action:

> Rabbi Zechariah said in the name of Rabbi Ishmael: God wanted to derive the priestly line from Shem, as it is said, "He was priest of God Most High" [Gen. 14:18]. But God derived (the priestly line) from Abraham, when Shem placed the blessing of Abraham before the praise of God, as it is said, "Blessed be Abram by God Most High, maker of heaven and earth; and blessed be God Most High" [Gen. 14:19].
>
> Said Abraham to him: "Does one place the blessing of a servant before that of his master?"
>
> Immediately (the priesthood) was given to Abraham, as it is said, "The Lord says to my lord: 'Sit at my right hand, until I make your

> enemies your footstool' " [Ps. 110:1]. And after this it is written, "The Lord was sworn and will not change his mind, 'Thou art a priest forever after the order of Melchizedek' " [Ps. 110:4]. This means, on account of what Melchizedek had said. And that is why it is written, "He was a priest of God Most High" [Gen. 14:18]. *He* was a priest, but his descendants were not priests.

While there may be "nothing more than innocent *midrashic* play in the identification of Melchizedek with Shem,"[12] the polemical tone is strong in the disparagement of Melchizedek's eschatological status and in the renunciation of his continuing priesthood. Perhaps also, on reevaluation, it is present as well in the Melchizedek-Shem equation. But against whom is the polemic directed? Louis Ginzberg, R. Travers Herford, Marcel Simon, and many others[13] have seen it as being against the Christian employment of Melchizedek in the Letter to the Hebrews and as continued in Justin Martyr's *Dialogue with Trypho* 19 and 33: Melchizedek, priest of the Most High God, a foreigner by birth, sees humbled before him one whom the chosen people claimed as their father and whom the Christians now recognized as such; he is the true father of the Gentiles, of whom the titles are in consequence older than those of Israel; in his person, the Gentiles are mingled with the church, which triumphs over the Jews.[14] Kaufmann Kohler, on the other hand, viewed the polemic as directed against "Jewish propagandists of Alexandria, who were eager to win proselytes for Judaism without submitting them to the rite of circumcisions," and who therefore appealed to Melchizedek in support of their "cosmopolitan monotheism."[15]

The problem with viewing the polemic of b. Nedarin 32*b* and its parallels as being directed initially or principally against Christians is, as Victor Aptowitzer and Hans Windisch noted long ago, that there is nothing in the statement of Rabbi Zechariah given in the name of Rabbi Ishmael that specifically interacts with the characterization of Melchizedek in the Letter to the Hebrews.[16] And to speak of a "cosmopolitan monotheism" among the Jews of Alexandria that was prepared to omit the practice of circumcision by appeal to a universal Melchizedekian figure is to deduce from later Christian sources what the arguments of the Jewish propagandists of Alexandria must have been—but totally without warrant. Certainly Philo never thought of an allegorical understanding of the Mosaic law as setting aside its literal practice; in De migratione Abrahami 92, in fact, he specifically insists that though circumcision should be understood allegorically, it must be practiced literally.

It therefore seems that we must interpret the Pharisaic stances with regard to Melchizedek as arising initially in opposition to the Hasmonean-Sadducean preemption of this Old Testament king-priest in support of their own priestly-kingly prerogatives—though, of course, it may also have been expressive of their attitude later toward the Christians. Or, as Jakob Petuchowski cogently suggests: "If, then, we find Rabbi Ishmael, in the second century C.E., making a statement the import of which is to make impossible the claim that the established levitical line can be superseded by another 'after the order of Melchizedek,' the Rabbi may well have given expression to the opposition voiced against the Hasmonean use of Psalm 110 by the early Hasidim, and transmitted by the Pharisees. . . . The Pharisaic-rabbinic attempts to put the old priest-king of Salem in his place considerably ante-date the second century polemics against Christianity."[17]

4. *The Evidence from Qumran.* Melchizedek is mentioned in two of the scrolls that represent the distinctive views of the covenanters of Qumran: the Genesis Apocryphon from Cave 1 (1QApoc) and the Melchizedek Scroll from Cave 11 (11QMelch). 1QApoc 22:14-17 retells the biblical story of Abraham's encounter with Melchizedek, without embellishment and with the inclusion of the ascription "Priest of God Most High." But beyond that, it adds nothing to our understanding of the person or significance of Melchizedek in Jewish sectarian circles. With 11QMelch, however, the situation is quite different.

In 1956 Bedouin shepherds found thirteen fragments of a single scroll in what is now known as Cave 11 at Qumran. When pieced together, the fragments were found to comprise the better part of one column of text made up of twenty-six lines, with extensive lacunae both within and between the lines. One third of the material in the reconstructed column consists of Old Testament quotations (i.e., Lev 25:9-10, 13; Deut 15:2; Ps 7:8-9; 82:1-2; Isa 52:7; 61:1), with the remainder being an exposition on these testimonia verses dealing with the final salvation of the elect and the retribution that will be meted out upon the wicked. The text was first published by A. S. van der Woude in 1965, together with a German translation and explanatory annotations.[18] Since then, of course, it has become the subject of extensive investigation and discussion.

Melchizedek (*mlky sdk*) first emerges in the scroll's portrayal of the final eschatological drama at line 5, and thereafter he appears repeatedly as the one who brings back the elect, who proclaims liberty, who makes atonement for those bound by the powers of wickedness, and who executes judgment on Belial and his band of perverse spirits. Lines 10 and 11*a,* however, constitute the most significant section of the scroll for our purposes and have become the focus of scholarly debate. Quoting Psalm 82:1-2, the lines read (*à la* van der Woude's translation): "as it is written [line 10] concerning him in the hymns of David, who says: 'The heavenly one (*'lwhym*) standeth in the congregation of God; among the heavenly ones (*'lwhym*) he judgeth', and concerning him he says: 'Above them [line 11] return thou on high; God shall judge the nations'." Van der Woude argues that here Psalm 82:1-2 is applied by the writer of the scroll to Melchizedek, with the first *'lwhym* designating Melchizedek himself and the second employment of *'lwhym* referring to angels of lower rank than Melchizedek. His reasons for so understanding the passage are basically four: (1) that the expression "concerning him" (*'lyn*) has as its logical antecedent the Melchizedek of lines 5 through 9 immediately preceding; (2) that God is consistently designated elsewhere in the column not by *'lwhym* but by *'l*; (3) that line 13 expressly differentiates Melchizedek from God in the activity of judging ("Melchizedek will avenge with the vengeance of the judgments of God"), which distinction allows for understanding a similar distinction in lines 10-11*a*; and (4) that the motif of the return to heaven by the *'lwhym* would have been understood by Jews of the day most readily in terms of a return of angels. As A. S. van der Woude therefore understands the lines, Melchizedek is depicted as a Heavenly Redeemer Figure ("ein himmlische Erlösergestalt") who functions as an Archangel Warrior with certain priestly characteristics. And in this judgment van der Woude has been substantially joined by such scholars as Martin de Jonge,[19] Yigael Yadin,[20] Joseph Fitzmyer,[21] and F. du Toit Laubscher[22]—though without always continuing the identification of Melchizedek with the archangel Michael, as van der Woude originally proposed.

Recently Jean Carmignac has arrived at an understanding of 11QMelch that is sharply at variance with the view proposed by van der Woude.[23] According to Carmignac, the principal theme of the so-called Melchizedek Scroll is not Melchizedek but rather the execution of judgment by God himself upon the powers of Belial and the consequent liberation of the righteous. Carmignac therefore insists that the lacuna of line 9 allows for another subject other than Melchizedek as the antecedent for the expression "concerning him" of line 10, which antecedent must be God himself. Further, by the double use of *'lwhym* in line 10 the writer is not referring first to Melchizedek and then to the angelic hosts but first to God and then to the saints of the congregation, who will be assumed into the Messianic Age with God's judgment upon the nations. The distinction made by many commentators between *'lwhym* and *'l* Carmignac believes to be both inexact and inappropriate, since the writer of the scroll is only utilizing *'lwhym* where the tetragrammaton appears in the biblical text and prefers to employ *'l* where he comments himself—without any intended difference of meaning or designation. In addition, Melchizedek is not portrayed in the scroll as the king-priest of Abraham's day but is thought of as someone existing within the Qumran community itself; he is not some sort of celestial being comparable to an angel, but was a historical person recognized by the sect as reproducing the character of the biblical Melchizedek. He was thought of by the convenanters at Qumran as a "King of Justice," probably a king or military leader, who may be identical with the "Messiah of the Spirit" (*mšyḥ hrwḥ*) of line 18 and who in turn may well be identical with one of the messiahs expected at Qumran.

Indeed, Carmignac may be right. There are just too many lacunae within and between the lines of the text to be dogmatic. Yet the bulk of scholarship to date has judged his case to be weak, and the more natural reading of the text in its present form supports the interpretation of A. S. van der Woude *et al.* It appears, therefore, that what we have in 11QMelch is a partial portrayal of the messianology of the Qumran sectarians at (probably) some later time in the history of the community, when such an intensive antagonism to the Melchizedekian figure as caused the scribe who copied Jubilees to omit 13:25*a* was somewhat abated and at a time roughly contemporaneous with the rise of Christianity. At such a time, it seems, Melchizedek was brought back into the messianic expectations of the covenanters at Qumran and thought of in terms of an Archangel Warrior-Redeemer from Heaven who in making atonement for sins was to exhibit certain priestly characteristics.

5. *Philo of Alexandria.* Philo (*ca.* 20 B.C.-A.D. 50) refers to Melchizedek in three of his extant writings: *Legum allegoriae* 3.79-82, *De congressu eruditionis gratia* 99 and *De Abrahamo* 235, though without naming him in the latter. In *De cong.* 99 and *De Abr.* 235, Melchizedek is presented as a historical personage; in *Leg. all.* 3.79-82, however, all of the details of his appearance in Genesis 14 are employed to portray him as a representation of the eternal Logos. Three matters in Philo's treatment deserve comment here. In the first place, the name "Melchizedek" is treated etymologically in *Leg. all.* 3.79-82 to mean "Righteous King" (βασιλεὺς δίκαιος) and the title "King of Salem" to mean "King of Peace" (βασιλεὺς τῆς εἰρήνης). Secondly, evidently building upon the fact that Melchizedek is the first priest mentioned in holy scripture, all three of Philo's references highlight the uniqueness of Melchizedek's priesthood. In *De cong.* 99 and *De Abr.* 235, his historical priesthood is described as being a "self-taught" (αὐτομαθῆ) and "instinctive" (αὐτοδίδακτον) priesthood; while in *Leg. all.* 3.79-82 the fact that he was the first priest in scripture and therefore without antecedents leads to the conclusion that he was the Logos. And thus, thirdly, Melchizedek became for Philo the manifestation of the high-priestly Logos who intoxicates the soul with esoteric virtues.

Many commentators, of course, have focused upon Philo's treatment of Melchizedek as a representation of the eternal Logos. Hans Windisch in 1913, for example, correlated the employment of Melchizedek in *Leg. all.* 3.79-82 with the priestly Logos speculation of *De vit. Mos.* 2.2-7 and argued that such a view must have been fairly widespread and should be seen as the primary basis for the Melchizedekian Christology of the Letter to the Hebrews.[24] But in 1970 Ronald Williamson demonstrated that though Logos speculations play a part in both Philo and Hebrews (more prominently in Philo, where the word λόγος appears some 1,300 times, than in Hebrews), "Philo and the Writer of Hebrews represent quite different (perhaps even entirely unconnected) strands in the intricate pattern of Jewish-Christian

Logos speculation."[25] In fact, as Williamson went on to show, Hebrews seems to owe little to Philonic thought beyond the rather common etymological treatment of the names "Melchizedek" and "Salem" and a general appreciation for the uniqueness of the person and priesthood of Melchizedek. In his employment of etymology and his general appreciation of Melchizedek's uniqueness, therefore, Philo seems to be reflecting attitudes that were fairly widespread among Jews of his day (as will be noted again in the discussion of Josephus below), though it may be questioned as to just how much he may have represented or influenced other Jews, whether Hebraic or Hellenistic, with respect to his Logos speculations and his treatment of Melchizedek along these lines.

6. *Flavius Josephus.* Josephus (*ca.* A.D. 37-100) speaks of Melchizedek in two passages of his four compositions: The *Jewish War* 6.10.1, §438 and *The Antiquities of the Jews* 1.10.2, §180-181. In relating the history of Jerusalem, Josephus says:

> Its original founder was a Canaanite chieftain (Χαναναίων δυνάστης, "a potent man among the Canaanites"), who was called in the native tongue "Righteous King" (βασιλεὺς δίκαιος), for such indeed he was. In virtue thereof he was the first to officiate as priest of God and, being the first to build the temple, gave the city, previously called Solyma [i.e., the biblical "Salem"], the name "Jerusalem."[26]

And in recounting the story of Abraham's encounter with Melchizedek in Genesis 14, he writes:

> He was received by the king of Solyma [Salem], Melchizedek; this name means "Righteous King" (βασιλεὺς δίκαιος), and such he was by common consent, insomuch that for this reason he was moreover made priest of God. Solyma was in fact the place afterwards called Hierosolyma [the Hellenized form of "Jerusalem"]. Now this Melchizedek hospitably entertained Abraham's army, providing abundantly for all their needs, and in the course of the feast he began to extol Abraham and to bless God for having delivered his enemies into his hand. Abraham then offered him the tithe of the spoil, and he accepted the gift.[27]

For Josephus, then, Melchizedek was a Canaanite chieftain who became a priest of Israel's God because of his uprightness of character. He was the first to officiate as a priest of God at Jerusalem, actually building there the first temple to God, and his name means etymologically "Righteous King." In addition, Josephus refers to Melchizedek's blessing first Abraham and then God, but he does not elaborate any Pharisaic polemic against Melchizedek on this basis.

The problem with Josephus' treatment of Melchizedek is, of course, determining to what extent the historian is adjusting first-century Jewish views for the ears of his Roman audience. How many Jews of that day, for instance, would have spoken of a Canaanite chieftain as the first to build a temple at Jerusalem? And is not the portrayal of Melchizedek's extolling Abraham, for which reason Abraham reciprocates by offering him a tithe of the spoil, more propaganda than conviction? Nevertheless, the fact that Josephus speaks of Melchizedek as a Canaanite chieftain, of the priority and uniqueness of his priesthood, and of the etymological significance of his name indicates that at least one first-century Jew thought of Melchizedek along these lines, and there may have been others who did as well.

Summation. What, then, can be said regarding Melchizedek in Late Judaism? No longer can it be assumed that "the normal idea in late Judaism" was that Psalm 110:1 describes a heavenly monarch, as has been commonly proposed,[28] or that Melchizedek was a quite insignificant figure during the first century, as has been sometimes stated.[29] Rather, Psalm 110 seems to have "entered the NT age trailing associations of the dusty glory of the Hasmoneans,"[30] and the person and significance of Melchizedek seem to have been hotly disputed on all sides. For the Hasmoneans and their Sadducean successors, he was the prototype of their priestly-kingly prerogatives; for certain quietists drawn from both Sadducean and Pharisaic backgrounds, such Hasmonean associations were personally revolting; for the Pharisees, he was to be identified with Shem and to be demoted from any continuing priestly succession because of his irreverence; for Philo, he was mainly the manifestation of the eternal Logos; for Josephus, he was an early Canaanite chieftain who became God's priest at Jerusalem because of his piety; and for the covenanters at Qumran, he was a heavenly and eschatological Archangel Warrior-Redeemer who exercised certain priestly characteristics in atoning for sin. The list could probably be extended if only more of the writings from Late Judaism were extant.[31] Nonetheless, though we know only in part, it is against such a background that we must consider the treatment of Melchizedek in the Letter to the Hebrews.

II

THE TREATMENT OF MELCHIZEDEK IN THE LETTER TO THE HEBREWS

A rather radical reevaluation of the Letter to the Hebrews has taken place during the past two decades, due principally to the discoveries at Qumran but also due in large measure to renewed study of the relation of Hebrews to Philo and Philonic thought. Based on the striking parallels between the distinctive tenets of the Qumran community and the argument of Hebrews, Yigael Yadin insisted in 1958 that "the addressees of the Epistle must have been a group of Jews originally belonging to the Dead Sea Sect who were converted to Christianity carrying with them some of their previous beliefs."[32] Shortly thereafter, Ceslas Spicq, impressed by Yadin's evidence, retracted in 1959 his earlier Philonic approach in favor of a position that lays emphasis upon such parallels, while still holding to a degree of Alexandrian influence on the letter through Apollos its author,[33] and John Wick Bowman sought to popularize what he calls an "Essene Thesis" in his 1962 "Layman's Bible Commentary" on the letter.[34] Running concurrent to such studies based on the Dead Sea materials, though working independently, C. K. Barrett argued in 1954 that with regard to eschatology "certain features of Hebrews which have often been held to have been derived from Alexandrian Platonism were in fact derived from apocalyptic symbolism,"[35] and G. B. Caird asserted in 1959 that the scriptural exegesis of Hebrews, rather than being "Alexandrian and fantastic," was in reality "one of the earliest and most successful attempts to define the relation between the Old and New Testaments, and that a large part of the value of the book is to be found in the method of exegesis which was formerly dismissed with contempt."[36] In fact, in what is probably the most extensive and penetrating analysis to date of the linguistic, conceptual, and hermeneutical affinities between Philo and Hebrews, Ronald Williamson has argued in a work published in 1970 that Hebrews "differs radically from the outlook and attitude of Philo. Neither in his basic judgment about the essential character of the O.T. nor in his chief method of scriptural exegesis does the Writer of Hebrews appear to owe anything to Philo."[37]

Not everyone, of course, agrees with what may be called "the Qumran hypothesis" for the Letter to the Hebrews. Some have overplayed it,[38] and some have denied it.[39] Nonetheless, I believe that it provides a better basis for the interpretation of Hebrews than any other proposed to date, and therefore I suggest in particular that in 11QMelch we have an important key for the understanding of the treatment of Melchizedek in the letter. Particularly is this so, I propose, in the following four areas.

1. *The Place of Melchizedek in the Structure and Thought of Hebrews.* The Letter to the Hebrews is unique both in the emphasis it gives to the priesthood of the Son and in its explication of this priesthood as being "after the order of (κατὰ τὴν τάξιν) Melchizedek." The focal point of and the watershed for the exposition of chapters 1-10, in fact, is the Melchizedekian argument of chapter 7, culminating, as it does, the discussion of the superior priesthood of Jesus that was mentioned in 2:17-3:1 and then developed in 4:14-5:10, and preparing the way for the detailing of Christ's high-priestly ministration in 8:1-10:39. The questions have always been, however: What gave rise to such a high-priestly Christology? and, further: Why did the writer climax his exposition with the Melchizedekian argument? Some commentators view these questions as only two parts of the same basic

issue, connecting the high-priestly motif and the Melchizedekian argument in such a fashion that what is said about the one applies also to the other. Others, rightly I believe, consider two matters to be involved here.

As for the high-priestly motif of 3:1*b* and 4:14-5:10, it may well be that Hebrews is unique only in the emphasis given. Olaf Moe has demonstrated that the idea of the priesthood of Jesus lies implicit, at least, elsewhere in the New Testament;[40] Hugh Montefiore has related the priestly ascription of Jesus in Hebrews to the consciousness of Jesus as portrayed in the Gospels;[41] and George Buchanan, following E. Brandenburger, has built a case for the confessional nature of Hebrews 5:7 ("Who during the days of his flesh offered up prayers and petitions. . . .") and of Hebrews 5:8-9, thereby rooting in the early church some consciousness of a high-priestly activity for the Christ.[42] Indeed, therefore, there are reasons to believe that the high-priestly motif of Hebrews is unique in the New Testament not in the fact of its appearance but in the emphasis it receives. But with regard to the Melchizedekian argument of Hebrews, its uniqueness resides not just in emphasis but in the very fact of its employment, for nowhere else does it appear in the New Testament materials.

With 11QMelch in hand, however, we now have a plausible explanation as to why the writer to the Hebrews built his argument in such a manner—if, that is, "the Qumran hypothesis" be anywhere close to the mark. As Delcor argues:

> Indeed, since Melchizedek played an eschatological and celestial role in the speculations of the members of the Qumran community, it was quite normal for the author of an epistle addressed to priests of an Essene origin to use this theologoumenon as a pivot for his argument. It was a proof of apologetic skill to take his starting-point for an exposition of Christ's priesthood in the very beliefs shared by those with whom he was discussing the question of Melchizedek who was to play a role at the time of the judgment in the eschatological age.[43]

What the writer to the Hebrews seems to be doing is not only climaxing his presentation of Jesus as high priest in 3:1*b* and 4:14-5:10 with the Melchizedekian argument, but also culminating his portrayal of the superiority of the Son to angels in chapters 1 and 2—and all with an eye to what his addressees may have held in great esteem prior to their conversion to Christianity, and now were being tempted to return to. In so doing, of course, he was speaking circumstantially. But also, in so doing, he was attempting to direct his readers' attention back to what he believed to be the true significance of the Melchizedekian figure of Genesis 14:18-20 and Psalm 110:4, though of this we must speak later in what follows below.

2. *The Initial Hesitancy of the Writer in Presenting his Melchizedekian Argument.* The first reference to Melchizedek in Hebrews is the quotation of Psalm 110:4 in Hebrews 5:6. Then, after two short confessional bits

in 5:7 and 5:8-9 (*à la* Brandenburger and Buchanan), the writer comes to the apex of his presentation in 5:10: "And he was designated by God to be high priest, 'after the order of [κατὰ τὴν τάξιν, perhaps best rendered "in line with" or "just like"] Melchizedek'." Yet though he has come to the climax of his argument, he immediately backs off from the discussion, saying "περὶ οὗ we have much to say, but it is hard to explain because you are slow to learn" (v. 11). There then follows a rebuke of the addressees' inability to understand and a warning regarding apostasy (5:12-6:20), after which the writer takes up the Melchizedek argument with great relish in chapter 7.

The question, of course, is: Why this initial hesitancy to enter directly into the full-blown portrayal of Melchizedek as given eventually in chapter 7? If the pronoun of περὶ οὗ in 5:11 is understood as a neuter relative pronoun, then the reference would be back to the whole discussion of high priesthood, and the writer would be saying, in effect, that the topic of the priestly nature of Jesus is difficult. But the use of the neuter relative pronoun to capture the entirety of a previous discussion is not really in the style of Hebrews elsewhere. If the οὗ is understood as masculine, Christ as typified by Melchizedek may be what he had in mind as that which is difficult to present—and many commentators would readily agree. But the masculine relative pronoun could just as readily refer to its immediate antecedent, "Melchizedek." Linguistically, this is preferable. And in light of the variety of attitudes toward Melchizedek in Late Judaism—and particularly in view of a possible early ambivalence toward him at Qumran, but a later near-veneration—such a reading has much to commend it. The writer is dealing not only with a topic about which there seems to have been a great many conflicting opinions in his day, but he is also addressing people who prior to their conversion probably held Melchizedek in very high esteem. He is at the heart of his argument, but he is also at a crucial point of difference between the Christian faith which he is calling his addressees to reaffirm and their old allegiances to which they are being enticed again. And in such a situation, his initial hesitancy to elaborate a Melchizedekian argument is somewhat understandable.

3. *The Biblical Argument of the Writer with Respect to Melchizedek.* The Letter to the Hebrews is structured along the lines of an "anticipation-consummation" theme. From the perspective of the Messiah's presence among his people in "these last days," Israel's life and worship are viewed as preparatory for the coming of the Lord's Christ. A more profound significance is seen in the prophetic words and the redemptive experiences recorded in scripture, and these words and events are understood to be looking forward to the consummation of God's salvific program in the work and person of Jesus. For the author of Hebrews, as B. F. Westcott has aptly pointed out, "the O.T. does not simply contain prophecies, but . . . it is one

vast prophecy, in the record of national fortunes, in the ordinances of a national Law, in the expression of a national hope. Israel in its history, in its ritual, in its ideal, is a unique enigma among the peoples of the world, of which the Christ is the complete solution."[44]

In spelling out this theme, the argument of the letter is built around five biblical portions: (1) a catena of verses drawn from the Psalms, 2 Samuel 7, and Deuteronomy 32 (LXX and 4QDeut), upon which Hebrews 1:3-2:4 is based; (2) Psalm 8:4-6, upon which Hebrews 2:5-18 is based; (3) Psalm 95:7-11, upon which Hebrews 3:1-4:13 is based; (4) Psalm 110:4, upon which Hebrews 4:14-7:28 is based; and (5) Jeremiah 31:31-34, upon which Hebrews 8:1-10:39 is based.[45] All the exhortations of Hebrews 11-13 depend upon the exposition of these five biblical portions, and all other verses quoted in the letter are ancillary to these.

In approaching each biblical portion, the writer to the Hebrews asks basically the same question—and always from a Christocentric perspective: What do these enigmatic passages really mean when viewed from a Christian perspective? What do the scriptures mean when they speak of God's Son (Ps 2:7; 2 Sam 7:14), of One whom all the angels of God are to worship (Deut 32:43 LXX and 4QDeut), and of One who is addressed as God by God, yet distinguished from God (Ps 45:6-7; 102:25-27; 110:1)? What does the psalmist mean when he talks about man's creatureliness and subordination, yet also of his destined glory, honor, and universal authority (Ps 8:4-6)? What does the psalmist mean when he speaks about entering God's rest (Ps 95:7-11)? What did Jeremiah mean by a New Covenant (Jer 31:31-34)? And in Hebrews 7 he does the same with respect to Melchizedek.

George Caird has somewhat overstated the case in arguing that "it is important to recognize that throughout his treatment of Melchizedek our author is concerned *solely* with the exegesis of Ps. 110,"[46] for the narrative of Genesis 14:18-20—both in what is said about Melchizedek and what is not—plays a significant role in the author's argument as well. But Caird is quite right to insist that "he carries us back to the story of Genesis 14 not to compose a fanciful and allegorical *midrash* on that chapter after the manner of Philo, but rather because he wishes to answer the very modern question: 'What did the words "priest for ever after the order of Melchizedek" mean to the psalmist who wrote them?' "[47]

The writer to the Hebrews is working with two traditions. In the first place, he accepts Psalm 110 as being messianic, as has become traditional within the church (e.g., Acts 2:34-35) and as credited to the impetus of Jesus himself (cf. Mark 12:36, par.), and he seeks to explicate verse 4 of that psalm along these lines. Secondly, he seems to have an eye toward the figure of Melchizedek as revered at Qumran. On the basis, therefore, of his Christian perspectives, in line with certain current and widespread Jewish exegetical procedures,[48] and probably with a view to his addressees' understanding of the enigmatic personage of Genesis 14:18-20, he asks: Who is this Melchizedek and what was the nature of his priesthood—particularly in view of the fact that the psalmist speaks of him in a messianic psalm? And, further: How does he serve as a prototype of the Christ? And how can Jesus, the Messiah and Son of God, be compared to him?

We need not here become diverted into a psychoanalysis of the psalmist's intention at this point, as though millennia later we could assemble the exact details of his consciousness when writing. Nor need we become carried away with the writer's allegorical-etymological treatment of the name "Melchizedek" and the title "King of Salem." As we have seen above, Josephus as well as Philo can treat Melchizedek's title in this fashion, which indicates something of the widespread nature of the practice, and, as Richard Hanson points out, our author's treatment of these names is "so simple and obvious" that their employment hardly signals anything specifically Alexandrian or Philonic.[49] For the writer to the Hebrews, the Melchizedek of Genesis 14 is an enigma that finds its solution in Psalm 110:4—but only when Psalm 110 is recognized as having messianic relevance. From this Christian view of the psalm, the typological correspondences that lie inherent in the redemptive history of Genesis 14 can be drawn out and a fuller sense in the narrative explicated by means of commonly accepted exegetical procedures.

The writer to the Hebrews, it seems, did not consider himself to be inventing a new interpretation or employing any deviant exegetical procedures. He was simply extending the application of a psalm that had already been identified within the church as having messianic relevance, and doing so with an eye to the interests and appreciation of his readers. In the process, of course, he employed a mild allegorical-etymological treatment of the name "Melchizedek" and the title "King of Salem" (7:2), but that seems to have been to some extent common in his day, and he argued for the eternality of Melchizedek on the basis of the silence of scripture as to his ancestors and descendants (7:3), but the principle *quod non in thora non in mundo* was also quite widespread in the hermeneutics of the day.[50] Given his presuppositions, his precedents, and his audience, in fact, our author's exposition of the Melchizedekian priesthood of Jesus may be judged to be quite straightforward and telling.

4. *The Theological Significance of the Melchizedek-Christ Comparison in Hebrews.* The writer to the Hebrews seems to have found himself confronted by two basic necessities: (1) the need to support a high-priestly acclamation of Jesus the Messiah on some explicit biblical basis, for certainly being from the tribe of Judah our Lord had no inherited priestly rights; and (2) the need to set out the superiority of Jesus the high-priestly Messiah over the Archangel Warrior-Redeemer figure of Qumran messianology, who was evi-

dently being turned to again by his addressees in their desperation to find something or someone upon whom to build their hopes. What priestly claims were made for Jesus prior to our writer's time were evidently made principally on a functional rather than a speculative basis (e.g., Gal 3:10-14; Rom 3:21-26; 2 Cor 5:18-21; Eph 5:2). But our writer was not willing to leave it at that. Having accepted Psalm 110 as possessing messianic relevance, he found in verse 4 the explicit biblical support he needed for a high-priestly Christology. This seems to have been his own contribution to the ongoing development of early Christian apologetic, which involved methodologically only a broadening of focus from verse 1 to include also verse 4 in an already accepted messianic portion. In so doing, of course, Melchizedek became important to him as a prototype of messianic redemption.

In agreement with his addressees, he acknowledges the legitimacy of considering Melchizedek a heavenly figure of continuing priestly significance.[51] This is indicated most clearly in the statements of 7:3, "Without father, without mother, without genealogy, without beginning of days or end of life, like the son of God he remains a priest forever." The verse may very well be poetic in structure, originally appearing in some such form as the following:

> ἀπάτωρ, ἀμήτωρ, ἀγενεαλόγητος,
> μήτε ἀρχὴν ἡμερῶν μήτε ζωῆς τέλος ἔχων,
> ἀφωμοιωμένος δὲ τῷ υἱῷ τοῦ θεοῦ,
> μένει ἱερεὺς εἰς τὸ διηνεκές.[52]

Such a structure suggests that these words were drawn, either wholly or in part, from some previous oral or written midrashic treatment of Genesis 14:18-20—perhaps even from a catechetical or hymnodic portion employed previously by his addressees. But whether our author used an earlier formulation which may have been known to his addressees or composed the wording himself, there can be no doubt from his manner of usage that he had at least some commitment to what is said. And though some have argued that the statements have reference to Melchizedek's priestly qualifications alone and not at all to his person,[53] it is by far more natural to read them as referring to his person. The whole discussion of 7:1-10 is, in fact, encapsulated in the exclamation of 7:4*a* : "Just think how great he was!" And thus the writer speaks of Melchizedek in 7:2 as the "King of Righteousness" (βασιλεὺς δικαιοσύνης) and the "King of Peace" (βασιλεὺς εἰρήνης), and in 7:4-10 as one who is greater than Abraham and the Levitical cultus in that both Abraham and Levi ("one might even say") paid tithes to him.

More than that, however, our author takes pains to point out in 7:11-

22 that Melchizedek was the priest of "God Most High" prior to and apart from the Aaronic priesthood, being appointed by God on the basis of his character, and that it is of such a priesthood as based on character rather than lineage that Psalm 110 speaks in connection with the Messiah. And it is at this point in his argument that the comparisons between Christ and Melchizedek are drawn, for Jesus' priesthood, too, is (1) based on "the power of an indestructible life" apart from any Aaronic lineage, and (2) given by divine oath apart from any Mosaic legislation. While our author agreed with his addressees in 7:1-10 as to the nature of Melchizedek's person, he did not attempt to correlate the person of Christ with the person of Melchizedek—rather, in fact, with respect to their persons, he did just the opposite in relating Melchizedek to "the Son of God." But now in 7:11-22 he employs Melchizedek as the precedent for and prototype of an eternal priesthood based on character apart from lineage and ordained by God apart from law. And having established the precedent and prototype, he goes on to elucidate Jesus' high priesthood in these terms.

Yet, while agreeing with his addressees as to the nature of Melchizedek's person, the writer to the Hebrews profoundly disagrees with them as to the place of Melchizedek in redemptive history and as to the significance of his ministry. For them, to judge by 11QMelch, Melchizedek would be involved in the Messianic Age as an Archangel Warrior-Redeemer figure who would in his priestly activities atone for sin and for whom the epithets *'lwhym* (line 10) and perhaps *mšyḥ* (line 18) apply. For our author, however, Melchizedek serves only as the precedent for and prototype of a greater high priesthood that is also based on character apart from lineage and ordained by God apart from law. In addition, in the warfare of the Son with the devil in 2:14-18, it is a fully human and suffering Messiah who became "a merciful and faithful high priest" in order to be able "to help those who are being tempted," which is in sharp contrast to the military figure of 11QMelch who bests Belial in the final cosmic battle.

The addressees of the Letter to the Hebrews were, it seems, beginning to think more of Melchizedek than of Christ in connection with redemption and fulfillment of God's promises. The writer to the Hebrews, however, convinced as to the messianic relevance of Psalm 110 and agreeing with his addressees as to the nature of their hero's person, finds in Psalm 110:4 the key to understanding the relationship between Melchizedek and Jesus the Christ: the one being the precedent for and prototype of the much greater One, the Messiah, who having been made "perfect through suffering" is the only "Pioneer (ἀρχηγός) of their salvation" (2:10). In so arguing, of course, our author speaks in ways that are circumstantially conditioned to meet his addressees' interests and appreciation. But he also, both through providential insight and challenge, develops the motif of the priestly nature and ministry of Jesus in ways beyond what was heretofore expressly stated in the

New Testament, or, presumably, explicitly taught by other Christian teachers of his day.

III

ON THEOLOGICAL DEVELOPMENT AND CIRCUMSTANTIAL EXPRESSION

Our interest in this article has been in the manner in which the writer to the Hebrews employed the Melchizedek argument, which required first that we sketch out such attitudes toward Melchizedek as are able to be discerned in the extant materials representative of Late Judaism and then that we attempt to understand our author's employment of the Melchizedek figure both in the light of his Christian commitments and *vis-à-vis* the situation he was addressing. The detailing of the background situation and of the argument itself, of course, has value of itself for exegesis and for biblical theology. But we have been primarily interested in these matters in order to gain from them some appreciation for the features of theological development and circumstantial expression as these appear generally throughout the New Testament and, more particularly, in one individual unit of material explicating one distinctive theme. Admittedly, we have selected for investigation one of the more difficult themes and one of the more perplexing units of material for our case study. But it is often true that the more difficult matter must be dealt with first if one is to have any direction in treating those issues which appear at first glance to be more easily understood.

I have therefore "taken the plunge" into what many will undoubtedly consider a most audacious enterprise, believing that any theory that seeks to explicate the factors of theological development and circumstantial expression in the New Testament must be able to fit the data of the most perplexing individual examples, and that, conversely, the study of the individual units of material must inform the overall theory as it begins to take shape. Any theoretic construct of what we might call "A Philosophy of Theological Development and Circumstantial Expression in the New Testament" is built up via the reciprocal interplay of a working hypothesis drawn from the broad mass of material and the intensive investigation of crucial individual units of that material. Having attempted such an investigation with respect to the Melchizedek argument of the Letter to the Hebrews, I would now like in what follows to hold up for examination one possible working hypothesis for understanding the flow of New Testament thought and then to indicate how the treatment of Melchizedek in Hebrews relates to that model.

The New Testament, of course, does not come to us as a treatise on theology or a compendium of ethics. It presents itself as the record of God's redemptive activity in first-century Palestine through the ministry, death, and resurrection of Jesus of Nazareth, and as the apostolic interpretation of that activity to various people in their varying cultural situations and ideological environments. As such it speaks in the language of the day to the issues and interests of the day, employing such exegetical methods and arguments in support as were then current, in order to win the allegiance of all those it addresses to Jesus, who is Israel's true Messiah and mankind's only Lord. The message it proclaims appears in the record in various stages of development and in various cultural forms, dependent not only upon the perception of the particular writer involved but also upon the interests, appreciation, and understanding of the particular addressees. The student of the New Testament, therefore, finds himself confronted by a multifaceted flow of thought and a variety of presentation in his primary materials which often seem to yield no clearly definable system of doctrine but from which he seeks to extract something approaching a coherent understanding. In addition, he is faced with the issue of how the normative principles of the gospel relate to the specific situations to which they were originally directed and to the particular forms into which they were first cast, asking always how to distill those principles from the cultural forms of that day—and then, by God's grace, how to recast them into forms that will speak to the interests, appreciation, and understanding of people today in their varying cultural situations and ideological environments, so that the same gospel might confront the thought and lives of people today with something of the same force as it did in apostolic times.

It is no mean task that the student of the New Testament takes upon himself. It requires all the scientific, artistic, and theological acumen that can be marshalled, together with a constant dependence upon God's Spirit for illumination and discernment. It necessitates as well interaction with the many and various attempts to understand the New Testament that have been advanced, both in the past and as proposed today. And as one current proposal, I would like to offer the following by way of understanding the flow of New Testament thought generally and the Melchizedek argument of Hebrews in particular.

It is possible to understand the multifaceted flow of New Testament thought and the variety of presentations within the New Testament canon along the lines of the following four captions: (1) revelational immediacy; (2) historical continuity; (3) theological development; and (4) circumstantial expression. Foundational to all New Testament preaching, and the ultimate rationale for the composition of the New Testament itself, is the fact that God has acted redemptively and revealed himself uniquely in the person and work of Jesus of Nazareth. Everything in the New Testament stems ultimately from this initial note of revelational immediacy: that in Jesus men have experienced the presence of God in their midst; that to know him is to know the One who sent him; that God was in Christ effecting man's redemption; and that by the Spirit relationship with the risen Christ is maintained. The proclamation of the earliest apostles was based upon and validated by their having been commissioned directly by Jesus—whether during his earthly ministry (Mark 3:13-19, par.; John 15:27), immediately after his ascension (Acts 1:21-26), or later on the road to Damascus (Gal 1:12, 15-16; 1 Cor 9:1)—and their business was to bear witness to the revelation they had received. But while their message was rooted in the revelation of God in Jesus Christ, it was to be filled out providentially through the continued ministry of the Spirit, just as the Lord had promised (cf. John 16:12-15). Thus they sought for continuity with the past redemptive activity of God by means of a Christocentric reevaluation of the scriptures, taking Jesus' own exegetical practice as the paradigm for their hermeneutical procedures. Thus they were led to explicate their convictions in ways that developed from a more functional manner of speaking to include more speculative and ontological affirmations, finding that the issues they faced in making the message intelligible often forced them to think in such ways. And thus they expressed their convictions in terminology suited to the interest, appreciation, and understanding of their audiences, discovering that the various cultural situations and ideological environments they confronted often caused them to refine the terms of that message so as better to convey its truth—and sometimes supplied them with certain vehicles of expression that could be appropriately employed in their proclamation.

In particular, as we have argued before and now formally propose, the Melchizedek argument of the Letter to the Hebrews is, to an extent, a good example of the general approach outlined above as to the flow of New Testament thought. It fails to do full justice to the theory in that, though he assumes a decidedly Christocentric perspective in treating the Old Testament, the writer does not root his presentation in any revelation which he has received personally himself. Rather, in 2:3-4 he explicitly speaks of having received the basic gospel traditions from the apostles, and he seems to reserve such revelational immediacy for the apostles alone. But in matters having to do with historical continuity, theological development, and circumstantial expression, our author reveals quite clearly how one early Christian leader—perhaps Apollos, who was associated with the apostolic ministry (cf. 1 Cor 1-4)—understood and explicated such features.

Throughout the letter the writer demonstrates his interest in historic continuity, particularly in highlighting the five biblical portions around which he builds his argument. Theological development, however, reaches its zenith in the Melchizedek argument itself, where our author expands on the theme of the high priesthood of Christ: first by bringing Psalm 110:4 explicitly into the orbit of messianically relevant passages; then by explicating our Lord's priestly ministry in ways that go beyond the dominantly functional statements of the earliest Christians and begin to move into more distinctly ontological and metaphysical realms; and finally by treating Melchizedek as the precedent for and prototype of Jesus' high priesthood. And it is in the Melchizedek argument that his circumstantial expression comes most to the fore: in agreeing with his addressees as to the nature of Melchizedek in order that he might then go on to draw such comparisons and contrasts between Melchizedek and Christ as to enhance the superiority and supremacy of our Lord's high priesthood and priestly ministry.

We may not today feel entirely comfortable with the writer's views regarding the nature of Melchizedek. Nor may we feel the same necessity to root the high priesthood and priestly ministry of Christ in some such explicit precedent and prototype. In accepting such a view regarding the enigmatic king-priest of Genesis 14 and in searching for such an explicit precedent, our author, it seems, was trying to tie into his addressees' views and to speak along the lines of their interests. In so arguing, of course, he committed himself as well (at least to some extent) to the correctness of such opinions—much like he does elsewhere in speaking of the Mosaic law as mediated by angels (2:2), or in acknowledging the tabernacle as Israel's ideal place of worship (8:5; 9:2-5, 21), or in referring to the post-biblical martyrs (11:35-37); or, for that matter, as Paul does with reference to the rock that followed the Israelites in the wilderness (1 Cor 10:1-4). But these are matters having to do with the circumstances of his argument and which he employs only to explicate within a specific ideological environment the priestly nature and ministry of Jesus the Messiah in a more developed manner.We can appreciate the circumstantial expression, but we must not become so weighted down by it as to lose the significance and impact of the theological development.

Notes to Chapter 11

1. For informed treatments of Melchizedek in the Old Testament, the patristic materials, and later Christian writings, see G. Bardy, "Melchisédech dans la tradition patristique," *RB* 35 (1926) 496-509, and 36 (1927) 25-45; G. Wuttke, *Melchisedech der Priesterkönig von Salem: Eine Studie zur Geschichte der Exegese* (Giessen: Töpelmann, 1927); M. Delcor, "Melchizedek from Genesis to the Qumran Texts and the Epistle to the Hebrews," *JSJ* 2 (1971) 115-135; F. L. Horton, Jr., *The Melchizedek Tradition. A Critical Examination of the Sources to the Fifth Century A.D.and in the Epistle to the Hebrews* (Cambridge: University Press, 1976); B. Demarest, *A History of the Interpretation of Hebrews 7, 1-10 from the Reformation to the Present* (Tübingen: Mohr, 1976).

2. Melchizedek's title "Priest of *'El 'Elyon"* (translated τοῦ θεοῦ τοῦ ὑψίστου, "of God Most High") suggests first of all the Phoenician deity *'El 'Elyon,* with the title being later employed by the Hebrews in attribution of Yahweh (Ps 78:35; Dan 3:26; 4:32; 5:18, 21) and by the Greeks of Zeus (cf. C. Roberts, T. C. Skeat, and A. D. Nock, "The Guild of Zeus Hypsistos," *HTR* 29 [1936] 39-88). While often debated, recent evidence tends to increase the probability that as "King of Salem" Melchizedek ruled over the Canaanite city-state the Hebrews later

called Jerusalem. This equation of Salem with Jerusalem is not only made in Psalm 76:2 and by Josephus in *Ant.* 1.10.2, §180, but has been more recently attested by the Genesis Apocryphon from Qumran (1QApoc 22.18) and by the Targums Onkelos and Neofiti on Genesis 14:18. Further, the Ebla texts speak of a Palestinian "Salem" as being in existence in the third millennium B.C. (see G. Pettinato, "The Royal Archives of Tell Mardikh-Ebla," *BA* 39 [1976] 46).

3. Recent scholarship has tended to push the date of Psalm 110 back to the time of the United Monarchy, favoring a provenance in the early days of David's reign (cf. H. H. Rowley, "Melchizedek and Zadok (Gen. 14 and Ps. 110)," *Festschrift für Alfred Bertholet zum 80. Geburtstag* [edd. O. Eissfeldt, K. Ellinger, W. Baumgartner, L. Rost; Tübingen: Mohr, 1950] 461-472; A. Weiser, *The Psalms: A Commentary* [Philadelphia: Westminster, 1962] 693; F. L. Horton, Jr., *The Melchizedek Tradition,* 29-34).

4. Though, admittedly, the qualifications of 14:41*b*, "until a faithful prophet should arise" (ἕως τοῦ ἀναστῆναι προφήτην πιστόν), seems somewhat out of harmony with the apparent "realized" messianology of the rest of the chapter.

5. Cf., e.g., D. B. Duhm, *Die Psalmen* (Tübingen: Mohr, 2nd ed., 1922) 398-399; R. H. Pfeiffer, *Introduction to the Old Testament* (New York: Harper, 1948) 161; *idem, History of New Testament Times, with an Introduction to the Apocrypha* (New York: Harper, 1949) 19 n.

6. Cf. D. M. Hay, *Glory at the Right Hand: Psalm 110 in Early Christianity* (Nashville: Abingdon, 1973) 19, 24.

7. Ibid., 24.

8. Ibid., 25.

9. *The Apocrypha and Pseudepigrapha of the Old Testament* (2 vols.; Oxford: Clarendon, 1913) II, 33 n.

10. Cf. A. Diez Macho, *Neophyti 1: Targum palestinense, Ms de la Biblioteca Vaticana.* Tomo I: *Genesis* (trans. R. Le Déaut, M. McNamara, and M. Maher; Madrid: Consejo superior de investigaciones cientificas, 1968).

11. Cf. J. Bowker, *The Targums and Rabbinic Literature* (Cambridge: University Press, 1969) 193-199.

12. As insists J. J. Petuchowski, "The Controversial Figure of Melchizedek," *HUCA* 28 (1957) 129.

13. L. Ginzberg, *The Legends of the Jews* (7 vols.; Philadelphia: Jewish Publication Society of America, 1909-1938) V, 226, n. 104; R. T. Herford, *Christianity in Talmud and Midrash* (London: Williams & Norgate, 1903) 265, 338-340; M. Simon, "Melchizedek dans la polémique entre Juifs et Chrétiens et dans la légende," *RHPhR* (1937) 58-93; *idem, Verus Israel* (Paris: De Boccard, 1948) 110-111. See also M. Delcor, "Melchizedek from Genesis to the Qumran Texts and the Epistle to the Hebrews," *JSJ* 2 (1971) 132.

14. To paraphrase M. Simon, ibid.

15. K. Kohler, "Melchizedek," *The Jewish Encyclopedia* (12 vols.; New York: Funk and Wagnalls, 1901-06) VIII, 450.

16. V. Aptowitzer, "Malkizedek," *MGWJ* 70 (1926) 93-113; H. Windisch, *Der Hebräerbrief* (*HNT;* Tübingen: Siebeck-Mohr, 1931) 61.

17. "The Controversial Figure of Melchizedek," *HUCA* 28 (1957) 136; see also 130-132.

18. A. S. van der Woude, "Melchisedek als himmlische Erlösergestalt in den neugefundenen eschatologischen Midraschim aus Qumran-Höhle XI," *OTS* 14 (1965) 354-373.

19. M. de Jonge and A. S. van der Woude, "11Q Melchizedek and the New Testament," *NTS* 12 (1966) 301-326.

20. Y. Yadin, "A Note on Melchizedek and Qumran," *IEJ* 15 (1965) 152-154.

21. J. A. Fitzmyer, "Further Light on Melchizedek from Qumran Cave 11," *JBL* 86 (1967) 25-41.

22. F. du Toit Laubscher, "God's Angel of Truth and Melchizedek," *JSJ* 3 (1972) 46-51.

23. J. Carmignac, "Le document de Qumran sur Melkisedeq," *RevQ* 7 (1970) 343-378.

24. Windisch, *Der Hebräerbrief.*

25. R. Williamson, *Philo and the Epistle to the Hebrews* (Leiden: Brill, 1970) 430.

26. *J.W.,* 6.10.1, §438.

27. *Ant.* 1.10.2, §180-181.

28. As, e.g., S. A. Cook, *The Old Testament: A Reinterpretation* (London: SPCK, 1936) 205-

206; C. H. Dodd, *According to the Scriptures* (London: Nisbet, 1952) 120; B. Lindars, *New Testament Apologetic* (London: SCM, 1961) 45-46.

29. As was affirmed just before the publication of 11QMelch in 1965 by H. Braun, "Qumran und das Neue Testament: Ein Bericht über 10 Jahre Forschung (1950-1959)—Hebräer," *TRu* 30 (1964) 20, and H. Montefiore, *The Epistle to the Hebrews* (*HNTC,* New York: Harper, 1964) 117-118.

30. To quote again D. M. Hay, *Glory at the Right Hand,* 25.

31. Mythical material preserved in the third and last part of Slavonic Enoch (i.e., 2 Enoch 21-23), entitled "The Priesthood of Methuselah, Noah and Melchizedek," depicts the miraculous conception of Melchizedek (i.e., his mother conceived "without having slept with her husband") and his birth from the corpse of his mother, Sophonim, the wife of Nir and sister of Noah, and goes on to predict that this Melchizedek will reign as a priest and a king in the middle of the earth as the prototype of the Messiah. But this is a Christian midrash upon the statements "without father, without mother, without beginning of days or end of life" of Hebrews 7:3, and need not detain us here. For the most recent treatment of the provenance of 2 Enoch, advocating Christian authorship in the ninth or tenth centuries A.D., see J. T. Milik, *The Books of Enoch. Aramaic Fragments of Qumran Cave 4* (Oxford: Clarendon, 1976) 110, 114-116.

32. Y. Yadin, "The Dead Sea Scrolls and the Epistle to the Hebrews," *Aspects of the Dead Sea Scrolls* (Scripta Hierosolymitana IV) (edd. C. Ragin and Y. Yadin; Jerusalem: Hebrew University, 1958) 38; cf. also the development of his thesis in his "A Note on Melchizedek and Qumran," *IES* 15 (1965) 152-154.

33. C. Spicq, "L'Épitre aux Hébreux, Apollos, Jean-Baptiste, les Hellenistes et Qumran," *RevQ* 1 (1959) 365-390; cf. his earlier *L'Épitre aux Hébreux* (2 vols.; Paris: Gabalda, 1952, 1953).

34. J. W. Bowman, *Hebrews, James, I & II Peter* (Richmond: John Knox, 1962), esp. 9-10 on "A New Solution."

35. C. K. Barrett, "The Eschatology of the Epistle to the Hebrews," *The Background of the New Testament and its Eschatology* (edd. W. D. Davies and D. Daube; Cambridge: University Press, 1954) 393.

36. G. B. Caird, "The Exegetical Method of the Epistle to the Hebrews," *CJT* 5 (1959) 45.

37. Williamson, *Philo and the Epistle to the Hebrews*, 538.

38. E.g., H. Kosmala, *Hebräer-Essener-Christen* (Leiden: Brill, 1959); cf. also J. Daniélou, *The Dead Sea Scrolls and Primitive Christianity* (Baltimore: Helicon, 1958).

39. E.g., J. Coppens, "Les Affinites qumranienes de l'Épitre aux Hébreux," *NRT* 84 (1962) 128-141 and 257-282; F. F. Bruce, " 'To the Hebrews' or 'To the Essenes'?," *NTS* 9 (1963) 217-232—though, unfortunately, usually on the basis of lumping together Yadin's thesis with that of Kosmala, and then easily demolishing the former by association with the latter. Bruce's later review of the question in light of 11QMelch is much more moderate, and contains a good summation of the current state of scholarly opinion: "Recent Contributions to the Understanding of Hebrews," *ExpTim* 80 (1969) 260-264.

40. O. Moe, "Das Priesterthum Christi im NT ausserhalb des Hebräerbriefes," *TLZ* 72 (1947) 335-337; cf. O. Cullmann, *The Christology of the New Testament* (Philadelphia: Westminster, 1959), esp. 104-107.

41. Montefiore, *Epistle to the Hebrews,* 95-96.

42. G. W. Buchanan, *To the Hebrews* (*AB;* Garden City, N.Y.: Doubleday, 1972) 98-100.

43. M. Delcor, "Melchizedek from Genesis to the Qumran Texts and the Epistle to the Hebrews," *JSJ* 2 (1971) 126-127.

44. B. F. Westcott, *The Epistle to the Hebrews* (London: Macmillan, 1889) 493.

45. Cf. Caird, "Exegetical Method," 47-51; also R.N. Longenecker, *Biblical Exegesis in the Apostolic Period* (Grand Rapids: Eerdmans, 1975) 174-185.

46. Caird, "Exegetical Method," 48 (italics his).

47. Ibid.

48. Cf. my *Biblical Exegesis in the Apostolic Period,* 28-50.

49. R. P. C. Hanson, *Allegory and Event* (London: SCM, 1959) 86.

50. The triad ἀπάτωρ, ἀμήτωρ, ἀγενεαλόγητος of 7:3 has often been viewed in the past as a strictly Philonic argument from silence (cf., e.g., J. Moffatt, *A Critical and Exegetical*

Commentary on the Epistle to the Hebrews [*MNTC;* New York: Scribner's, 1924] 92). Paul Billerbeck, however, has demonstrated that for the Rabbis—and, presumably, also for the earlier Pharisees—what is not said in the Torah was just as significant as what is said, and that therefore rabbinic hermeneutics also laid stress on such an argument from silence (H. L. Strack and P. Billerbeck, *Kommentar zum Neuen Testament aus Talmud und Midrasch* [5 vols.; Munich: Beck, 1922-56] III, 694-695). A further example comparable somewhat to Hebrews' treatment of Melchizedek can be found in Targum Pseudo-Jonathan's treatment of the parentage of Cain, where on Genesis 4:1 it speaks of Eve having "conceived from Sammael the angel, and she became pregnant and bare Cain" and on Genesis 5:3 it says that Eve bore Cain "who was not like Adam." The biblical rationale that is invoked for Cain being a child of Sammael, from whom he inherited his evil character, and not Adam's own son, is the statement in Genesis 5:3 which says that Adam "begat a son in his own likeness, after his image; and called his name Seth." Such a direct statement of lineage is not given earlier with respect to the birth of Cain, and therefore the targumist drew from that silence the conclusion that Cain was not Adam's true son (cf. Bowker, *The Targums and Rabbinic Literature,* 132, 136).

51. Agreeing with M. de Jonge and A. S. van der Woude, "11QMelchizedek," 321; though Horton, *The Melchizedek Tradition,* has lately (1976) argued that "the Epistle to the Hebrews should not be reckoned with the literature in which Melchizedek is considered a divine or heavenly figure" (p. 164).

52. Cf. de Jonge and van der Woude, "11QMelchizedek," 319. O. Michel, *Der Brief an die Hebräer* (MeyerK; Göttingen: Vandenhoeck & Ruprecht, 11th ed. rev., 1960) 164, also considers verse 3 to be poetic. In verse 3 Melchizedek is compared to "the Son of God," whereas elsewhere in the chapter the reverse is true.

53. As Michel, *Brief an die Hebräer,* 162-163; Horton, *The Melchizedek Tradition,* 162-163.

12: The God of Abraham, Isaac, and Jacob in New Testament Theology

Bo Reicke

In the night of November 23, 1654, the famous French scholar Blaise Pascal had a vision which lasted from *ca.* 10:30 to *ca.* 12:50, and dominated his mind for the rest of his life. He described his experience on a parchment which he always carried with him under the lining of his doublet, and this so-called "Mémorial" was discovered when he died in 1622. Pascal saw a fire which he understood as representing "the God of Abraham, the God of Isaac, the God of Jacob, not of the philosophers and scholars," and he said the experience gave him "certainty, feeling, joy, peace." He had met that God who long ago, in the burning bush, had presented himself to Moses as the God of Abraham and the other patriarchs (Exod 3:6). Pascal also thought of the fact that Jesus had defined his Father as the God of Abraham, Isaac, and Jacob (Matt 22:32 par.). With ecstatic joy he addressed this "God of Jesus Christ" as "my God and your God" (John 20:17), and declared that knowledge of the real God is only possible in the way indicated by the gospel, that is, by the knowledge of Jesus Christ (John 17:25).[1]

In his *Pensées,* a collection of maxims published after his death, Pascal emphasized again this difference between human understanding and divine reality. Whereas the heathen seek in God the source of geometric truths and natural order, and whereas the Jews expect from him a permanent succession of agreeable years, the God of the Christians is the God of Abraham, Isaac, and Jacob. This implies that he is a God of love and consolation, a God who fills the minds and hearts of those who belong to him. People who seek God independently of his love in Jesus Christ find no light which can satisfy them. And without Jesus Christ the world must appear worthy of being destroyed or becoming like hell.[2]

Pascal's experience and his interpretation of it give concrete expression to a fundamental principle of biblical theology which is not always recognized: the belief in a God who acts in redemptive history and permits this history to culminate in Jesus Christ.[3]

I

According to all narratives and utterances of the Bible, God is no abstract being, but a living, active subject. His holy, ardent energy requires in the first instance veneration and obedience (Gen 2:16-17; Exod 20:5; Lev 19:2; Isa 6:3; Matt 4:10 par.Luke 4:8; John 4:24; Rom 12:1; Heb 10:31; Jas 4:4-10; Rev 4:8). But as the God of Abraham, Isaac, and Jacob he is also eager to bestow freedom and peace upon his people (Exod 3:7-10; Acts 7:32-34; Rom 9:7-13).

In the first instance, this gracious will of God finds an expression in his *covenant* with the patriarchs (Gen 15:18; Exod 2:24; Luke 1:72; Acts 3:25; Rom 4:17; 9:4; Heb 6:14). Here, within the framework of his covenant, God's majestic energy reveals itself as mercy, grace, and love (Gen 24:27; Exod 15:13; Ps 23:6; Isa 54:7-10; Luke 1:72; Acts 7:46; Rom 1:7; 4:4-8, 16; 9:13, 16). Within the New Covenant, the experience of God's mercy and grace is sublimated and intensified, since all dispensations in favor of the elect people are found concentrated in the person, word, and work of Jesus Christ, who is the perfect expression of God's wonderful grace and love. A few references to representative New Testament passages will be sufficient to confirm this well-known fact (Matt 1:21, 23; Mark 1:11; Luke 4:21; John 1:14-18; Rom 3:24; Heb 1:1-4; Rev 1:4-6).

But what is the specific character of this progression from the Old to the New Covenant?

Jesus, the apostles, the evangelists, and other New Testament writers regarded the Old Testament as the *active mediator* of God's revelation in the Old Covenant. Scripture was not supposed to be an objective document or a textbook in which different insights or principles should be sought and found, but a dynamic testimony of God's activity in the past insofar as this is an evidence of his activity in the present time, here and now.

It is this dramatic relation between the Old and the New Covenants that forms the principle of biblical theology. Paul has given it an instructive expression by his words in 1 Corinthians 10:11: "In a typological way (τυπικῶς) this happened to them [Israel in the desert]. But it was recorded in order to warn us to whom the final moments of the ages have come."

This typological relation between the units found in the Old and the New Covenants is often misunderstood. It is not fair to let it mean a mere contraposition of two analogous events or utterances, as if two isolated facts belonging to different historical contexts would have some intrinsic right to be combined. One should not overlook the common factor, that is, God's permanent activity. The facts compared are merely the expression of the energy of that God who is the supreme ruler of history and therefore called the God of Abraham, Isaac, and Jacob. His firelike holiness is so powerful that his actions—positive or negative—have an effect far beyond any primary historical situation.

In biblical thinking, the fact that God delivered his people from bondage "with an outstretched arm and with great acts of judgment" (Exod 6:6) was regarded as historical, as referring to an event that really took place in the past. Yet it was never treated in the retrospective way of modern historiography or even that of national celebrations, but felt as something permanently and presently effective. This was not so because the event itself was supposed to have a power of expansion. Rather, it depended on the experience of a God who is such a powerful ruler of his people and of the nations that he permits a historical event like the exodus of Israel to receive enduring importance. In this sense every Old Testament report of God's activity or revelation has the function of a receiver which takes in the energy of God found behind his past act or word and makes that same energy present and meaningful in the situation of the Christian believer.

II

Thus for example when Matthew interpreted Christ's birth as the fulfillment of Micah 5:1, the well-known prophecy of a ruler and shepherd coming from Bethlehem (Matt 2:6), the evangelist did not merely select an Old Testament passage mentioning Bethlehem in order to get a scriptural background for Christ's birth in the same city. In the first instance he was aware of the fact that Jesus was of David's family (Matt 1:20), and so he realized that Micah's prophecy referred to a David redivivus. His further consideration was this: In the past God gave his people a great ruler in the person of David, and that will be the case again on a higher level in the person of Jesus, which is confirmed by the detail that Bethlehem is the background of both. Micah lived between David and Jesus, and was allowed to be mediator by announcing that God's gracious sending of David will be renewed and made sublime by the sending of Jesus.

Matthew's version of the Sermon on the Mount is another example. It does not imply that isolated utterances of Moses and Jesus were to be confronted with each other. Jesus did not come to dissolve or replace the commandments of God revealed to Moses on Mount Sinai, but to proclaim their fulfillment in the present kingdom (Matt 5:17). He gave each commandment a wider meaning (5:21-22, 27-28, 31-32, 33-37, 38-42, 43-44), and at the same time concentrated everything on the commandment of love (5:43-44; 7:12). It is not a question of two units, but of the same revelation of God's will, first on the level of the law ("it was said to the ancestors"), then on the level of the gospel ("I say to you").

Mark represents a corresponding typological perspective, but this is somewhat reduced because the second evangelist was more concerned with concrete narratives. Nevertheless he also emphasized the reference of the Old Testament to the New Covenant. This is already confirmed by the prophecy quoted as introduction (Mark 1:2): "I send my messenger before thy face, who shall prepare thy way" (cf. Mal 3:1). God was here said to have informed the Son before his birth about the sending of John as his predecessor, and the Old Testament prophet was supposed to have forwarded this revelation to the members of the New Covenant. A word of Jesus on the Sabbath, quoted only by Mark, is another illustration of the progression in question (Mark 2:27): In the Old Covenant God established the Sabbath for the benefit of man, and so in the New Covenant the Son of man is the Lord of the Sabbath because his entire ministry is for the benefit of man. The sublimation of Old Testament units in the New Covenant is also evident from the acclamation of the multitude accompanying Christ into Jerusalem (Mark 11:10): "Blessed is the kingdom of our father David that is coming!" This quotation is only found in Mark. It implies that the glory of David's kingdom is reestablished on a higher level, when Jesus ascends the Mount of Zion. Other examples of Mark's view on the progressive movement between the two covenants are found in sayings of Jesus quoted in accordance with the triple tradition, for instance, the parable of the wicked husbandmen (12:1-12) and the reference to God revealing himself to Moses as the God of Abraham, Isaac, and Jacob (12:26).

According to Luke, the kingdom of David was to be reestablished by the birth of Christ (Luke 1:32), and this also meant fulfillment of the promise given to Abraham (1:55, 73). When the prophecy of Isaiah, mentioning the Spirit of the Lord "upon me" (Isa 61:1-2), had been read by Jesus in Nazareth, he proclaimed its present fulfillment in his own person (Luke 4:16-21). Thus the Master of Nazareth identified himself with the person speaking in the prophecy about his eschatological ministry, which in fact implies an awareness on Jesus' part that he had already spoken to Israel by the mouth of Isaiah about the year of grace now to be welcomed. But this awareness in turn depended on his consciousness of being the direct instrument of God, so that his proclamation first in Isaiah and then in the synagogue of Nazareth was the result of God's activity in favor of his people. The subsequent references to Elijah and Elisha (4:25-27) confirm the idea of God's progressive activity in the Old and the New Covenants. Israel's earliest prophets were sent to help foreigners, and Jesus is sent to save the nations. In accordance with these and other examples of salvation history, Jesus says at the conclusion of Luke's Gospel (24:44): "These are my words which I spoke to you, while I was still with you, that everything written about me in the law of Moses, the prophets and the psalms must be fulfilled." The reason was not supposed to be any preestablished harmony between the period of the Old Testament and the days of Jesus, but the permanent activity of God, who has revealed himself to Moses and in Jesus.

John represents an even more elaborate picture of the progression from the Old Testament to the New Covenant. At the beginning of the universe (Gen 1:1-2) the Logos or Word of God created initial light (John 1:1, 4), and this Word which brings light is now present in Christ (1:9, 14). The fulness of Christ inspired all God's messengers in the past, including

Moses and John the Baptist (1:16-17). Moses and the prophets actually wrote about Christ (1:45; 5:39, 46). God also demonstrated his love to Israel when Moses lifted up the healing serpent in the desert, and so he proves his love to mankind by the elevation of Christ on the cross (John 1:14-16). This classical example of a typology does not imply a mere comparison of two events which look similar. Behind the healing miracle in the desert there was already that active love of God which has found its full expression in the sending of his beloved Son. In a time even more remote, Abraham was looking forward to seeing the Day of the Lord, and rejoiced when he saw its coming with Jesus (8:56). In the days of David, the Logos of God sent to Israel was permitted to call the elect people "divine" (John 10:34; cf. Ps 82:6), and so there should be no objection to addressing Jesus as the Son of God, for he is this divine messenger (10:35-36). When the prophet Isaiah was called in the temple, God let him see the glory of the Lord sitting upon his throne (Isa 6:1), and since this Lord is Jesus Christ, the prophecies of Isaiah refer to him (John 12:41), including the lamentation on Israel's unbelief (12:38-40). In this context the evangelist did not disregard the historical situation of Isaiah's vision in the temple, but indicated that God had given the prophet's experience in the temple a transparency which enabled him to foresee the realization of the vision in the church. Finally, attention may be drawn to several emphatic remarks on the fulfillment of scripture found in the passion story of John (13:18; 17:12; 19:24, 28, 36-37; 20:9). The details should not be understood as scattered analogies between Old and New Testament items. John meant them as selected examples of the fact that God's dynamic activity in the Old Covenant was a purposeful totality, a magnificent preparation for the salvation drama experienced in the New Covenant. This fundamental aspect of the fourth Gospel has been underestimated by those who have endeavored to impose Hellenism, Gnosticism, or Existentialism on it.

With regard to Paul, his thinking in terms of salvation history is acknowledged by most interpreters. It must be observed, however, that Paul did not regard the line drawn from Old Testament circumstance to New Testament reality as being the reason for their coherence, nor did he ascribe independence to salvation history. Paul also considered the powerful activity of God as the fundamental element of all the connections between Old and New Testament items. This will be illustrated by a few examples.

God promised Abraham that he would make him the father of a numerous people, and justified him on the basis of his faith so that he became a model for Christian believers of all nations (Gal 3:8-9; Rom 4:3, 16). It was God who justified Abraham, and it is God who justifies Christians. God's covenant with Abraham has not been changed by the law of Moses (Gal 3:17), but is still valid, that is, in the New Covenant.

In spite of his own and Sarah's advanced age Abraham was convinced that God would fulfill the promise to give him a son, and this faith was "reckoned to him as righteousness" (Rom 4:20-22). Paul added the remark that God let this be recorded not only with regard to Abraham, but also for the information of Christians, who believe in a God who has raised Jesus from the dead (4:23-25). The common factor is the activity of that God who introduced himself as the God of Abraham, Isaac, and Jacob. He made the barren womb of Sarah give birth to Isaac, and compelled Hades to let Jesus be raised from the dead. He justified Abraham because of his faith, and justifies Christians on the basis of their faith. Abraham was an instrument of God by which he demonstrated his power and grace for generations to come. Because of Abraham's faith, God made this patriarch of Israel the father of all Jewish and heathen believers within the church (4:11-12, 16-17). Then his freeborn son Isaac (Gal 4:22) was begotten according to God's promise, and through him Christians are Abraham's true descendants since their life also depends on God's promise (Rom 9:7-9). Isaac's younger son Jacob was elected by God even before his birth, and thus called to experience God's love before having an opportunity to do anything good or evil; on the basis of such a free choice Christians are called to become heirs of the promise (9:10-13).

III

Paul did not ignore the fact that God's providential dealing with Abraham, Isaac, and Jacob would not have been known without the revelation found in the law of Moses. Foreseeing the fulfillment of the promise and the righteousness that is presently offered to all nations by the gospel, Moses anticipated the gospel by quoting the word of God to Abraham that all nations would receive blessing through him (Gal 3:8).

It is a question of a prophetic function which Paul ascribed to the law, and he regarded this *usus propheticus legis* as primary. The essential task of the law as well as of the prophets was to bear witness to the righteousness and salvation that would come with Jesus. Characteristic passages of the Letter to the Romans illustrate this positive understanding of Moses and the prophets. God has used his prophets for previous announcements in the holy scriptures about the ministry of his Son (Rom 1:2-3). Justification is granted to all believers since they are the real doers of the law (2:13). The divine righteousness now available by faith was already testified by the law and the prophets (3:21). Paul was absolutely convinced that he, by his prophetic interpretation of the law as being referred to faith, was able to restore the proper meaning of the law (3:31), and this is demonstrated by the faith of Abraham (4:3). Israel wanted to fulfill the law of righteousness, but had the impudence to attempt it by works instead of doing it by faith (9:31). The purpose (τέλος) of the law is Christ, and its effect is righteousness for every believer (10:4). Moses explained this in Leviticus when he wrote about Christ as "the man who has fulfilled" the law (ὁ ποιήσας, Gal 3:12), and when he prophesied that Christ would rise to life through it (10:5). And in Deuteronomy Moses has further characterized the righteousness available through faith, first by referring it to Christ's incarnation and resurrection as becoming historical facts, then by connecting it with the matter of faith now preached and confessed in the church (10:6-10).

Nevertheless, Paul was profoundly discouraged upon seeing that the the positive function of the law had been suppressed by many Jews, namely, those who sought to establish their own righteousness by works instead of accepting God's righteousness in faith (9:32; 10:3). For if the law is not seen as information about the God of Abraham and the patriarchs, the God of promise and salvation, the God who acts though his Son Jesus Christ, then it contains nothing but numerous demands, accusations, and judgments. Everybody is thus exposed to the convicting function of the law, although this *usus elencticus legis* is secondary in relation to its prophetic meaning (see the reference to Rom 3:31 above). It is man's general refusal to accept the goodness of God (Rom 2:4) that brings about the judgment announced by the law (2:5-6, 12). Under these circumstances the law has also to inform man that he is a sinner (3:19), to convey knowledge of sin to mankind (3:20; 4:15*b*; 7:7-8), to expose the sinner to wrath and curse (Gal 3:10; Rom 4:15*a*), and even to increase the power of sin (Gal 3:19; Rom 5:20; 8:2) and the slavery under death (Gal 2:19; Rom 7:5; 8:2).

However, just as the elenctic function of the law is not primary, but so to say an expression of God's "strange work" (Isa 28:21, *opus alienum)* when he punishes the disobedient, so this function of the law is not meant to be definitive. It leads to a final judgment of the stubborn unbelievers (Rom 2:8, 12), but is actually meant to bring man to confess his sinfulness and to accept God's righteousness in Christ. The elenctic function of the law is what compels man to exclaim: "Wretched man that I am! Who will deliver me from this body of death?" (7:24). Such despair leads to the insight that Christ offers the only chance of salvation. This means that the elenctic function of the law is to be fulfilled by its prophetic function so that belief in Christ becomes the proper effect or "work" of the law (2:14-15).

Vice versa, Paul declared belief in Christ to be what enables man to replace the elenctic by the prophetic function of the law. He saw the christological understanding of the law as the result of belief and illumination by the Holy Spirit, and therefore characterized the replacement of the elenctic by the prophetic function of the same divine law in this way: "For the law of the Spirit as being connected with life in Christ Jesus has delivered you from the law as being connected with sin and death" (8:2).

Because of the weakness of the flesh, the law had in the latter context to be replaced by God's work of reconciliation in Christ (8:3), and this permitted the law's commandment of righteousness to be fulfilled now by Christians who are walking in spirit and life (8:4, 10).

The relation between the elenctic function of the law and its christological fulfillment can also be illustrated by Paul's remarks on the difference between the ministry of condemnation represented by Moses and the ministry of justification represented by the apostles (2 Cor 3:9). In this context Paul characterized the Mosaic law as confined to letters and connected with death, whereas the New Covenant and the apostolic ministry imply spirit and life (3:6-8). Nevertheless there was such a glory on the face of Moses that he was obliged to cover it with a veil, and so the children of Israel did not see the consummation (τέλος) of his ministry, namely, that it was due to be replaced in Christ (3:13-14). This veil is still over the eyes when the Old Testament is read in the synagogue. It is removed only "when you turn to the Lord," that is, when a person is converted to Christ (3:15-16). The contact with the Lord also implies the presence of the Holy Spirit, who enables believers to reflect the glory of the Lord in scripture without that veil (3:17-18).

Faith, however, is only the framework in which the negative function of the law is replaced by its positive meaning. The active factor, by which this sublimation of the perspective is made possible, is the redemptive work of Christ. Paul made this clear in his discussion with the Galatians: "Christ redeemed us from the curse of the law, having become a curse for us—for it is written, 'Cursed be everyone who hangs on a tree.' " (Gal 3:14; cf. Deut 21:23). Thus the blessing of Abraham should come over the nations through Jesus Christ, so that we should "receive [the fulfillment of] the promise concerning the Spirit through faith" (Gal 3:13-14).

Here Paul has given a summary of his covenant theology. It is the Old Covenant offered to Abraham that is restored in the New Covenant present in Jesus Christ. The two covenants are identical, for nobody changes a covenant already established (Gal 3:15), and their contents are promise and fulfillment (3:16). Between the promise given to Abraham and its fulfillment in Jesus the law was inserted to exercise pressure upon sin (3:17-23). But it represents the function of a servant who leads the children to a school where they are "justified by faith" and then are no more under the servant (3:24-25).

IV

A homiletic synopsis of these conceptions about the promise given to Abraham and its fulfillment in Jesus Christ is found in a sermon of Peter summarized by Luke in Acts. Peter introduces his message by saying: "The

God of Abraham, Isaac and Jacob, the God of our fathers, has glorified his Servant Jesus" (Acts 3:13). Later he refers to Moses and the prophets, emphasizing the prophetic function of the law and the preliminary revelations of the prophets about the days of Christ (3:21-24). The conclusion is another reference to Abraham and the covenant with the patriarchs, implying that its blessing is now available in Jesus, the Messiah and Servant of God (3:25-26).

Notes to Chapter 12

1. B. Pascal, "Mémorial: Oeuvres de Blaise Pascal, publiées par L. Brunschwicg" 12 (1904) 4-5: "Feu. Dieu d'Abraham, Dieu d'Isaac, Dieu de Jacob, non des philosophes et des savants. . . . Père juste, le monde ne t'a point connu, mais je t'ai connu. . . ."
2. Pascal, *Pensées,* VIII, 556: "Oeuvres" (n. 1) 14 (1904) 5-6: "Le Dieu des Chrétiens ne consiste pas en un Dieu simplement auteur des vérités géométriques et de l'ordre des éléments. . . . Sans Jésu-Christ le monde ne subsisterait pas; car il faudrait, ou qu'il fût détruit, ou qu'il fût comme un enfer."
3. G. E. Ladd, *Jesus and the Kingdom: The Eschatology of Biblical Realism* (New York: Harper, 1964) xii.

13: Biblical Theology and the Analogy of Faith

DANIEL P. FULLER

Every theology regarding itself as Christian, it seems, would want to affirm that it was in agreement with the Bible. There may be another authority alongside the Bible, as in Roman Catholicism, which regards church tradition as a separate source of authority. But since Roman Catholicism never regards these two sources as clashing with each other, it would always affirm heartily that its theology is biblical.

It is noteworthy, however, that the term "biblical theology" first appeared in the followers of the Reformation, among those who espoused the principle of *sola scriptura*. This principle affirmed that since the church was founded upon the teachings of the prophets and apostles, the authority for its teaching and practice must be derived only from the Bible. To support the legitimacy of a claim to know what the prophets and apostles taught, the reformers made several radical departures from the way theologians had been content to interpret the Bible in preceding centuries.

For one thing they rejected the medieval practice of finding in a biblical passage a fourfold sense: the literal, the allegorical, the moral, and the anagogical (or mystical, ultimate) sense. At the end of his life Luther summarized this hermeneutical principle in these words:

> [The Holy Spirit's] words cannot have more than one, and that the very simplest sense, which we call the literal, ordinary, natural sense. . . . We are not . . . to say that the Scriptures or the Word of God have more than one meaning. . . . We are not to introduce any . . . metaphorical, figurative sayings into any text of Scripture, unless the particulars of the words compel us to do so. . . . For if anyone at all were to have power to depart from the pure, simple words and to make inferences and figures of speech wherever he wished . . . [then] no one could reach any certain conclusions about . . . any article of faith. . . .[1]

Studying the Bible in the original Greek and Hebrew was another way the reformers earned the right to make claims about what the Bible taught. Both Luther and Calvin strove to master the language conventions of the biblical Hebrew and Greek so they could more readily grasp the meaning the biblical writers attached to their own terms, and be less apt to impute current meaning back onto those ancient words. But they also wanted their conclusions about the Bible's meanings to be made available to as many people as possible, and so they stressed the need for translating the Bible into contemporary language. The more people could read the Bible for themselves, the more the Bible itself *(sola scriptura!)* would directly teach individual Christians, and consequently there could be a priesthood of all believers.

The reformers also realized that theologians had kept the Bible from speaking for itself because they were so prone to construe its statements in terms of medieval scholasticism, which drew so heavily upon the philosophy of Aristotle. Luther said, "This defunct pagan [Aristotle] has attained supremacy [in the universities]; [he has] impeded, and almost suppressed, the Scripture of the living God. When I think of this lamentable state of affairs, I cannot avoid believing that the Evil One introduced the study of Aristotle."[2] And in arguing against the Roman Catholic view of transubstantiation, Calvin said, "The doctrine which we have put forward has been drawn from the pure Word of God, and rests upon its authority. . . . Not Aristotle, but the Holy Spirit teaches that the body of Christ from the time of his resurrection was finite, and is contained in heaven even to the Last Day."[3]

Seeking in these ways to let the Bible speak for itself, the reformers demonstrated how much of the principle of *sola scriptura* they had grasped. Ebeling has remarked, "Reformation theology is the first attempt in the entire history of theology to take seriously the demand for a theology based on scripture alone. Only among the followers of the Reformation could the concept 'biblical theology' have been coined at all."[4]

I

"THE ANALOGY OF FAITH" IN LUTHER AND CALVIN

But the reformers also emphasized a hermeneutical principle that is commonly called "the analogy of faith." This principle was used when the time came to combine what two or more biblical writers said about some article of faith like the law (Moses or Paul), or justification (Genesis, Paul, and James). In general, the analogy-of-faith principle of hermeneutics affirms that the norm for interpreting other parts of the Bible is certain passages in the Pauline letters, which supposedly set forth biblical teachings with the greatest clarity and precision.

In stating this principle Luther said, "It is the attribute of Holy Scripture that it interprets itself by passages and places which belong together, and can only be understood by a rule of faith."[5] On the surface, the statement that "scripture interprets itself" seems to be another pillar upholding the principle of *sola scriptura*. But Luther's additional statement that "passages . . . can only be understood by a rule of faith" raises the question of how anyone acquires the authority for knowing just what that rule is. As we consider how Luther and Calvin elaborated on this principle of the analogy of faith, it becomes clear that, in the final analysis, the subjective preference of the theologian himself is the only basis upon which this all-important norm for interpreting the rest of scripture is established. Consequently, the analogy-of-faith principle does not undergird but undermines the *sola scriptura* principle.

In elaborating this principle in another place Luther said, "Every word [of scripture] should be allowed to stand in its natural meaning, and that should not be abandoned *unless faith forces us to it* [italics added]."[6] Luther's readiness to let faith force him to suppress the natural meaning of a text becomes evident from his famous statement made in his Disputation thesis, *De fide,* September 11, 1535. There he affirmed, "Scripture is to be understood not contrary to, but in accordance with Christ. Therefore Scripture is to be referred to him, or else we do not have what represents Scripture. . . . If adversaries urge Scripture against Christ, we will urge Christ against Scripture." Likewise, "If it is to be a question of whether Christ or the Law is to be dismissed, we say, Law is to be dismissed, not Christ."[7]

Commenting on these statements of Luther, Ebeling says,

> Luther was no biblicist. . . . No biblicist speaks like that. . . . [Luther] had not thoroughly thought [the hermeneutical problem] through from the methodological point of view and therefore the methodology of theology in general remained obscure in decisive questions of fundamental importance. It was not made clear what the principle of *sola scriptura* means for the procedure of theology as a whole.[8]

For Luther there really were places where Christ should be urged against scripture. In his thinking, the term "Christ" often represented the whole of his understanding of justification by faith. Luther was convinced that what James said about justification could not be reconciled with Paul's teaching on that subject. In the conclusion to an introduction to Hebrews, James, Jude, and Revelation, Luther said, "Many sweat hard at reconciling James with Paul . . . but unsuccessfully. 'Faith justifies' [Paul] stands in flat contradiction to 'Faith does not justify' [James 2:24]. If anyone can harmonize these sayings, I'll put my doctor's cap on him and let him call me a fool."[9] Consequently Luther put James and these other books, each of which, in his view, had objectionable features, at the end of his New Testament of September, 1522. In his introduction to James itself, Luther said, "[This book] cannot be defended against [its] applying to works the sayings of Moses in Genesis 15, which speaks only of Abraham's faith, and not of his works, as St. Paul shows in Romans 4. . . . Therefore I cannot put him among the chief books."[10]

In another place he singled out the books of the New Testament which did properly "urge Christ."

> To sum it all up . . . St. John's Gospel [not the synoptics!], and his first epistle, St. Paul's epistles, especially those to the Romans, to the Galatians, and to the Ephesians, and St. Peter's first epistle—these are the books which show you Christ and teach everything which is needful and blessed for you to know even if you don't see or even hear any other book. . . . Wherefore St. James' epistle is a true epistle of straw compared with them, for it contains nothing of an evangelical nature.[11]

The foregoing statements indicate what Luther meant by his assertion, "Scripture interprets itself by passages and places which belong together, and [scripture as a whole] can only be understood by a rule of faith."[12] They give concrete examples of how the analogy, or rule, of faith justified singling out certain parts of scripture as the norm by which other parts of the canon were to be judged. Surely Luther's submission to the Bible, implied in his rejection of the fourfold meaning, scholasticism, and church tradition, enabled him to learn and transmit many scriptural teachings that have greatly profited the church. But when he set up his understanding of justification by faith as the basis for suppressing such books as the Synoptic Gospels, Hebrews, and James, he then made it impossible for theses books to deepen or improve his understanding of this doctrine. He also made it harder for these books to inform him on other subjects which they taught. So his use of the analogy of faith undercut the *sola scriptura* principle not only for himself but for all those who have followed his hermeneutical lead ever since.

This conclusion is confirmed by what Matthaeus Flacius (a Lutheran) said about the analogy of faith in his *Key to the Scriptures* (1567), the first hermeneutics book to emerge from the Reformation. According to Flacius,

> Every understanding and exposition of Scripture is to be in agreement with the faith. Such [agreement] is, so to speak, the norm or limit of a sound faith, that we may not be thrust over the fence into the abyss by anything, either by a storm from without or by an attack from within (Rom. 12:6). For everything that is said concerning Scripture, or on the basis of Scripture, must be in agreement with all that the catechism declares or that is taught by the articles of faith.[13]

This statement of Flacius shows how Luther's use of the analogy-of-faith principle had made church tradition, fixed in creeds and catechisms, the key for the interpretation of scripture. Even though this tradition was now of a Protestant rather than of a Roman Catholic variety, yet the barrier which it erected against letting biblical exegesis improve or correct that tradition was exceedingly hard to surmount.

John Calvin followed the same hermeneutical procedure as Luther. In his "Prefatory Address to King Francis," designed to gain recommendation for his *Institutes of the Christian Religion,* Calvin appealed to Romans 12:6 and its phrase "according to the analogy of faith"[14] as his best argument for why his teaching should be regarded as true. He said,

> When Paul wished all prophecy to be made to accord with the analogy of faith [Rom 12:6], he set forth a very clear rule to test all interpretation of Scripture. Now, if our interpretation be measured by this rule of faith, victory is in our hands. For what is more consonant with faith than to recognize that we are . . . weak, to be sustained by [Christ]? To take away from us all occasion for glorying, that he alone may stand forth gloriously and we glory in him?[15]

There are, to be sure, many passages where scripture teaches that "no human being should boast in the presence of God," but "Let him who boasts, boast of the Lord" (1 Cor 1:29, 31). Those who are committed to *sola scriptura* want their understanding of such passages as well as those setting forth all other biblical teachings, to be deepened and corrected by a careful exegesis of all of them.

But *sola scriptura* was threatened when Calvin, like Luther, made the Gospel of John the "key" for understanding the Synoptic Gospels. Concerning the Gospel of John, Calvin said, "The doctrine which points out to us the power and fruit of Christ's coming appears far more clearly in [John] than in [Matthew, Mark, and Luke]. . . . For this reason I am accustomed to say that this Gospel is the key to open the door to the understanding of the others."[16] The problem, however, is that one who is convinced that John's teaching is the key for understanding the other Gospels will devote more energy to learning what John teaches than he will to learning what a Synoptic Gospel teaches. This in itself would be contrary to *sola scriptura,* which requires one to be equally docile to all of scripture.

Calvin also required Exodus through Deuteronomy to be understood in terms of Paul's view of the law. Indeed, Calvin concluded, just from the exegesis of the Pentateuch itself, that "the *same* [italics added] covenant, of which Abraham had been the minister and keeper, was repeated to his descendants by the instrumentality of Moses." But then when he considered what Paul said about the Mosaic law, he said, "Paul opposes [the Mosaic law] to the promise given to Abraham, because as [Paul] is treating of the peculiar office, power and end of the law, he separates it from the promises of grace [that are found in Abraham and Moses]. . . ."[17]

Thus, according to Calvin, the message of Exodus through Deuteronomy could not be properly grasped simply by studying these books. One must first know about the antithesis Paul drew between Abraham, on the one hand, and parts of Moses, on the other, before his study of Exodus through Deuteronomy would produce accurate results. For Calvin, unless one knew that the promises in these books constantly shift back and forth between conditional and unconditional ones,[18] he would be led astray in his study of them. So Calvin concluded the introduction to his harmony of Exodus through Deuteronomy by saying, "I have thought it advisable to say this much by way of preface, for the purpose of directing my readers to the proper *object* [italics added] of the history. . . ."[19]

But there are numerous passages in scripture where such blessings as eternal life, and inheriting the kingdom of God, are given because of the good works men have done. According to Matthew 25:34-36, 46, the blessed will inherit the kingdom of God and eternal life because they have done such things for "Jesus' brethren" as feeding them when they were hungry. Likewise, Paul commands, "Whatever your task, work heartily, as serving the Lord and not men, knowing that from the Lord you will receive the inheritance as your reward . . ." (Col 3:23-24). In his *Institutes,* Calvin interpreted these two passages by calling in statements from such remote contexts as Ephesians 1:5-6, 18 and Galatians 4:7. According to Calvin, these affirm that "the Kingdom of heaven is not servants' wages but sons' inheritance, which only they who have been adopted as sons by the Lord shall enjoy, and that for no other reason than this adoption." So, "even in these very passages [Matt 25:34-46 and Col 3:23-24] where the Holy Spirit promises everlasting glory as a reward for works, [yet] by expressly terming it an 'inheritance' he is showing that it comes to us from another source [than works]."[20]

Here is a concrete example of how analogy-of-faith hermeneutics worked in Calvin's thinking. He has to construe Matthew 25 and Colossians 3 in terms of other passages drawn from such distant contexts as Ephesians 1 and Galatians 4. These he selects because they accord well with his understanding of the analogy of faith, that only God, and not men, should be glorified.[21] Then he applies these remote-context passages to the ones in Matthew and Colossians, whose own terminology does not affirm so clearly that God alone is glorified in man's salvation. They even say, on Calvin's own admission, that "the Holy Spirit [!] promises everlasting glory as a reward for works. . . ." But this statement of theirs must be suppressed and replaced by the passages from Ephesians and Galatians, so that the passages in Matthew 25 and Colossians 3 will make it clear that the *inheritance* spoken of there "comes to us from another source [than works]."[22]

So long as the exegesis of biblical passages is conducted by such analogy-of-faith hermeneutics, it would be difficult for systematic theology to be nourished and corrected by exegetical considerations from the biblical text. But this was the course which the reformers left for theology to steer. While the reformers themselves introduced into biblical exegesis many practices which greatly furthered the cause of *sola scriptura,* yet because they did not grasp how their analogy-of-faith principle clashed with *sola scriptura,* they gave a strong impetus for Reformation theology also to revert to a scholasticism not unlike the medieval sort against which they had rebelled. Thus Ebeling argues,

> This lack of clarity became apparent in the degree to which Reformation theology, like medieval scholasticism, also developed into a scholastic system. What was the relation of the systematic method here [in the post-Reformation]

> to the exegetical method? Ultimately it was the same as in medieval scholasticism. There, too, exegesis of holy scripture went on not only within systematic theology but also separately alongside of it, yet so that the possibility of a tension between exegesis and systematic theology was *a priori* excluded. Exegesis was enclosed within the frontiers fixed by systematic theology.[23]

There was one big difference, however. The post-Reformation era could not completely forget the several strong impulses which the reformers had given toward *sola scriptura.* So the more post-Reformation theology became scholastic, the more it clashed with these latent *sola scriptura* impulses. Consequently, it was inevitable that a methodology would arise which (whatever its name) would seek that full conformity with *sola scriptura* that systematic theology, with its analogy-of-faith principle, could not achieve.

II

THE RISE OF BIBLICAL THEOLOGY

A century after the Reformation the term "biblical theology" was first used. At the outset the term signified a corrective which certain precursors of Pietism felt Protestant Orthodoxy sorely needed. Philip Spener, one of the founders of Pietism, remarked in his *Pia Desideria* (1675) how two court chaplains in the parliament at Regensburg had complained some years earlier that "scholastic theology," expelled by Luther through the front door, had now come in at the back door to suppress "biblical theology."[24] In his later writings Spener drew an antithesis between "biblical theology" and "scholastic theology." But in making this contrast Spener was not trying to discard systematics in favor of another theological method. He merely wanted to encourage theological students to spend less time mastering philosophical subtleties and more time learning the "simple" teachings of Christ and the apostles. As a result of Spener's plea there appeared a number of books which assembled proof-texts from all over the Bible to substantiate the affirmations of systematic theology.[25]

It was a century later that Johann Gabler used the term "biblical theology" to designate a method for ascertaining Christian teaching which should supersede systematic theology. In his inaugural address as a professor at Altdorf in 1787 he drew a sharp distinction between biblical and systematic theology. "Biblical theology," he said, "always remains the same since its arguments are historical."[26] What was "historical" had an unvarying quality about it, since "what the sacred writers thought about divine things" was something fixed in the past and represented to us today by an unchanging text of scripture. Dogmatic theology, on the other hand, "is subjected along with other human disciplines to manifold change." "It teaches what every theologian through use of his reason philosophizes about divine things in accordance with his understanding, with the circumstances of the time, the age, the place, the school [to which he belongs]. . . ." "Therefore," Gabler argued, "we are carefully to distinguish the divine from the human and to undertake a separation between biblical and dogmatic theology."

Thus biblical theology should be pursued in order to grasp exactly how each of the biblical writers thought. To do this, Gabler recommended that two steps be taken. First, every effort must be directed to "what each of [the biblical writers] thought concerning divine things . . . only from their writings." A vital requisite for this is to learn "the time and place" where any single literary unit was composed. Second,

> We must carefully assemble all ideas of the several writers and arrange them in their proper sequence: those of the patriarchs, those of Moses, David, and Solomon, those of the prophets—each of the prophets for that matter. . . . And as we proceed we are for many reasons not to despise the Apocrypha. In similar fashion, from the epochs of the new form of doctrine, [we must carefully assemble and arrange in proper sequence] the ideas of Paul, Peter, John and James.

After accomplishing these two steps, the interpreter's third step is

> . . . to investigate which ideas are of importance to the permanent form of Christian doctrine and consequently apply to us, and which were spoken only for the people of a given age or were intended for a given form of instruction. . . . Who, I ask, would relate the Mosaic regulations, long since done away with by Christ, to our time, and who would insist on the validity for our time of Paul's exhortations that women should veil themselves in the sacred assembly? The ideas of the Mosaic form of instruction, which are confirmed neither by Jesus and his apostles *nor by reason itself* [italics added], can therefore be of no dogmatic value. We must zealously examine . . . what we must regard as belonging to the abiding doctrine of salvation; what in the words of the apostles is truly divine and what is fortuitous and purely human. . . . Then the consequence is in fact a "biblical theology." . . . And when such solid foundations of "biblical theology" . . . have been laid after the manner we have described . . . we shall have no wish to follow uncertain ideas set forth by a dogmatic theology that is conditioned by our own times.[27]

In Gabler's first two steps there is the implication that each biblical spokesman should be studied with equal diligence. But then came his third step of drawing a distinction between "the permanent form of Christian doctrine," and "ideas . . . for the people of a given age." Later revelation (that of Jesus and his apostles) as well as "reason" were the criteria for making this distinction. The problem with Gabler, and with all biblical theology for the next century, was that the criteria for carrying out the third step, and especially "reason," were so amenable to the prevailing philosophy of a certain age that in the teaching produced by biblical theology, the prophets, Christ, and the apostles sound very similar to current modes of thinking.

An example of this is Bernhard Weiss's *Biblical Theology* (1868), which argued that the kingdom of God proclaimed by Jesus existed to the degree that the disciples surrounding Jesus made progress in living up to his ethical principles. Weiss said that "the dominion of God begins to be fulfilled when a company of disciples gather around Jesus, in whose midst is the kingdom of God."[28] Although Weiss conceded that "Jesus nowhere directly designates the fellowship of his adherents as the kingdom of God," yet on the basis of verses like Matthew 21:31, "tax collectors and harlots precede you [Pharisees] into the kingdom of God," he confidently affirmed that "in [the disciples'] fellowship [the kingdom] begins to be realized. . . . [Its] success depends on the condition of men's hearts."[29] It was the kingdom of God understood in these terms which "must spread over the whole nation, like the mustard seed which grows from small beginnings to a disproportionate greatness."[30]

Such an understanding of the kingdom of God, however, was saying scarcely anything different from ethical idealism, the prevailing philosophy of that time. And this understanding was a virtual reduplication of the theology of Albrecht Ritschl, who stressed that the kingdom which Jesus founded was a community committed to the practice and furtherance of his ethical ideals.

We recall how Gabler had confidently predicted that as his three-step program for a biblical theology was carried out, the result would be ideas that belonged to the permanent form of Christian doctrine. These would replace the teachings of dogmatic theology, which have no permanence in that they are always conditioned by the thinking of their own times. But when a man as deeply committed to biblical authority as Bernhard Weiss practiced biblical theology and came up with an understanding of Jesus' teaching about the kingdom of God that accorded so well with the prevailing philosophy and theology, it seemed that biblical theology was as vulnerable to the influence of current thinking as was dogmatic theology. The ideal of *sola scriptura* would be achieved only when the exegetical method left the interpreter with no alternative but to let the text speak for itself in its own terms.

III

THE IMPACT OF *RELIGIONSGESCHICHTE*

About the middle of the last century, certain biblical scholars became aware of many parallels between Jesus' language in the Gospels and the Jewish apocalyptic literature. The use of such writings as an aid for understanding what Jesus meant in his frequent references to "the kingdom of God" would be an example of one application of the exegetical procedure of *Religionsgeschichte,* or "the history-of-religions school."

In 1892 Johannes Weiss included this procedure in his exegetical method in which, as he put it, "we attempt once more to identify the original historical meaning which Jesus connected with the words 'Kingdom of God,' and . . . we do it with special care lest we import modern, or at any rate alien, ideas into Jesus' thought-world."[31]

J. Weiss noted his father's concession that nowhere did Jesus equate the kingdom of God with his disciples.[32] Indeed, Jesus did say, in Matthew 12:25-28, that the kingdom had already come, but the meaning here is that the kingdom was present in that Jesus had power to cast out demons and to dismantle Satan's realm. So while Jesus was on earth, the kingdom of God was invisible and only indirectly evident through Jesus' miracle-working power. But according to Luke 17:20-24, what is now invisible will come, *in the future,* with the highest visibility when Jesus returns as the "Son of man" spoken of in Daniel 7 and in numerous places in the Jewish apocryphal book of Enoch.

On the basis of many other statements of Jesus about the futurity of the kingdom, and a rather constant allusion to similar thinking about the kingdom of God in Jewish apocalyptic literature—The Assumption of Moses, The Testament of Daniel, Enoch, and 4 Ezra—J. Weiss concluded,

> The kingdom of God as Jesus thought of it is a wholly supernatural entity that stands completely over against this world. It follows from this that in Jesus' thought there cannot have been any place for a development of the kingdom of God *within the framework of this world.* On the basis of this result it seems to be the case that the dogmatic religio-ethical use of this idea in recent theology, which has divested it completely of its originally eschatological-apocalyptic meaning, is unjustified.[33]

Weiss's conclusion regarding Jesus' understanding of the kingdom of God was much better established than his father's conclusion, because the son argued not only from a mass of evidence in the Synoptic Gospels, but also from evidence provided by *Religionsgeschichte,* that is, from similar ideas in Jewish apocalyptic literature, which were pertinent because they stemmed from the same general milieu in which Jesus lived. Faced with such double evidence, it became virtually impossible for a modern man to understand Jesus' statements about the kingdom of God in terms of cherished contemporary concepts.

This is why J. Weiss's *Die Predigt Jesu vom Reiche Gottes* (Göttingen: Vandenhoeck and Ruprecht, 1892) represents a great turning point in the history of biblical interpretation. It was this book and Wilhelm Wrede's *Das Messiasgeheimnis in den Evangelien* (Göttingen: Vandenhoeck and Ruprecht, 1901) that provided Albert Schweitzer with the key for showing that nineteenth-century liberalism could no longer find support for its teachings from the Jesus of the Synoptic Gospels. As Krister Stendahl has said,

> The alleged biblical basis for what has been called "liberal theology" in the classical form . . . was not shattered by conservatives but by the extreme radicals of the *religionsgeschichtliche* Schule ("history-of-religions school"). [The exponents of this school] could show, on the basis of the comparative material, that such a picture of Jesus or of the OT prophets was totally impossible from the historical point of view and that it told more about the ideals of bourgeois Christianity in the late nineteenth century than about the carpenter from Nazareth or the little man from Tekoa.[34]

So the history-of-religions school presented biblical theology with an exegetical tool which made it virtually impossible for the Bible's message to be molded according to the current philosophy of a given culture. Now the Bible had to speak in terms of the meanings which the biblical writers had intended by the words they used. *Sola scriptura* was now within the reach of all those who would work with the biblical text to grasp its intended meanings and who were not obligated to shape those meanings to conform to some analogy of faith.

But as *Religionsgeschichte* forced one back to the way the Bible thought in its own times and cultures, the relevance of the biblical message seemed, for many, to vanish. As Johannes Weiss expounded the Gospels' own view of the kingdom, he observed that "most people will neither be satisfied with this more negative description of the concept [of the kingdom of God as that which triumphs over Satan], nor want to understand it in this completely supernaturalistic way of looking at things, which is mythological from our standpoint."[35] And Stendahl observes that "the resistance to the *religionsgeschichtliche Schule* was openly or unconsciously against its disregard for [contemporary] theological meaning and relevance."[36]

Indeed, *Religionsgeschichte* had made it possible for biblical theology to tell "what it meant," but there is little market for exegetical labors which merely describe, with an antiquarian interest, the thoughts of a by-gone age. There is, however, a very strong desire to know "what the Bible means,"[37] and this desire has sought fulfillment in two very distinct theological procedures.

IV

TWO ALTERNATIVES

Karl Barth's procedure for affirming "what the Bible means" begins with the presupposition that though the biblical writers and the present-day interpreter are far removed from each other in terms of their culture, yet they have very much in common in that both have immediate access to the "subject matter" of the Bible. At the beginning of the *Church Dogmatics* Barth affirmed,

> Language about God has the proper content, when it conforms to the essence of the Church, i.e., to Jesus Christ. . . . *eite prophetēian kata tēn analogian tēs pisteōs* (Rom. 12:6). Dogmatics investigates Christian language by raising the question of this conformity. Thus it has not to discover the measure with which [dogmatics] measures, still less to invent [that measure]. With the Christian Church [dogmatics] regards and acknowledges [that measure] as given (given in its own thoroughly peculiar way, exactly as the man Jesus Christ is given us . . .). . . .[38]

Since Christ is given for us today, just as he was for the writers of the New Testament, it is understandable why Barth, at the very outset of his theological career, recommended an interpretational procedure which regarded all exegetical labors with a text's historical and philological data as mere "preliminary work," which was to be followed quickly by a "genuine understanding and interpretation," which means

> . . . that creative energy which Luther exercised with intuitive certainty in his exegesis; which underlies the systematic interpretation of Calvin . . . [who] having first established what stands in the text, sets himself to re-think the whole material and to wrestle with it, till the walls which separate the sixteenth century from the first become transparent! Paul speaks, and the man of the sixteenth century hears. The conversation between the original record and the reader moves around the *subject matter* [italics added], until a distinction between today and yesterday becomes impossible.[39]

An example of how this all-important "subject matter" (which in another place in the *Church Dogmatics* is stated as "revelation remains identical with Jesus Christ"[40]) controlled Barth's interpretation of the text is his handling of passages like 1 Corinthians 15:51-54, which affirms that believers "shall all be changed, from mortality into immortality" (vv. 51, 52, 54). But Barth said that in the Christian hope, "there is no question of a continuation into an indefinite future of a somewhat altered life . . . [but, rather] an 'eternalizing' of this ending life." His reasoning behind this suprising statement is, it seems, that if believers did actually undergo the inherent change of being resurrected, then something of what is revealed in Jesus Christ would be transposed from Christ over to created beings. But since Barth's *Sache,* or analogy of faith, bars revelation from extending itself beyond Jesus Christ, and since this *Sache* confronted both Barth and Paul, despite great cultural differences between them, therefore Barth regarded it as proper to restate 1 Corinthians 15:51-54 from his knowledge of it, even though his words communicated a different meaning from Paul's. As Stendahl puts it,

> Orthodoxy never had repristination as its program in the periods of its strength. The possibility of translation was given—as it is for Barth—in the reality of the *subject matter* [italics added], apart from the intellectual manifestations in the thought patterns of the original documents. God and Christ were not Semites in such a sense that the biblical pattern of thought was identified with the revelation itself.[41]

The problem with Barth's procedure is that even though Christ might be regarded as given to all believers in church proclamation, yet this Christ will be preached somewhat differently from church to church, and so each interpreter will read the text in a different light. Hence this procedure will produce as many interpretations of the text as there are interpreters, and not even as profound and wise a thinker as Barth has any basis for claiming that his interpretation of a biblical text should be taken seriously. Stendahl observes that

> . . . Barth speaks as if it were a very simple thing to establish what Paul actually meant in his own terms. . . . [But] biblical theology along this line is admittedly incapable of enough patience and enthusiasm for keeping alive the tension between what the text meant and what it means. [In Barth] there is no criteria by which they can be kept apart; what is intended as a commentary turns out to be a theological tractate, expanding in contemporary terms what Paul should have said about the subject matter as understood by the commentator.[42]

In contrast, biblical theology, controlled only by philological and historical considerations, regards its first order of business to be to construe an author's intended meaning *in his own terms.* Stendahl argues that biblical exegesis has reached a point where this is now possible for much of the biblical material:

> Once we confine ourselves to the task of descriptive biblical theology as a field in its own right, the material itself gives us the means to check whether our interpretation is correct or not. . . . From the point of view of method it is clear that our only concern is to find out what these words meant when uttered or written by the prophet, the priest, the evangelist, or the apostle—and regardless of their meaning in later stages of religious history, our own included.[43]

Stendahl regards Oscar Cullmann's procedure for establishing Christian teaching as representing the alternative to Barth's way. Cullmann is distressed with Barth for not subjecting his theological thinking to the meaning of the text as determined by philological and historical considerations. "Barth is particularly open to this danger, not only because of the richness of his thought, but because systematically he seems to treat philological and historical explanations as too exclusively *preliminary* in character."[44] Cullmann argues that the Holy Spirit who inspired the biblical writings

> . . . can only speak in human language, and that language must always bear the stamp of the period and of the individuality of the biblical writer. For this reason . . . [all philological and historical considerations] help to provide us with a "transparency" through which, by an effort of theological concentration, we may see *with* the writer the truth which he saw and *with him* may attain to the revelation which came to him. We must thoroughly understand this historic "transparency"; our vision through it must be so clear that at any moment we may become the actual contemporaries of the writer.[45]

In contrast to Barth, Cullmann wants to find the subject matter of any literary unit in scripture simply by submitting himself to the pertinent historical and philological data, and by means of these alone to construe an author's intended meaning. Only as the interpreter is thinking along "*with* the writer [of the text]" will he have access to the author's subject matter. Cullmann rejects Barth's idea that the interpreter should have prior access to the subject matter through the church's proclamation of Christ. He says,

> When I approach the text as an exegete, I may not consider it to be certain that my Church's faith in Christ is in its essence really that of the writers of the New Testament. . . . In the same way, my personal self-understanding [*contra* Bultmann], and my personal experience of faith must not only be seen as exegetical aids, but also as possible sources of error.[46]

How then does Cullmann proceed where the Reformation foundered, namely, in the matter of avoiding subjectivity when the time comes to bring all the teachings of the Bible together? He answers that with the closing of the canon,[47]

> . . . the thing that is new in this concluding new interpretation is the fact that not just individual excerpts of salvation history are presented, as was the case [prior to the composition of the last book in the canon], but that now, through the *collection together* of various books of the Bible, the whole history of salvation must be taken into account in understanding any one of the books of the Bible. When we wish to interpret some affirmation coming from early Christianity not merely as an isolated phenomenon, but as an actual *biblical text,* as a part belonging to a totality, we must call upon salvation history as a hermeneutical key, for it is the factor binding all the biblical text together.[48]

Thus Cullmann affirms that "a dogmatics or ethics of salvation history ought to be written some day."[49]

To the objection that making redemptive history the perspective for understanding any given passage of scripture is just as subjective as any of the other rules, or analogies, of faith, Cullmann answers that salvation history is what called forth certain writings as canonical in the first place, and therefore only salvation history can provide the perspective from which they are to be interpreted. "I simply do not see any other biblical notion [besides salvation history] which makes a link between all the books of the Bible such as the fixing of the canon sought to express."[50] It should also be observed that, for Cullmann, salvation history never allows the thinking of one writer to be suppressed in favor of another (as the various analogies of faith do). He says,

> . . . [the scholar] must . . . resist the temptation to bring two texts into harmony when their affirmations do not agree, if he is convinced that such a synthesis is incompatible with the critical control exercised by philology and history; this he must do, however painful the biblical antinomy with regard to one point or another, once the synthesis has been rejected.[51]

Cullmann, however, does have statements where he speaks of later events in redemptive history as providing "reinterpretations" of earlier ones. For example, when the Old Testament kerygma passes on into the New Testament, he says, "This *kerygma* passes through new interpretations more radical than all those undertaken within the sphere of the Old Testament, because they are all subsequently oriented toward the Christ event." Furthermore, "The evangelists [Matthew, Mark, Luke, and John] still offer their reinterpretation of the form of a life of Jesus at a relatively late stage in the formation of the primitive Christian *kerygma*."[52]

But this "reinterpretation" does not mean that older interpretations of a redemptive event are discarded as no longer useful. The "correction" of the interpretation of a past saving event ". . . never happens in such a way that an earlier account is disputed. Rather, aspects formerly unnoticed are by virtue of the new revelation now placed in the foreground, creating a correspondingly wider horizon."[53] Elsewhere he uses such words as "completed" and "refined"[54] to define what he means by "reinterpretation," and he also expressly criticizes Von Rad's understanding of later interpretations in redemptive history as invalidating earlier ones.[55] Therefore older interpretations of a redemptive event continue to make valid contributions to our understanding of that event, even though later revelation adds new information about it so that the perspective by which we view it shifts from that provided merely by the earlier interpretations.

On the basis of such an approach Cullmann argues that one hears what the Bible itself is trying to say, and the very objectivity of this message, arising from the sequence and meaning of the Bible's redemptive events, constitutes the proper object to which faith responds. The very "otherness," or "strangeness," of the biblical message increases, rather than detracts from, the Bible's applicability to life. In that the biblical message is so out of step with human thinking in any age, it calls for a response from men that involves a complete break with the ways they are prone to view things. Cullmann affirms,

> The "application of the subject matter to myself" [paraphrasing the famous statement of Bengel given in the eighteenth century] presupposes that in complete subjection to the text (*te totum applica ad textum* [Bengel]), silencing my question, I struggle with the *"res"*, the subject matter. But that means that I must be ready to hear something perhaps foreign to me. I must be prepared to hear a faith, an address, running completely contrary to the question I raise, and in which I do *not* at first feel myself addressed.[56]

At this point George Ladd criticizes Cullmann for not having taken the "second step in biblical theology—that of interpreting how the theology of salvation history can be acceptable today. . . . Biblical theology must be alert to this problem and expound reasons why the categories of biblical thought, admittedly not those of the modern world, have a claim upon our theological thinking."[57] One reason Ladd gives for why men should welcome the claim made in the Bible's history of salvation is that because "Christ is now reigning as Lord and King," and will continue to reign until he has put all enemies under his feet (1 Cor 15:25), therefore "his reign must [eventually] become public in power and glory and his Lordship universally recognized (Phil. 2:10-11)."[58] A salvation history in which so many promises already have been fulfilled and which now promises that all the enemies that presently bring us such woe will someday be banished, inspires a confidence for the future which, it would seem, all men would most readily welcome.

Notes to Chapter 13

1. Quoted by W. G. Kümmel, *The New Testament: The History of the Investigation of its Problems* (Nashville/New York: Abingdon, 1972) 22-23.
2. M. Luther, *An Appeal to the Ruling Class: Martin Luther; Selections from His Writings* (ed. J. Dillenberger; Garden City, New York: Doubleday, 1961) 470-471.
3. J. Calvin, *Institutes of the Christian Religion (LCC* 20, 21, ed. J. McNeill; Philadelphia: Westminster, 1960) 21, 1393 (IV, xvii, 26). All further references to the *Institutes* follow this edition.
4. G. Ebeling, "The Meaning of 'Biblical Theology'," *Word and Faith* (London: SCM, 1963) 82.
5. Quoted by C. Briggs, *Biblical Study* (New York: Scribner's, 1884) 332. A century later the Westminster Confession (I, ix) used similar language in enunciating this hermeneutical principle: "The infallible rule of interpretation of Scripture is the Scripture itself, and therefore when there is a question about the true and full sense of any Scripture (which is not manifold but one), it must ["may" in the American edition] be searched and known by other places that speak more clearly."
6. Briggs, *Biblical Studies,* 332.
7. Taken from the Latin given by Ebeling, "Meaning of Biblical Theology," 82.
8. Ebeling, "Meaning of Biblical Theology," 82.
9. Quoted by Kümmel, *History of Investigation,* 26.
10. Ibid., 24-25.
11. Quoted by E. Reuss, *History of the Canon of the Holy Scriptures in the Christian Church* (Edinburgh: Hunter, 1891) 322, 329.
12. *Supra,* n. 5.
13. Quoted by Kümmel, *History of Investigation,* 30. We note Flacius' reference to Romans 12:6, where Paul exhorts his readers that if they have the gift of prophecy, they are to exercise this gift "according to the analogy of faith" (κατὰ τὴν ἀναλογίαν τῆς πιστέως). Paul's point is that each Christian should exercise his spiritual gift in accordance with the appropriate inner faith, or inclination, that he has by virtue of that particular gift. So it is clear that "faith" in this passage does not represent some objective body of truth. But that is the sense in which this passage was taken by Flacius, and by Origen, who as nearly as I can determine was the first to use the words "according to the analogy of faith" to urge people to conform their language and thinking about a passage of scripture to an *a priori* understanding of what God's Word must be like *(De principiis* 4.26).
14. Cf. *supra,* n. 13.
15. Calvin, *Institutes,* 20, 12-13.
16. J. Calvin, *The Gospel according to John, 1-10* (edd. D. and T. Torrance; Grand Rapids: Eerdmans, 1959) 6.
17. J. Calvin, *Commentaries on the Four Last Books of Moses* (4 vols.; Grand Rapids: Eerdmans, repr. 1950) I, 314.

18. In my opinion, however, Calvin never demonstrated the existence of an unconditional promise in the Pentateuch, or anywhere in the Bible. A major emphasis of his system is that the gospel calling for faith comprises *un*conditional promises, whereas law appears in every conditional promise. See *Institutes,* 20, 575 (III, ii, 29) where he makes his most basic statement regarding this distinction.
19. Calvin, *The Four Last Books of Moses,* I, 316.
20. Calvin, *Institutes,* 20, 822 (III, xviii, 2).
21. *Supra,* n. 15.
22. To the objection that we must remain with analogy-of-faith hermeneutics or else we will let passages like Matthew 25 and Colossians 3 lead us right back to Rome and salvation by works, my answer is twofold. First, we must determine, regardless of consequences, what the intended meaning of each of the biblical writers is. We must let each one speak for himself and avoid construing him by recourse to what another writer said. Otherwise there is no escape from subjectivism in biblical interpretation. Since the Bible itself does not point to certain parts as the norm to which other parts must conform, one would be free to set up any analogy of faith that he chooses so long as he can adduce a handful of verses, preferably from the New Testament, to support it.

Second, when we cannot quickly escape from passages running counter to our theological presuppositions by an analogy-of-faith procedure, then we are driven to hear out a biblical writer with an intensity that is not otherwise possible. I am convinced that the whole problem of faith and works, which analogy-of-faith hermeneutics is most often called in to solve, evaporates as one probes more deeply into biblical theology. A good starting-point for solving this problem is an understanding of what Paul meant by a "work of faith" (1 Thess 1:3; 2 Thess 1:11). Works done from the motivation of faith preclude the possibility of any boasting and give all glory to God, yet these works are so vital to a saving faith that those lacking them are not saved. On this line of reasoning Colossians 3:23-24, Matthew 25, and many other passages could speak for themselves without having to be muzzled by the analogy of faith.
23. Ebeling, "Meaning of Biblical Theology," 82-83.
24. Ibid., 83-84.
25. F. C. Baur, *Vorlesungen über neutestamentliche Theologie* (Darmstadt: Wissenschaftliche Buchgesellschaft, repr. 1973) 3, provides a list of these books.
26. This and subsequent quotes from Gabler are taken from Kümmel, *History of Interpretation,* 98-100.
27. Ibid., 99-100.
28. B. Weiss, *Biblical Theology of the New Testament* (2 vols., 3rd ed.; Edinburgh: T. & T. Clark, 1882) I, 67.
29. Ibid., 68.
30. Ibid., 69.
31. J. Weiss, *Jesus' Proclamation of the Kingdom of God* (Lives of Jesus Series; Philadelphia: Fortress, 1971) 60.
32. Ibid., 68.
33. Quoted by Kümmel, *History of Interpretation,* 228.
34. K. Stendahl, "Contemporary Biblical Theology," *IDB* (4 vols.; Nashville/New York: Abingdon, 1962) I, 418.
35. J. Weiss, *Jesus' Proclamation,* 81.
36. Stendahl, "Biblical Theology," 419.
37. I am indebted to Krister Stendahl, in his article on "Biblical Theology," cited above, for this apt way of stating the difference between the exposition of a text's meaning and its application for today.
38. K. Barth, *Church Dogmatics* (Edinburgh: T. & T. Clark, 1936) I/1, 11-12.
39. K. Barth, *The Epistle to the Romans* (6th ed.; New York/Toronto: Oxford, 1933) 7. This is a statement Barth made in his foreword to the second edition of this book in 1921.
40. K. Barth, *Church Dogmatics* (Edinburgh: T. & T. Clark, 1956) I/2, 118.
41. Stendahl, "Biblical Theology," 427.
42. Ibid., 420.
43. Ibid., 422. Barth opposes letting biblical theology have this sovereignty in determining Christian teachings. He regards it as having an equal share of the responsibility along with

dogmatic history, systematic theology, and practical theology. "Biblical and exegetical theology can become a field of wild chasing and charging when it bows to the idol of a supposedly normative historicism and when therefore, without regard to the positively significant yet also warning ecclesiastical and dogmatic history, or to its co-responsibility in the world of systematic theology (in which it may perhaps make a dilettante incursion), or to the fact that ultimately theology in the form of practical theology must aim to give meaningful directions to the ministry of the community in the world, it claims autonomy as a kind of Vatican within the whole" (Barth, *Church Dogmatics* [Edinburgh: T. & T. Clark, 1962] IV/3, 881). But in reply we ask, How else can the principle of *sola scriptura* be realized unless we seek to remain silent and let each biblical writer speak for himself, in his own terms? In the earlier parts of this essay we have heard the warning, we believe, from what happened at the Reformation and afterwards when analogy-of-faith hermeneutics, such as Barth advocates, led theology down the road to scholasticism.

44. O. Cullmann, "The Necessity and Function of Higher Criticism," *The Early Church* (ed. J. Higgins; Philadelphia: Westminster, 1956) 16.

45. Ibid., 13. Note Cullmann's use of Barth's key word, "transparency" *(supra,* n. 38).

46. O. Cullmann, *Salvation in History* (New York: Harper, 1967) 68-69. A Lutheran, Cullmann nevertheless believes Luther's rule of faith ("What urges Christ," *supra,* n. 7) needs to be modified to include the whole of redemptive history (*Salvation in History,* 297-298).

47. For Cullmann's understanding that the canon imposed itself upon the church and was not established by some arbitrary bias in the early church, see *Salvation in History,* 293-304, and his essay, "The Tradition," *The Early Church,* 55-99.

48. Cullmann, *Salvation in History,* 297.

49. Ibid., 292. There is, I believe, a similarity between the sort of theological treatise which Cullmann envisions, and that which Jonathan Edwards hoped to live long enough to develop from his *History of the Work of Redemption,* which was a series of sermons he gave in 1739. His son re-edited this series after his father's death so they would read as a continuous treatise. It begins with God's creation of the world (and even his purpose in creating it) and inquires how each successive redemptive event, such as the call of Abraham, the Exodus, and so on, makes its distinctive contribution to the realization of God's one great purpose in history. At the beginning of this work Jonathan Edwards said, "In order to see how a design is carried on, we must first know what the design is. . . . Therefore that the great works and dispensations of God that belong to this great affair of redemption might not appear like confusion to you, I would set before you briefly the main things designed to be accomplished in this great work, to accomplish which God . . . will continue working to the end of the world, when the work will appear completely finished" (J. Edwards, *The Work of Redemption: The Works of President Edwards* [4 vols.; New York: Leavitt & Allen, 1858] I, 302). In the editorial introduction to this work, the son remarked that his father ". . . had planned a body of divinity, in a *new* method, and in the form of a *history* . . ." (ibid., I, 296. Italics added).

50. Cullmann, *Salvation in History,* 298.

51. Cullmann, "The Necessity and Function of Higher Criticism," 15. Cullmann believes that such antinomies exist in scripture because he says, "That there were distorting influences involved in the interpretation of the historical character and the kerygmatic meaning of the event should certainly not be disputed" *(Salvation in History,* 96). He thinks, however, that he can detect which interpretation is a distortion and can correct it by looking more closely at the event which it was trying to interpret. My problem with this is that redemptive events in scripture are always so inextricably bound up with interpretations that I despair of ever separating an event from the interpretation given it by the one reporting it. Furthermore, even if one could remove all interpretive features from a reported event, one could not then work back from this bare event to decide which interpretation was more valid. For example, knowing only that a man named Jesus rose from the dead carries with it no implication of its significance.

52. Cullmann, *Salvation in History,* 113.

53. Ibid., 88.

54. Ibid., 112, 136.

55. Ibid., 88.

56. Ibid., 70.

57. G. Ladd, "The Search for Perspective," *Int* 25 (1971) 48. Stendahl ("Biblical Theology," 421) voices the same criticism. It should be noted, however, that Cullmann deliberately avoids pointing to any psychological or existential need which the biblical message fulfills, because of the danger that such a need would become an "analogy of faith" by which every biblical line of thought would then be interpreted. This is what has happened in Bultmann's thinking, and Cullmann wants none of that.
58. G. Ladd, *A Theology of the New Testament* (Grand Rapids: Eerdmans, 1974) 630.

A Select Bibliography of George Eldon Ladd

1952

Crucial Questions About the Kingdom of God (Grand Rapids: Eerdmans).
"The Kingdom of God in the Jewish Apocryphal Literature": *BibS* 109 (1952) 55-62, 164-174, 318-331; 110 (1953) 32-49.

1956

The Blessed Hope (Grand Rapids: Eerdmans).

1957

"Biblical Theology, History, and Revelation," *RevExp* 54: 195-204.
"Eschatology and the Unity of New Testament Theology," *ExpTim* 68: 268-271.
"The Modern Problem of Biblical Scholarship," *Bethel Seminary Quarterly* 5:10-20.
"The Rapture Question," *Eternity* (May) 8-10.
"The Revelation and Jewish Apocalyptic," *EvQ* 29: 94-100.
"Revelation, History and the Bible," *Christianity Today* (Sept. 30) 5-8.
"Revelation of Christ's Glory," *The Journal of the American Scientific Affiliation* 9 (Sept.) 15-18.
"RSV Appraisal: New Testament," *Christianity Today* (July 8) 7-11.
"Why Not Prophetic-Apocalyptic?" *JBL* 76: 192-200.

1958

"Justification," *Eternity* (July) 10.
"The Origin of Apocalyptic in Biblical Religion," *EvQ* 30: 13-15; 75-85.

1959

The Gospel of the Kingdom (Grand Rapids: Eerdmans). Spanish ed., *El Evangelio del Reino* (Editorial Caribe, 1974).
"Dispensational Theology," *Christianity Today* 4 (Oct. 12) 38-40.
"More Light on the Synoptics," *Christianity Today* 3 (March 2) 12-16.

1960

"Age," *Baker's Dictionary of Theology* (ed. E. F. Harrison; Grand Rapids: Baker) 31-33.
"Apocalyptic, Apocalypse," *Baker's Dictionary of Theology* (ed. E. F. Harrison; Grand Rapids: Baker) 50-54.
"Kingdom of God," *Baker's Dictionary of Theology* (ed. E. F. Harrison; Grand Rapids: Baker) 307-314.
"Matthew," *The Biblical Expositor* (ed. C. F. H. Henry; Philadelphia: Holman) 23-72.
"The Greatness of the Kingdom," *EvQ* 32: 48-50.

"Revelation 20 and the Millennium," *RevExp* 57 (April) 167-175.

1961

"The Lord's Return," *His* (April) 9-11.
"Pondering the Parousia," *Christian Century* 78 (Sept. 13) 1072-1073.

1962

"The Acts of the Apostles," *The Wycliffe Bible Commentary* (edd. C. F. Pfeiffer and E. F. Harrison; Chicago: Moody) 1123-1178.
"Apocalyptic," *The New Bible Dictionary* (ed. J. D. Douglas; Grand Rapids: Eerdmans) 43-44.
"Eschatology," *The New Bible Dictionary* (ed. J. D. Douglas; Grand Rapids: Eerdmans) 386-394.
"The Knowledge of God: The Saving Acts of God," *Basic Christian Doctrines* (ed. C. F. H. Henry; New York: Holt, Rinehart and Winston) 7-13.
"Consistent or Realized Eschatology in Matthew," *Southwestern Journal of Theology* 5 (Oct.) 55-63.
"Doctrinal Purity and Visible Unity," *Eternity* (June) 7-9.
"The Kingdom of God—Reign or Realm?" *JBL* 81: 230-238.
"The Resurrection and History," *Dialog* 1 (Autumn) 55-56.
"What Does Bultmann Understand by the Acts of God?" *Bulletin of the Evangelical Theological Society* 5: 91-97.
"What Is Rudolph Bultmann Trying To Do?" *Eternity* (May) 26-28.

1963

"Apocalyptic Literature," *Zondervan Pictorial Bible Dictionary* (ed. Merrill C. Tenney; Grand Rapids: Zondervan) 49-50.
"He Shall Come Again," *Things Most Surely Believed* (ed. Clarence S. Roddy; New York: Revell) 63-75.
"Kingdom of God," *Zondervan Pictorial Bible Dictionary* (ed. Merrill C. Tenney; Grand Rapids: Zondervan) 466-467.
"Faith and History," *Bulletin of the Evangelical Theological Society* 6: 86-91.
"The Life-Setting of the Parables of the Kingdom," *JBR* 31 (July) 193-199.
"The Resurrection and History," *Religion in Life* (Spring) 3-12.
"The Theology of the Apocalypse," *The Gordon Review* 7 (1963-64) 73-86.

1964

Bultmann (Chicago: Inter-Varsity).
Jesus and the Kingdom (New York: Harper and Row; Waco: Word Books, 1968; London: SPCK, 1966).
Jesus Christ and History (Chicago: Inter-Varsity). Spanish ed., *Vendré Otra Vez* (Buenos Aires: Ediciones Certeza, 1964).
The Young Church (London and New York: Lutterworth and Abingdon).
"The Resurrection of Christ," *Christian Faith and Modern Theology* (ed. C. F. H. Henry; New York: Channel Press) 261-284.
"History and Faith," *Foundations* 7: 5-14.
"Israel and the Church," *EvQ* 36: 206-214.
"Is There a Future for Israel?" *Eternity* (May) 44.
"The *Sitz im Leben* of the Parables of Matthew 13: the Soils," *SE* 2: 203-210.

1965

"The Lion is the Lamb," *Eternity* (April) 20.
"The Role of Jesus in Bultmann's Theology," *SJT* 18 (March) 57-68.
"Unity and Variety in New Testament Faith," *Christianity Today* 10 (Nov. 19) 21-24.

1966

"History and Theology in Biblical Exegesis," *Int* 20 (Jan.) 54-64.
"Searching for the Historical Jesus," *Eternity* (Oct.) 17-19.

1967

The New Testament and Criticism (Grand Rapids: Eerdmans).
"The Christian and the State," *His* (Dec.) 2ff.

1968

"Paul and the Law," in *Soli Deo Gloria: Festschrift for William Childs Robinson* (ed. J.M. Richards; Richmond: John Knox).
"The Christology of Acts," *Foundations* (Jan.-March) 27-41.
"The Problem of History and Faith in Contemporary New Testament Studies," *TU: SE V* (Berlin: Akademie Verlag) 88-100.

1969

The Pattern of New Testament Truth (Grand Rapids: Eerdmans).

1970

"Revelation and Tradition in Paul," in *Apostolic History and the Gospel: Festschrift for F. F. Bruce* (edd. W. W. Gasque and R. P. Martin; Grand Rapids: Eerdmans).

1971

"The Search for Perspective," *Int* 25: 41-62.

1972

Commentary on the Book of Revelation (Grand Rapids: Eerdmans).

1973

"Kingdom of God," "Interim Ethics," "Eschatology and Ethics," in *Baker's Dictionary of Christian Ethics* (ed. C. F. H. Henry; Grand Rapids: Baker)

1974

I Believe in the Resurrection of Jesus (London and Grand Rapids: Hodder & Stoughton and Eerdmans). Swedish ed., *Jag tror på Jesu uppståndelse* (Orebro: Bokforlaget Libris, 1977). German edition in preparation.
The Presence of the Future (Grand Rapids: Eerdmans [2nd ed. of *Jesus and the Kingdom*]).
A Theology of the New Testament (Grand Rapids and London: Eerdmans and Lutterworth).

"The Parable of the Sheep and the Goats in Recent Interpretation," in *New Dimensions in New Testament Study* (ed. R. N. Longenecker; Grand Rapids: Zondervan).
"The Role of Apocalyptic in New Testament Theology," in *Reconciliation and Hope: Festschrift for Leon Morris* (ed. Robert Banks; Grand Rapids: Eerdmans).

1975

"The Holy Spirit in Galatians," in *Current Issues in Biblical and Patristic Interpretation: Festschrift for Merrill Tenney* (Grand Rapids: Eerdmans).
"The Revival of Apocalyptic in the Churches," *RevExp* 72: 263-270.

1976

"Righteousness in Romans," *Southwestern Journal of Theology* 19: 6-17.

1977

"Historic Premillennialism," in *The Meaning of the Millennium: Four Views* (ed. Robert G. Clouse; Downers Grove: Inter-Varsity).
"The Kingdom of God," in *Dreams, Visions and Oracles: The Layman's Guide to Biblical Prophecy* (edd. C. E. Amerding and W. W. Gasque; Grand Rapids: Baker).

1978

The Last Things: An Eschatology for Laymen (Grand Rapids: Eerdmans).
"Why Did God Inspire the Bible?" in *Scripture, Tradition, and Interpretation* (edd. W. Ward Gasque and William S. LaSor; Grand Rapids: Eerdmans).

Tabula Gratulatoria

Achtemeier, Paul J.
Adrian, Victor
Alcorn, Wallace
Allen, Ronald Barclay
Anderson, Hugh
Archer, Gleason L.
Armerding, Carl Edwin

Baarda, T.
Baird, J. Arthur
Barbour, R. S.
Barclay, W.
Barker, Glenn W.
Bartchy, S. Scott
Bass, Clarence B.
Beardslee, William A.
Beasley-Murray, G. R.
Bell, Jr., William E.
Benoit, P.
Best, Ernest
Betz, Hans Dieter
Betz, Otto
Bilezikian, Gilbert
Birdsall, J. Neville
Black, Matthew
Borchert, Gerald L.
Borgen, Peder
Bornkamm, Guenther
Bower, Robert K.
Bromiley, Goeffrey W.
Brown, Raymond E.
Buehler, Wm. W.
Burdick, Donald W.
Bush, Frederic Wm.

Campbell, Robert J.
Cannon, George
Carlston, Charles E.
Charles, Howard H.
Charlesworth, James H.
Cranfield, C. E. B.
Cullmann, Oscar
Culver, Robert D.

Daane, James
Dalton, William J.
Danker, Frederick W.
Davies, W. D.
Demarest, Bruce A.
Derrett, J. Duncan M.
Donfried, Karl Paul
Drane, John W.
Dungan, David L.
Dunn, James D. G.
Dunnett, Walter McGregor

Earle, Ralph
Ellis, E. Earle
Elwell, W. A.
Enslin, Morton S.
Erickson, Millard
Erwin, Dan R.
Evans, Robert

Farrell, Hobert K.
Fee, Gordon O.
Feinberg, Charles Lee
Feinberg, Paul D.
Filson, Floyd V.
Fitzmyer, Joseph A.
Fowler, Paul B.
Fuller, Daniel P.
Fuller, R. H.
Funk, Robert W.

Gaebelein, Frank E.
Gasque, W. Ward
Gerhardsson, Birger
Gerig, Wesley L.
Giacumakis, Jr., George
Gibbs, John G.
Glasson, T. Francis
Green, E. M. B.
Grudem, Wayne
Gundry, Robert H.
Guthrie, Donald

Hagner, Donald A.
Hamerton-Kelly, R.
Hammer, Paul L.
Harris, Murray J.
Hawthorne, Gerald F.
Hayden, Roy E.
Hengel, M.
Henry, Carl F. H.
Hestenes, Roberta
Hill, David
Hoehner, Harold W.
Hoekema, Anthony A.
Hooker, Morna D.
Howe, E. Margaret
Hubbard, David A.
Hughes, Philip E.

Inch, Morris A.

Jeremias, Joachim
Jewett, Paul K.
Johnson, Alan F.

Kaiser, Jr., Walter C.
Kalland, Lloyd A.
Keck, Leander E.
Kee, H. C.
Kerr, William F.
Kerr, William Nigel
Kingsbury, Jack Dean
Kistemaker, Simon J.
Knight III, George W.
Kraft, Robert A.
Kuhn, Harold B.
Kümmel, Werner Georg

Lake, Donald M.
Lane, William L.
Larson, Clifford E.
LaSor, William Sanford
Leaney, A. R. C.
Lehman, G. Irvin
Leonard, Paul E.
Lewis, Arthur H.
Liefeld, Walter L.
Lincoln, Andrew T.
Lindars, Barnabas
Lindsell, Harold
Lyon, Robert W.

MacRae, George W.

Madvig, Donald H.
Mare, W. Harold
Marshall, I. Howard
Martin, Ralph P.
McArthur, Harvey K.
McComiskey, Thomas E.
Meeks, Wayne A.
Metzger, Bruce M.
Michel, Otto
Mitchell, Donald R.
Montefiore, H. W.
Morgan, Robert
Morosco, Robert E.
Moule, C. F. D.
Munger, Robert B.

Nicole, Roger

Obitts, Stanley

Paine, Stephen W.
Pannell, William E.
Pinnock, Clark H.
Piper, John
Piper, Otto A.
Powell, Ralph E.

Reumann, John
Richardson, Peter
Ridderbos, Herman
Riesenfeld, Harald
Rigaux, B.
Robinson, James M.
Rogers, Jack
Roloff, Juergen

Schaper, Robert N.
Scharlemann, Martin H.
Schnackenburg, R.
Schoonhoven, Calvin R.
Schultz, Samuel J.
Scott, Jr., J. Julius
Schroeder, David
Smalley, Stephen S.
Smedes, Lewis B.
Smick, Elmer B.
Smith, Jr., D. Moody
Snyder, Graydon F.
Stanton, Graham N.
Stein, Robert H.
Stek, John H.
Stendahl, Krister

Tenney, Merrill C.
Tinder, Donald
Turner, George Allen

Van Elderen, Bastiaan
Van Groningen, G.
Van Unnik, W. C.
Via, Jr., Dan O.

Wagner, Guenther
Wead, David W.
Wilder, Amos N.

Yamauchi, Edwin
Young, Warren C.
Youngblood, Ronald